UNIVERSITY OF IOWA

HUMANISTIC STUDIES

ORIGINS OF POE'S CRITICAL THEORY

ORIGINS OF POE'S CRITICAL THEORY

by

MARGARET ALTERTON

NEW YORK

RUSSELL & RUSSELL · INC

1965

FIRST PUBLISHED IN 1925

REISSUED, 1965, BY RUSSELL & RUSSELL, INC.

BY ARRANGEMENT WITH THE UNIVERSITY OF IOWA

L. C. CATALOG CARD NO: 65-13946

PRINTED IN THE UNITED STATES OF AMERICA

PREFACE

This paper, dealing as it does with the genesis of Poe's critical theory, lays no claim to an appreciation of the writer's art, nor does it attempt to suggest any degree of local or foreign commendation that time has awarded him or has withheld from him. From the nature of the problem, it has from necessity sought to discover, first, what were Poe's readings; secondly, what were the particular parts of those readings which interested him to the exclusion of the rest of the matter he read; thirdly, what broad lines of thought grew up in his mind as a result of these congenial interests; fourthly, what original researches they prompted him to make; fifthly, what use these interests were to him in ways of subject-matter; and, finally, what working-principle applicable to the needs of a writer evolved itself from his methods of thinking.

Poe's own literary work,—criticism, poetry, and short story,—points by its variety to the fact that he was a prodigious reader. Magazine literature, both of America and of Europe, of his own day, and of periods preceding, fell under his eye. Scientific and philosophic material, much of which appeared in these periodical issues, and also literary critical opinions both in magazines and in their authors' volumes, were objects of his study. To mention only a few of these readings, it is plain that he shows himself a student of *Blackwood's Edinburgh Magazine,* of the *Edinburgh Review,* of a certain part of the work of Augustus Wilhelm von Schlegel, of Coleridge, of Plato, and of the *Philosophical Transactions of the Royal Society of London.* And it was from such readings that there arose his particular congenial interests, such as law, dramatic procedure, scientific problems concerning the motions of the heavenly bodies, and philosophic ideas, principally those of Plato, of Aristotle and of the Christian philosophers. And in many striking instances, he betrays a following of these readings in his subject-matter, especially whenever philosophic reasoning and scientific experimentation appear in his text.

Moreover, as evidence that in this dependence he was possessed also with the spirit of originality, he is seen to extend his study to a point where he combines these different lines of interest into one consistent way of thinking. Thus it can be made apparent that

3

the idea of unity grew and developed in his mind until he reached what to his sense was a writer's reliable standard of criticism and a writer's working-principle; and that he derived a technical method from the themes he had chosen. Cases of pathological interest for example, offer suggestions for method in their scientific diagnoses. Furthermore, the perfect working of physical law, he insists, should be the model for the writer of a story or a poem. I shall try to show that natural processes lay back of all Poe's theory and practice.

Watching thus the growth of Poe's literary principles and noting how he endeavored to use his own dicta, I have been tempted to propose for consideration some additional material for the Poe canon. In some cases, since various pieces in periodicals of his time not hitherto attributed to Poe, bear in idea so striking a resemblance to his own productions and stand the test of such external evidence as exists, I have not hesitated to attribute them to Poe. In other instances, I have only suggested the remote possibility that certain pieces came from his pen.

The thesis was undertaken and written under the direction of Professor Hardin Craig. In all the work connected with its start, progress, and completion, Professor Craig has been both inspiring and helpful. I am therefore glad to take advantage of this opportunity to give public and grateful expression of the debt that I owe him.

MARGARET ALTERTON

CONTENTS

CHAPTER I
BLACKWOOD AND OTHER BRITISH PERIODICALS

Although British periodical literature was well known and accessible to American readers during the period of Poe's critical work, and Poe's interest in the "brief article" coming from the mother country was, therefore, by no means an interest peculiar to him, yet a study of what may be said to be his rather unusual familiarity with the text of the foreign magazine, reveals him as being a more serious reader than he has perhaps been generally considered.[1]

One of the earliest influences on Poe's conscious method was his knowledge of *Blackwood's Edinburgh Magazine* and other British periodicals. Evidence points to the fact that he was an indefatigable student of their contents. In the first place, he testifies himself to his habit of "poring over foreign files."[2] In the early days of his editorship of the *Southern Literary Messenger*,[3] he pub-

---

[1]Republishing of British periodicals in America was carried on extensively. Advertising notices for publishing foreign magazines occur frequently in the *North American Review*. See vol. 18, p. 219; p. 438; vol. 19, p. 484. Allen and Ticknor of Boston "propose to republish *Blackwood's Edinburgh*, and the *London New Monthly Magazine*, at a cost so moderate, as to bring them within the reach of a large class of readers who cannot afford the expense of importing the English copies."—*New York Mirror*, 1832, vol. 10, p. 190. Lilly, Wait, Coleman and Holden, also of Boston, were said according to the *New York Mirror*, vol. 10, p. 159, to be "conferring a favor on literary circles on this side of the Atlantic by their American editions of the *Edinburgh Review* and the *London Quarterly Review*." Foreign periodicals, in addition to being reprinted in America, had also their contents republished in part. Charles Bowen of Boston planned to give in the *Select Journal of Foreign Periodical Literature* a selection of the most interesting articles and the most important information contained in the principal foreign literary journals." *New York Mirror*, vol. 10, p. 254. The "intelligent conductor" of the *Albion* also "reflects from his columns, with peculiar taste and skill, the wit, eloquence, information and general spirit of the British periodical press."—*New York Mirror*, vol. 10, p. 222. *Littell's Museum*, published in Philadelphia, 1835, planned, according to the *Southern Literary Messenger*, to reprint in the same way:—"The plan of the *Museum* is certainly most excellent. It is to select and republish from all the British periodicals of high reputation, everything which is either of *present* or *permanent* value, omitting the vast mass of

7

lished reviews from contemporary foreign magazines. From his own remarks it can be seen[4] that he was following the trend of British criticism.

He condemns the general tone of criticism written by British reviewers. He thinks that British critics were too apt to discuss the subject-matter under review rather than to weigh the merit of the article according to any standard of criticism. Of the review of Article XIV, "The Mythology of Ancient Greece and Italy," by Thomas Keightley, in the *Westminster Review*,[5] he says:

"This is an interesting and able paper, but has no pretensions to the name of Review. The position of the Bacchanalians in Greek and Roman History, and their progress, together with the dangers and impediments encountered in their course, forms the subject of the Essay—for *it is* an Essay, although an admirable one."

The *Westminster Review* of the same date errs, he considers, in having the greater part of what was supposedly a critical article, taken up in reviewing some of the leading features in Scottish history.[6] He finds the same fault with "The Memoirs of John Napier," by Mark Napier, as reviewed in the same magazine. He considers that British criticism has adopted an arrogance of tone that is by no means justifiable; and he defends Coleridge against the abuse of the *Edinburgh Review,* saying how little different in spirit that abuse was from the "cold and brief compliments with the warm *regrets* of the *Quarterly.* If there be any one thing more

---

matter which is local to Great Britain or not interesting to an American reader."—*Southern Literary Messenger,* vol. 1, p. 251. The *Living Age,* Boston, 1844, speaks of "feeling bound to give all that is very good in the foreign Magazines and Reviews." *Littell's Living Age,* vol. 1, p. 130. Foster reprinted, according to the *Messenger* of August, 1835, in cheap and valuable form, the *London, Edinburgh,* and *Westminster Reviews.* Cf. *Southern Literary Messenger,* vol. 1, p. 651.

[2]*Broadway Journal,* vol. 1, p. 349.

[3]Poe seems to have had various connections with the *Southern Literary Messenger.* Thomas White, the editor, apparently employed him as purveyor for the magazine since Poe's letters of 1835 reveal that he was securing contributions. He writes to White, June 12, 1835: "I suppose you have rec'd Mr. Calvert's communication. He will prove a valuable correspondent."— Harrison, James A., *Complete Works of Edgar Allan Poe,* (New York, 1902), *Letters,* p. 7. Cf. also *Letters,* p. 18. He was likewise useful, it appears, in increasing the circulation of the *Messenger. Ibid.,* p. 6. Hereafter *S. L. M.* will denote *Southern Literary Messenger;* Harrison's edition will be referred to as *Works* or *Letters.*

than another which stirs within us a deep spirit of indignation and disgust, it is that damnation of faint praise which so many of the Narcissi of critical literature have had the infinite presumption to breathe against the majesty of Coleridge."[7] Occasionally, however, Poe expresses himself as pleased with a British review. He commends a criticism in the London Quarterly[8] as being "one of those exceedingly rare cases in which a British critic confines himself strictly to his text."

Poe likewise appears to have been in the habit of comparing the opinions of different reviewers on the same subject. In the case of the "Journal of Frances Anne Butler," which was the subject of comment in the whole round of periodical literature, Poe thus compares two reviewers on the merit of the work, adding his own opinion to the others: "The tone of this Notice[9] is very similar to that of the Article on the same subject in the Edinburgh for July. . . . The Reviewer is of the opinion that 'Master Fanney's Journal' was from an early period, if not from the first line, intended for publication, and that the entire thing is arranged for stage-effect. Both these suppositions are highly probable. Indeed, for our own part, we never had a doubt about the matter." He also compares the Edinburgh and the Quarterly Review in their handling of the "Memoirs of the Life of the Right Honorable Sir James MacIntosh."[10]

---

[4]S. L. M., vol. 2, p. 139. Publishers Notice.—Poe was criticized for printing reviews of reviews and discontinued the practice. In the Supplement to the S. L. M. that Poe issued containing complimentary notices from various magazines concerning the success of the Southern Literary Messenger, occur the following strictures on his printing the reviews of foreign magazines. The Norfolk Beacon says: "The critical notices in the present number of the Messenger, particularly of the North American and the British Reviews, are in bad taste." The Lynchburgh Virginian makes much the same comment: "Too much space is allotted to 'Critical Notices' in the December No. of the Messenger." The critical department, in the opinion of this paper, should not "be occupied with reviews of Reviews—a dish of hash newly warmed, and served up, in all its insipidity, to an already palled appetite."

[5]Ibid., vol. 2, p. 61.

[6]Ibid., p. 59.

[7]Ibid., vol. 2, p. 451, June, 1836. Review of Letters, Conversation and Recollections of S. T. Coleridge.

[8]Ibid., p. 62.

[9]Ibid., vol. 2, p. 61. Review of London Quarterly Review.

[10]Ibid., vol. 2, p. 63.

In the second place, Poe shows that he is familiar with the contents of British periodicals other than their critical matter. He speaks of Boz, the author of "Watkins Tottle and Other Sketches," as being a "far more pungent, more witty, and better disciplined writer of sly articles than nine-tenths of the Magazine writers in Great Britain—which is saying much, it must be allowed, when we consider the great variety of genuine talent, and earnest application brought to bear upon the periodical literature of the mother country."[11] And, again, showing his familiarity with the British periodical press, he says that the English as far excell us in writing the "brief article" as "Hyperion" does a "Satyr." He would recommend British stories as models to those who turn their attention to magazine writing.[12] Poe apparently "pored over" files of early foreign periodicals as well as over those of contemporary interest. In a critical essay written in May, 1835,[13] he mentions a review in an Edinburgh magazine of an early date. He would gladly, he says, appropriate the introductory remarks of the article were it fair to do so; but "honor among thieves!" And in his famous review of Hawthorne's "Twice-Told Tales," he refers to the existence of good tales of effect in "the early numbers of *Blackwood*."[14]

Poe's stories likewise prove him to be a student of foreign magazines. In "Lionizing" he asserts that he placed no confidence in their critical power,[15] characterizing them in the following way:

"As I felt within me the divine *afflatus*, I considered this accident rather fortunate than otherwise. I resolved to be guided by the paternal advice. I determined to follow my nose. I gave it a pull or two upon the spot, and wrote a pamphlet on Nosology forthwith.

"All Fum-Fudge was in an uproar.

'Wonderful genius!' said the *Quarterly*.

'Superb Physiologist!' said the *Westminster*.

'Clever fellow!' said the *Foreign*.

---

[11]*Ibid.*, vol. 2, p. 457. Review of *Watkins Tottle, and Other Sketches.*

[12]*Ibid.*, p. 458.

[13]*Ibid.*, vol. 1, p. 520. Review of *I Promessi Sposi.* Poe speaks of the review being one which welcomed *Waverly* as a new type of novel. He may be referring to the review of *Waverly* in the *Edinburgh Review*, vol. 24, p. 208.

[14]*Graham's Magazine*, vol. 20, p. 299.

[15]*Lionizing* was one of the tales submitted for a prize by Poe in 1833 to the *Baltimore Visitor.* An account of Poe's winning this prize with his story, *The MS. Found in a Bottle*, appears in *Works I*, pp. 101-106.

'Fine writer!' said the *Edinburgh*.
'Profound thinker!' said the *Dublin*.
'Great man!' said *Bentley*.
'Divine soul!' said *Fraser*.
'One of us!' said *Blackwood*.''

Poe also gave to his story, "Loss of Breath,"[16] the sub-title of "A Tale neither in nor out of Blackwood." But perhaps the most convincing proof that Poe was an ardent student of foreign magazines is in his sketch of "How to Write a Blackwood Article." In this sketch,[17] whose satire we must disregard for the present, he gives the titles of several stories that occur through the pages of *Blackwood*. The tales which he mentions are "The Dead Alive,"[18] "The Involuntary Experimentalist,"[19] "Passages from the Diary of a Late Physician,"[20] and "The Man in the Bell."[21]

Poe's letters are further evidence that he had his attention fixed on foreign quarterlies. He discusses with Judge Beverley Tucker the value of the general tone of British criticism and the relative merits of certain of the chief English reviewers, Jeffrey and Wilson in particular.[22] He writes to Mr. J. P. Kennedy that by "Loss of Breath" he intended to satirize the extravagance of *Blackwood*.[23]

Christopher North, the editor of *Blackwood*, seems always to have been to Poe a type of the extravagant in critical commendation or blame. Poe maintained that North owed his tremendous popularity in the critical world more to his great exuberance of spirits and "dashing audacity" than to any very profound knowledge of critical principles.[24] In fact, he seems to be generally of the opin-

---

[16]*S.L.M.*, vol. 1, p. 735. As the story appeared in the *Messenger*, it was entitled *Loss of Breath, a Tale à la Blackwood*.

[17]*American Museum*, vol. 1, p. 375.

[18]Later it will be shown how similar Poe's tale is to the *Buried Alive* in *Blackwood's Edinburgh Magazine*, vol. 10, p. 262.

[19]*Ibid.*, vol. 42, p. 487.

[20]*Ibid.*, vol. 28, pp. 322, 474; vol. 32, pp. 279, 42, 248; vol. 29, p. 105.

[21]*Ibid.*, vol. 10, p. 373.

[22]*Letters*, p. 23. Professor Trent gives an interesting account of Judge Beverley Tucker's correspondence with aspiring men of letters; of his interest in Southern literature, especially as that interest touched William Gilmore Simms. Trent, William P., *William Gilmore Simms*. (Boston and New York, 1896) p. 176.

[23]*Letters*, p. 30.

[24]*Graham's Magazine*, vol. 20, p. 72. Review of *Critical and Miscellaneous Essays* by Christopher North. Also, *Broadway Journal*, vol. 2, p. 136. Review of Wilson's *Genius and Character of Burns*.

ion that Judge Tucker was correct in deeming North arrogant in critical matters.[25] He intended, as has just been noted, to satirize in "Loss of Breath" the extravagance in *Blackwood*. He probably meant a satirical attack more particularly on *Blackwood's* criticism, and in the figure of Windenough he designed a satire on Christopher North. The author of "Lights and Shadows of Scottish Life," who was noted for his extravagance of critical judgments, for his caustic wit, who was elected to the professorship of Moral Philosophy in the University of Edinburgh,[26] may possibly be seen in the "gaunt, tall, and peculiar looking form" which Mr. Lackobreath drags from the tomb, saying:

". . . here is a wretch entitled to no earthly commiseration. . . . Who indeed would think of compassionating a shadow? Besides, has he not had his full share of the blessings of Mortality? He was the originator of tall monuments, shot-towers, lightening rods, Lombardy poplars. His treatise upon 'Shades and Shadows' has immortalized him. He edited with distinguished ability the last edition of 'South on the Bones'. He went early to college and studied pneumatics. He then came home and talked eternally and played upon the French horn. He patronized the bagpipes. Captain Barclay, who walked against Time, would not walk against *him*. Windham and Allbreath were his favorite writers; his favorite artist, Phiz."

Of all the foreign magazines which Poe knew, *Blackwood* is perhaps the one with which he was most familiar.[27] He appears to

This opinion of North was, according to Mrs. Oliphant in her work *William Blackwood and his Sons*, the general opinion of all readers of English periodicals of North's time. She cites as an instance of his tremendous wrath his expression of disgust at Henry Mackenzie's unfavorable criticism of his *Lights and Shadows of Scottish Life*. Oliphant, Mrs. T. K., *William Blackwood and his Sons*, Edinburgh and London, 1897, vol. 1, p. 269.

[25]*Letters*, p. 23.

[26]Oliphant, *op.cit.*, vol. 1, p. 259.

[27]The popularity of *Blackwood's Edinburgh Magazine* is attested in the columns of American periodicals. The *New York Mirror* speaks familiarly, though in a critical vein, of the *Noctes Ambrosianae*, saying that the absence of notes and explanations in that series of articles makes the meaning not always apparent to the American reader.—*The New York Mirror*, vol. 10, p. 198.

R. Shelton Mackenzie also testifies to the popularity of *Blackwood's Edinburgh Magazine* in the United States: "For one reader of *Blackwood's Magazine* in the old country," he says, "there cannot be less than fifty in the new."—*Noctes Ambrosianae*, by John Wilson (New York, 1863) vol. 1, p. XVI.

have derived from *Blackwood* suggestions for his own work in regard to both subject-matter and technique.[28] Considering the probability of his indebtedness, first, in subject-matter, one is struck
by the similarity of Poe's tales of effect to *Blackwood* material.
Both *Blackwood* and Poe agree, using very much the same phraseology, that the horrible and terrible is a legitimate sphere for effective work for the writer of fiction. Poe is of the opinion that
impressions produced by the tales of effect in *Blackwood* were
"wrought in a legitimate sphere of action and constituted a legitimate, although sometimes an exaggerated interest."[29] Compare
with Poe's remark, that of a reviewer in *Blackwood*, commenting
on "The Devil's Elixir" by E. T. A. Hoffmann. The English critic
makes the point that "the *horrible* is quite as legitimate a field
of poetry and romance, as either the pathetic or the ludicrous."[30]
In fact, the English magazines are filled with discussions of the
advantages of the terrible in fictional writing, and doubtless furnished Poe with many ideas on the subject.[31] The same *Blackwood*
reviewer explains that we delight in being horrified, that "the
earth does not at this moment contain one individual who has not
a superstitious shudder when he passes a church yard at midnight."
He thinks that, this fact being true, the human mind will continue

[28]Palmer Cobb, in his work on the influence of E. T. A. Hoffman on Poe,
quotes the French critic, Barine, to the effect that a distinction must be made
between Poe's indebtedness to sources for his subject-matter, and for his
technique. Cobb, Palmer. *The Influence of E. T. A. Hoffman on the Tales
of Edgar Allan Poe.* Published under the direction of The Philological Club
of the University of North Carolina, 1908, p. 11. Barine, it seems, had said
that Poe owed his *Idées générales* to Coleridge and his technique to "*des
romantiques allemands*"; adding, "*Il* [Poe] *possédait son Hoffmann sur le
bout du doigt.*" Palmer Cobb, however, is of the opinion that Poe owed
many of his themes to Hoffmann, but as far as technical method of writing
is concerned, he does not, in his conclusion, state that Poe has any debt to
pay his German source. He says, "Finally, Hoffmann's influence on Poe
did not extend to the latter's style. It was solely a borrowing and adaptation
of motives." *Ibid.*, p. 104.

[29]*Graham's Magazine*, vol. 20, p. 299. Review of Hawthorne's *Twice-Told
Tales.*

[30]*Blackwood's Edinburgh Magazine*, vol. 16, p. 55. The *Blackwood* critic
of *Popular Tales of Northern Nations* recommends the "doing into English"
of little German stories of *diablerie.* Vol. 14, p. 293.

[31]Both Palmer Cobb and Professor Gruener are doubtless right in thinking
that Poe must have read Walter Scott's essay on the *Supernatural* in the
Foreign Quarterly Review for July, 1827. Cobb, op.cit., p. 7.

to receive a tragic pleasure from the skilful use made of these fears in fiction. The author of the story, "Le Revenant," also in *Blackwood,* maintains that it is a human instinct to wish for a first-hand experience of the sensations that would attend the laying down of life. He considers that it is this strange desire to experience that greatest of all sensations that has led painters and poets to make the "estate of a man condemned to die a favorite theme of comment or description."[32] A further critic sees in the strangely fascinating records of physicians good material for "polite and popular literature."[33] The *Edinburgh Review,*—the writer in this case is Hazlitt,—is of the opinion that Shelley is catering to this taste for the horrible:

"He (Shelley) mistook the nature of the poet's calling, which should be guided by involuntary, not by voluntary impulses. He ransacked his brain for incongruities, and believed in whatever was incredible. Almost all is effort, . . . subjects are chosen because they are repulsive: the colours of his style, for their gaudy, changeful, startling effect, resemble the display of fireworks in the dark."[34]

The *Indicator* is of the belief that a writer's purpose should be to satisfy this craving for excitement; Leigh Hunt, the editor, says in his "How to Write a Grim Story":

"A man who does not contribute his quota of grim stories now a-days seems hardly to be free of the republic of letters. ' . . . If he does not frighten everybody, he is nobody."[35]

Poe and *Blackwood* writers also agree in the type of terror. They both seem to make a distinction between German and English types of terror. Although much favorable comment may be read in *Blackwood* on the merits of German devilry, on the value of Hoffmann's tales in particular,[36] there is yet a strong plea for a terror that arises from some real experience. One critic thus states the difference: "Fairy tales please; but (in England) they do not

---

[32]*Blackwood's Edinburgh Magazine,* vol. 21, p. 409. *Le Revenant.*

[33]*Ibid.,* vol. 28, p. 322. *Passages from the Diary of a Late Physician.*

[34]*Edinburgh Review,* vol. 40, p. 495.

[35]The *Indicator,* December 15, 1819.

[36]One critic exclaims enthusiastically: "We like to be horrified; we like *The Devil's Elixir.*" Kemperhausen, in the *Noctes Ambrosianae,* approves of Washington Irving's intention of giving "us a German Sketch Book." *Blackwood,* vol. 13, p. 610. Another critic later expresses bitter disappointment that *The Tales of a Traveller* have nothing characteristically German about them. *Blackwood,* vol. 16, p. 295. *Letters of Timothy Tickler, Esq., to Eminent Literary Characters.*

touch the soul. . . . the German terrible, besides that it wants
this our national *locus in quo*, takes a course commonly that the
English do not pleasantly fall in with. Almost all the northern
legends set out with a man's taking the bounty money of the devil;
so that we guess pretty well, in the beginning, how he is to be disposed of in the end. And we feel but little interest about a man,
after he has made a bargain of this sort. He is above (or below)
our sphere."[37] Another reviewer, although he is approving of the
power of the German writer, Ernst von Houvald, to produce a
"frightful sketch," yet appears to base his commendation on the
reality of the horror: "When this author published his first attempt—a frightful sketch, of which the scene was laid in a charnel-
house,—we predicted that he would rise to eminence."[38] A third
critic, Sir Walter Scott in this case, also distinguishes between
English and German types of terror.[39] He does not think the German school have handled the field of horror with any great appreciation of its power for effect. "Fantastic extravagances"
bring down his censure. Indeed, he says, stories of fiends, ghosts,
and prodigies produce not that "shuddering interest approaching
to fear"; they impress by little else than their oddity. The English language contains, he thinks, but one example of this fantastic style, "The Bold Dragoon," by Geoffrey Crayon. Translations into English, however, especially those from the German, he
considers present many instances, and of these he names in particular "The Devil's Elixir" by E. T. A. Hoffmann. But such
pieces of fantastic extravagance, he says, are ill-suited to "English
severity of taste." He feels a more compelling power in the Scottish tales told by the *Littérateur*, who was at the same time a scientist, of the strange though apparently natural disappearance of
a man into the depths of a mountainous wilderness; and more terror
from the "night-shriek" than from any ghost or goblin.

Another reviewer stresses the power of the real experience to hold
the attention. He gives it as his opinion that works on Medical
Jurisprudence detail cases of unquestioned authenticity, the horror
of which fascinates and haunts the mind of the reader. In a piece
entitled "Hints for Jurymen" he comments on a book on Medical

[37]*Ibid.*, vol. 14, p. 641. *A Chapter on Goblins.*
[38]*Ibid*, vol. 13, p. 3. *Horae Germanicae.*
[39]*Foreign Quarterly Review*, vol. 1, p. 72. *On the Supernatural in English
Fiction.*

Jurisprudence by Dr. Paris, an eminent physician, and Mr. Fonblanque, a no less eminent lawyer, giving in the words of the authors the definition of their work. It is, he quotes, that "science by which medicine, and its collateral branches are made subservient to the construction, elucidation, and administration of the laws."[40] And he suggests that in the next edition of this valuable work should well be included appalling examples drawn from the "facts" of M. Fodoré. Still another critic, also commenting on *médicine légale*, the theme of the work entitled "Elements of Medical Jurisprudence," by T. R. Beck, M.D., asserts that he has found in the book real "tales of terror." He considers that the horror in these sketches, many of them Scotch and American, have not their equal in power of morbid fascination.[41]

Poe as well as Scott and other British critics discredits for effectiveness the German tale of terror. Although it has been suggested that Poe, with Hoffman for a model, crossed and recrossed the boundary between the real and the supernatural,[42] yet evidence points to the probability that he followed not Hoffman, but a "severity of taste" affirmed to be more strictly English; that he caught the idea from *Blackwood* writers, particularly from critics commenting on Medical Jurisprudence, that real horror arises from contemplating diseased conditions, both mental and physical. And, even where he seems to go beyond the bounds of the rational, he is still treating horrible cases of pathological interest, nervous diseases and insanity.

Poe denies that he has modelled his pieces after the "phantasy pieces" of the Germans. "The truth is," he says in his Preface to "Tales of the Grotesque and Arabesque," a title which, by the way, he probably owes as Prof. Greuner and as Palmer Cobb suggest, to Scott's essay on the supernatural, noted above, "that, with a single exception, there is no one of these stories in which the scholar should recognize the distinctive features of that species of pseudo-horror which we are taught to call Germanic, for no better reason than that some of the secondary names of German literature have been identified with its folly." Then, apparently quoting the critic in *Blackwood* who had affirmed the "German

---

[40]*Blackwood's Edinburgh Magazine*, vol. 13, p. 673.

[41]*Ibid.*, vol. 17, p. 352. Review entitled *Beck and Dunlop on Medical Jurisprudence*. T. R. Beck's work was published in Albany, 1823.

[42]Cobb, *op.cit.*, p. 8.

terrible" to be incapable of touching the soul, he asserts: "If in
any of my productions terror has been the thesis, I maintain that
terror is not of Germany, but of the soul."[43]

Added to Poe's denial that the nature of the terror he sought
to produce was German in its origin, is the testimony of the Tales.
Perhaps in no way does the distinction between the fantastic and
rational show itself more clearly than in contrasting "The Fall of
the House of Usher" with its supposed prototype,[44] Hoffmann's
"Das Marjorat"; for the culminating point of terror in the German piece is undoubtedly the uncanny scratching on the bricked-
up door by the spirit of the dead domestic; whereas in Usher, horror reaches its culminating point when one hears Lady Madeline,
awakened from her cataleptic trance, knock on her tomb, and the
madman's shriek as he sees her standing, still enshrouded, at the
door.   And the distinction may be further noted when Poe presents the doctrines of personal identity and metempsychosis as
hallucinations of some disordered brain.   Thus, in "William Wilson" he tries to arouse horror by describing Wilson as the victim
of hereditary insanity.   A case in a medical journal might have
had Poe's wording:

"I am the descendant of a race whose imaginative and easily
excitable temperament has at all times rendered them remarkable;
and, in my earliest infancy, I gave evidence of having fully in-
herited the family character.   As I advanced in years it was more
strongly developed; becoming, for many reasons, a cause of serious
disquietude to my friends, and of positive injury to myself.   I
grew self-willed, addicted to the wildest caprices, and a prey to
the most ungovernable passions.   Weak-minded, and beset with
constitutional infirmities akin to my own, my parents could do but
little to check the evil propensities which distinguished me."[45]

And this case of incipient madness, developing with alarming
rapidity, takes the form of the victim's believing that his steps are
dogged by a double.   In "Morella" and in "Ligeia" Poe also explains metempsychosis as it might appear in the records of medical
cases.   Take, for instance, a case of insanity detailed in the *Medico-
Chirurgical Review* for 1838.   At least a germ of belief in this
doctrine is seen in the delusion of a madman who thinks that the
devil lives in the form of his wife and also in the form of his cat.
Haunted by this belief, and irritated beyond all power of self-

---

[43] *Works*, vol. 1, p. 151.
[44] Cobb, *op.cit.*, p. 8.
[45] *Works*, vol. 3, p. 300.

control, he puts them both to a horrible death.[46] Of course it
cannot be affirmed that Poe drew on the medical record for the
horror that he worked out in "The Black Cat"; yet for certain
reasons, one is tempted to put the two cases in juxtaposition. One
can recall Poe's familiarity with medical journals. He speaks of
the "high authority and merit" of the *"Chirurgical Journal of
Leipsic."* He speaks, too, with more than ordinary interest of
the *London Lancet* as being the most authoritative medical serial in
existence.[47] He welcomes its republication in America, for it gives,
he says, facts that concern not only the physician, but those concerning human vitality.[48] Moreover, the details of the cases related
in the *Chirurgical Review* are strikingly similar to those in "The
Black Cat." The insane man in Poe's story maltreats his cat whom
he has named Pluto, deliberately cutting one of its eyes from the
socket. Then, irritated beyond endurance by the continual reproach of its presence, he kills the cat by hanging it. A growing
belief takes possession of his mind, a belief for which he tries to
offer rational explanation, that Pluto returns to upbraid him, and,
in a fit of more than usual madness he attempts to kill the second
black cat; but, instead, he buries the axe in the brain of his wife.
Poe's story is, as the medical case, a horrible record of insanity.

Besides agreeing in the type of terror best adapted to the purposes of effective writing, the authors in *Blackwood* and Poe also
work out specific themes in common. *Blackwood* has an interesting treatment of the *life-in-death* theme, a theme which includes
the attendant horrors of suspended animation and premature
burial. "Buried Alive" reads in part as follows:

"I had been for some time ill of a low and lingering fever. My
strength gradually wasted, but the sense of life seemed to become
more and more acute as my corporeal powers became weaker. I
could see by the looks of the doctor that he despaired of my re-
covery; and the soft and whispering sorrow of my friends, taught
me that I had nothing to hope.

"One day towards the evening, the crisis took place.—I was
seized with a strange and indescribable quivering,—a rushing in
my ears, . . . the power of motion had departed.—I heard

---

[46]*The Medico-Chirurgical Review, and Journal of Practical Medicine,* vol.
28, p. 245.

[47]*Broadway Journal,* vol. 2, p. 275.

[48]*Ibid.,* vol. 1, p. 210. Compare, too, his appreciative critical comments on
the American edition of the *British and Foreign Medical Review. S. L. M.*
vol. 2, p. 785.

the sound of weeping at my pillow—and the voice of the nurse say, 'He is dead'.—I cannot describe what I felt at these words.— I exerted my utmost power of volition to stir myself, but I could not move even an eyelid. The world was then darkened, but I still could hear, and feel, and suffer.

"When my eyes were closed, I heard by the attendants that my friend had left the room, and I soon after found, the undertakers were preparing to habit me in the garments of the grave. . . . The day of interment arrived. . . . The hearse began to move. —Dreadful was the effort I then made to exert the power of action, . . . This is death, thought I. . . . I heard a low and undersound in the earth over me, and I fancied that the worms and reptiles of death were coming."

"Hints for Jurymen," the title of the review on *Medical Jurisprudence,* likewise makes suggestions on the theme of life-in-death:

"We shall now pass on to a subject . . . which must always command the most lively interest—that of *Suspended Animation.* . . . 'hence it is, as Cuvier has remarked, that the poetic fictions best calculated to insure our sympathy, are those which represent sentient beings enclosed with immovable bodies; . . . there is a propensity in the human mind to believe in these horrors, because between credulity and fear there is an inherent affinity and alliance'."

And again from "Hints for Jurymen" is the same theme developed; in this instance a living man actually showing all the symptoms of death:[49]

"On the following morning, the patient was examined by M. Battaglia, who found the integuments of the right arm almost entirely detached and pendant from the flesh; . . . and on the right hand, the part most injured, mortification had already commenced. . . . A short time previous to his decease, M. Battaglia observed with astonishment, that putrefaction had made so much progress that the body already exhaled an insufferable odour, worms crawled from it on the bed, and the nails had become detached from the left hand."

And, further, in the "Diary of a Late Physician":

"All these circumstances,—which terrified the servant who was shaking at my elbow, and muttering, 'She's possessed! . . . Satan has her!', convinced me that the unfortunate young lady was seized with *Catalepsy;* that rare mysterious affection, so fear-

---

[49]*Blackwood's Edinburgh Magazine,* vol. 13, p. 675. The example here alluded to is drawn, according to the reviewer of *Medical Jurisprudence,* from Fodoré's more extensive work on the same subject. It also appears in Beck's book, already referred to, vol. 2, p. 87.

fully blending the conditions of life and death—presenting—so
to speak—life in the aspect of death, and death in that of life!''[50]
Let us see in what way Poe reflects this *Blackwood* background.

He calls one of his stories ''Life-in-Death''; he gives also his
opening sentences somewhat in the manner of the commencement of
''Buried Alive,'' from *Blackwood*.

Buried Alive	*Life-in-Death*[51]
''I had been for some time ill of a low and lingering fever. My strength gradually wasted, but the sense of life seemed to become more and more acute as my corporeal powers became weaker. I could see by the looks of the doctor that he despaired of my recovery; . . . ''	''My fever had been excessive and of long duration. All the remedies attainable . . . had been exhausted to no purpose . . .''

In ''The Case of M. Valdemar,'' Poe makes the patient bear a
striking resemblance to the patient of M. Battaglia, as detailed in
''Hints for Jurymen.'' The unfortunate man is, with the help of
mesmerism, kept seven months from total extinction, even though
his body manifests the conditions that only death can produce.
One recalls the former loathsome case in the following:

''For what really occurred, however, it is quite impossible that
any human being could have been prepared. As I rapidly made
the mesmeric passes, amid ejaculations of 'dead! dead!' absolutely
bursting from the tongue and not from the lips of the sufferer, his
whole frame at once—within the space of a single minute, or even
less, shrunk—crumbled—absolutely *rotted* away beneath my hands.
Upon the bed, before that whole company, there lay a nearly liquid
mass of loathsome—of detestable putridity.''[52]

[50]*Blackwood's Edinburgh Magazine*, vol. 32, p. 283.

[51]*Graham's Magazine*, 1842, p. 200. The title of Poe's story *Life-in-Death*
was later changed to *The Oval Portrait*. The dropping of the title *Life-in-Death* and the taking of a more realistic one appears to be quite consistent
with Poe's idea of the power of realism as he attempted to work it out scientifically; see Chapter V below.

[52]*Works*, vol. 6, p. 154. George W. Eveleth writes to Poe that he believes
this condition, i.e., ''*the crumbling, rotting away into a loathsome liquid*,''
consistent with fact, and cites Bell's *Anatomy*, p. 245, as his authority. Mabbott, Thomas Ollive, *The Letters from George W. Eveleth to Edgar Allan Poe*,
p. 12. Poe may have known of the work of which Eveleth speaks, since, as
Mr. Mabbott says, it was a work often reprinted. Moreover, another treatise,
also by Bell, *Essays on the Anatomy of Expression in Painting*, reviewed in
the *Edinburgh Review*, vol. 8, p. 365, may have attracted Poe to the subject;
but the Blackwood case I have cited may doubtless be judged the most likely

Premature burial, as Poe treats it, appears likewise to follow *Blackwood's* development of the *Life-in-Death* theme. In his article entitled "Premature Burial"[53] he agrees with the author of "Hints for Jurymen" that the subject they have chosen lies in a legitimate sphere for fiction. He says:

"To be buried alive, is beyond question, the most terrific of these extremes which has ever fallen to the lot of mere mortality. That it has frequently, very frequently, so fallen will scarcely be denied by those who think. The boundaries which divide Life from Death are at least shadowy and vague. Who can say where the one ends and the other begins? We know that there are diseases in which occur total cessations of all the apparent functions of vitality, and yet in which these cessations are merely suspensions, properly so called. They are only temporary pauses in the incomprehensible mechanism."

The *Life-in-Death* theme in Poe's stories is an essential part of the plot; sometimes it occurs as suspended animation, sometimes as premature burial, and again, as a combination of the two. Poe seems to have used it as a foundation upon which to build a more extensive story, weaving around the horrors of the theme almost equally great attending horrors until the effect was one of overwhelming terror. For example, in "Berenice,"[54] the horror of the cataleptic trance and premature burial are intensified and more fully developed by the peculiar disease to which the character Egaeus was a victim. This disease, a sort of monomania, which consisted in a mad desire to stare at Berenice's teeth, and, after her trance and interment, to obtain them, adds a gruesomeness to the already gruesome and horrible theme. As can be seen, neither *Blackwood* nor Poe has depended in the least on the supernatural for the effect of horror from the *Life-in-Death* theme. Coleridge, on the contrary, though he, too, is dealing with life-in-death, presents the theme from the supernatural standpoint. Leigh Hunt is of the opinion that the most appalling personage in the "Ancient Mariner" is the Spectre Woman who is called Life-in-Death. He explains this awful character, however, as Death-in-Life, and there

---

source, since the passage from Bell's *Anatomy*, as Eveleth quotes it, gives only a slight general statement, while *Hints for Jurymen* enumerates, quite in Poe's manner, a list of loathsome details.

[53] In the text of his story, Poe gives the *Chirurgical Journal of Leipsic* as his source for the cases he cites. Palmer Cobb doubts that Poe ever saw this magazine. *Op.cit.*, p. 28.

[54] *S. L. M.*, vol. 1, p. 333.

seems to be a diminution in the effect of terror. He says, in his *Indicator:*

"He, (Coleridge) renders the most *hideous abstraction* more terrible than it could have otherwise been by embodying it in its own reverse. Death not only lives in it; but the unuttered becomes uttered."

In the same way, re-animation as Coleridge gives it in the "Ancient Mariner," implies a supernatural element, and, in spite of what Leigh Hunt considers its power to terrorize, it does not appear to equal in power of producing horror the power of *Blackwood's* more realistic method. Leigh Hunt, himself, though he speaks in favor of Coleridge's development of re-animation, yet testifies to the power of re-animation to terrorize when by a galvanic battery a dead body is made to undergo contortions. In the main, however, he considers the supernatural element necessary for the production of terror. He says in his article "How to Write a Grim Story":

"A ghost-story, to be a good one, should unite as much as possible objects such as they are in life with a praeternatural spirit. And to be a perfect one,—it should *imply some great moral sentiment,* something that comes out of the next world to remind us of our duties in this; or something that helps to carry on the idea of our humanity into after life, even when we least think we shall take it with us."[55]

It seems reasonable to think, therefore, that *Blackwood,* rather than Coleridge or Leigh Hunt, suggested the realistic method that Poe adopted for working out this theme. It is necessary to add, however, that Poe's "MS. Found in a Bottle" appears to embody somewhat Coleridge's method, and therefore does not seem to be dependent on *Blackwood,* as does the realism of the life-in-death theme in the other tales.

A second theme that Poe and *Blackwood* have in common is the galvanic battery associated with the knife of the anatomist. A discussion on the subject in *Blackwood* gives several cases where they have been used as efforts to resuscitate a supposed corpse. "Philippe Peu," says this article, "relates himself the case of a woman . . . where the first incision betrayed the awful fallacy under which he operated." And the same article adds:

"With respect to the instance of Vesalius we would make the general observation, which will probably apply to most of the cases on record; that the movements which have been observed on such

---

[55]The *Indicator,* December 15, 1819. Leigh Hunt, "How to Write a Grim Story."

occasions are not to be received as demonstrations of life, they merely arise from a degree of muscular irritability which often lingers for many hours after dissolution, and which, on its apparent cessation, may be even re-excited by the application of galvanic stimuli.''[56]

Among the stories in *Blackwood* that develop this theme are "Buried Alive," "Diary of a Late Physician," and "Le Revenant," all of which have a strongly realistic tone; for example, consider the following from "Buried Alive":

"Presently I felt the hands of some dreadful being working about my throat. They dragged me out of the coffin. . . .

"Previous to beginning the dissection, he proposed to try on me some galvanic experiment—and an apparatus was arranged for that purpose. The first shock vibrated through all my nerves; they rung and jangled like the strings of a harp. The students expressed their admiration of the convulsive effect. The second threw my eyes open, . . . But still I was as dead."

A third theme in which both the writers in *Blackwood* and Poe concur, is the coupling of beauty with disease; the viewing of the horrors, often the repulsive forms of diseased conditions, as they work to the final destruction of some beautiful young woman. It may not be too much to say that from passages from "The Diary of a Late Physician," in which *Blackwood* exploits this idea, Poe caught the suggestion which led him to choose as "the most poetic topic in the world," the death of a beautiful woman. In order to show that Poe was indebted to writers in *Blackwood* for this theme on which he built the dread disease and beauty of his Berenice, Ligeia, Madeline, Eleanora, it may be well to add to what has already been noted in regard to the fascination for the reading public which lies in a physician's records detailing diseased conditions.

Poe doubtless knew[57] that the series created a sensation among London readers, since the articles are prefaced by remarks which

---

[56]*Blackwood's Edinburgh Magazine*, vol. 13, p. 679. *Hints for Jurymen.*

[57]Poe's knowledge of this series of articles is testified to not only by his reference to the series in his *How to Write a Blackwood Article*, and the similarities between them and his work already alluded to, but also by the fact that he mentions them in several reviews. In one instance he says they were "shamefully ill-written". Review of "Ten Thousand a Year" by the Author of "Passages from the Diary of a Late Physician," *Graham's Magazine*, vol. 18, page 252. In another instance he considers that there is strong evidence in the series of a straining for effect and that this blemish disfigures what would otherwise have been admirable. *S. L. M.*, vol. 2, p. 287. Review of *Georgia Scenes.*

show that they touched a chord of interest. He announces that, in his opinion also, "Passages from the Diary of a Late Physician" holds fascinating material. Dr. Warren, he says, in choosing bodily health as the basis of his series of articles, has touched on a topic which comes home to the bosoms of all humanity; that he has, in fact, opened up a vein of universal interest.

In the second place, Poe apparently sees that if the element of beauty is added to the details of the diseased conditions, a greater fascination will result.[58] Both *Blackwood* and Poe appear to be striving to produce a morbid pleasure through analyzing the effects that disease has worked on the beautiful woman before them. Dr. Warren tells of his visits to a young woman of rare physical beauty who is stricken with the dread disease of cancer. The physician notes details of her condition, apparently with an almost morbid pleasure. He says himself that "the interviews were long and painfully interesting."

"I (the physician) found her, one morning, stretched on the crimson sofa in the drawing room; and though her pallid features, and gently corrugated eye-brows, evidenced the intense agony she was suffering,—on my enquiring what sort of night she had passed, she replied in a calm but tremulous tone, ... her pale features irradiated with a smile—sad, however, as the cold twilight of October. . . . Her hair was light auburn, and hung back neglectfully over a forehead and neck white as marble. Her full blue eyes . . . were now lighted with the glitter of a restlessness and agitation, ... Indeed, an eminent medical writer has re-

---

[58]Poe may have caught added suggestions for coupling beauty with disease, or, as he expresses the same idea elsewhere, for the conviction that the "imagination is exalted by the moral sentiment of beauty heightened in dissolution," from Archibald Alison's *Essays on the Nature and Principles of Taste*, Edinburgh, 1825, vol. 1, pp. 16 and 17. (Alison was reviewed in *Blackwood*, vol. 13, p. 385; vol. 45, p. 142; vol. 25, p. 542; vol. 27, p. 819; vol. 30, p. 94.) Alison makes the point that "the beauty of autumn is accompanied by . . . appearances of decay;" appearances leading "to the solemn imagination of that . . . fate which is to bring on . . . the decay of life."

Quite as probable a source, may be Edmund Burke's *A Philosophical Enquiry into the Origin of our Ideas on the Sublime and Beautiful*, London, 1798, p. 204. Burke is here of the opinion that a beautiful woman in distress has "much the more affecting beauty."

Prof. Prescott has already noted that Poe may have been influenced by A. W. von Schlegel's "Several inquiries . . . have placed the essence of the northern poetry in melancholy." *Selections from the Critical Writings of Edgar Allan Poe* by F. C. Prescott, New York, 1909, p. 327.

marked that the most beautiful women are generally the subjects of this terrible disease.''

Again, in ''Thunder Struck'' from the same series of articles, Dr. Warren notes the fascinating effect resulting from coupling beauty with disease. In this case the disease is catalepsy and the physician is now concerned with the changes that this fatal affliction has worked. The face that was, but a short time ago, of such rare beauty, now presents a fearful spectacle. You feel the artistic effect as you read the record of this interview:

''As it was now nearly nine o'clock, and getting dark, I ordered candles . . . . 'Beautiful, unfortunate creature!' thought I, as I stood gazing mournfully on her, with my candle in my hand, leaning against the bed-post. 'What mystery is upon thee? What awful change has come over thee?—the gloom of the grave and the light of life—both lying upon thee at once!' ''

And elsewhere in the story:

''Heavens! can I describe what I saw! Within less than a yard of me stood the most fearful figure my eyes have ever beheld. It was Agnes!—with both arms extended, as if in a menacing mood. Her hair was partially dishevelled. Her face seemed whiter than the white dress she wore. Her lips were of a livid hue. Her eyes, full of awful expression—of supernatural lustre, were fixed with a petrifying stare, on me. Oh, language fails me—utterly!—Those eyes have never since been absent from me when alone! I felt as though they were blighting the life within me . . . .''

Various other reports from the physician's diary are equally detailed. In ''The Scholar's Death-bed'' the disease is consumption, and there the analysis of the disease and its symptoms is so carefully made that the effect is one of morbid terror.

Poe, as well as the physician, seems to be attempting to produce a morbid pleasure by analyzing with much care the changes that disease is working in the beautiful woman. The beauty of the surroundings he also stresses. He sees Berenice, stricken as she was by the fatal disease ''not as a thing to admire, but to analyze; not as an object of love, but as the theme of the most abstruse although desultory speculation . . . .'' ''But uplifting my eyes, Berenice stood before me. . . .

''I remained for some time breathless, and motionless, with my eyes riveted upon her person. Alas! its emaciation was excessive, and not one vestige of the former being lurked in any single line of the contour. My burning glances at length fell upon the face.

''The forehead was high, and very pale, and singularly placid;

and the once golden hair fell partially over it, and overshadowed the hollow temples with ringlets.''[59]

And from ''Ligeia'': ''The wild eyes blazed with a too—too glorious effulgence; the pale fingers became of the transparent waxen hue of the grave; and the blue veins upon the lofty forehead swelled and sank impetuously with the tides of the most gentle emotion. I saw that she must die, and I struggled desperately in spirit with the grim Azrael.''[60]

Poe appears to be following Dr. Warren not only in the similarities just noted, but in his critical explanations in ''The Philosophy of Composition,'' to the effect that he has designedly chosen the death of a beautiful woman as the topic that will be of universal interest to humanity. He explains the idea in the following way:

''Now never losing sight of the object, *supremeness*, or perfection, at all points, I asked myself—'Of all melancholy topics, what, according to the *universal* understanding of mankind, is the most melancholy?' Death—was the obvious reply. 'And when,' I said, 'is this most melancholy of topics most poetical?' From what I have already explained at some length, the answer, here also is obvious—'When it most closely allies itself to *Beauty:* the death, then, of a beautiful woman is, unquestionably, the most poetical topic in the world. . . .''[61]

In a further consideration of Poe's dependence on *Blackwood* in subject-matter, a similarity of several of Poe's plots with those in *Blackwood* may be noted. In one case a *Blackwood* story furnishes part of a plot. Comparing Poe's ''Fall of the House of Usher'' with the story ''Thunder Struck'' in ''Passages from the Diary of a Late Physician,'' one finds many points in the two that are almost identical. One notices—

(1)   Identity in theme:

A beautiful young woman falls into a cataleptic trance.

(2)   Identity in plot:

Granting that the idea of the gloomy house of Usher is the symbol of the family being destroyed with the destruction of the surviving members,—granting that this idea does not appear in ''Thunder-Struck,'' and that these points do appear in Hoffmann's ''Das Marjorat,'' as Palmer Cobb has pointed out, the outline of the incidents

---

[59]*S. L. M.*, vol. 1, p. 333. *Berenice.*
[60]*American Museum*, vol. 1, p. 25.
[61]*Works*, vol. 14, p. 201. *The Philosophy of Composition.*

that develop the theme may be seen to be identical in both, *e.g.*—

  (a)   The action takes place in a storm.

  (b)   Detailed analysis of the disease is made in both cases.

  (c)   Both Lady Madeline and Agnes P— are placed in coffins. (This point is applied to the latter only in the dream that the physician has.)

  (d)   An apprehensive waiting for sound.

  (e)   The listener could not sleep—he leaps out of bed.

  (f)   A wild shriek is heard. (In *Blackwood* this was suggested.)

  (g)   A faint knock at the door.

  (h)   A death-like figure comes to life and, in Usher, appears at the door, and in *Blackwood* sits up in bed, presenting, however, in each case a horrible spectacle covered with blood.

The plot of Poe's "Pit and the Pendulum" appears to be gathered from several *Blackwood* stories. "The Iron Shroud," published in the twenty-eighth volume of *Blackwood,* details the horrors of a dungeon; the iron walls and ceiling of which, working by secret machinery, day by day close closer upon their victim.[62] The *Blackwood* material reads thus:

[The dungeon] "had the semblance of a vast cage, for the roof, and floor, and sides, were of iron, solidly wrought, and spaciously constructed. High above there ran a range of seven grated windows, guarded with massy bars of the same metal . . . . he surveyed his gloomy dungeon . . . . he noticed two circumstances . . . . The other circumstance which has attracted his notice, was the disappearance, as he believed, of one of the seven grated windows that ran along the top of the prison. . . . The remaining four windows looked as the seven had originally looked; that is, occupying at irregular distances, the top of the wall on that

---

[62]*Blackwood's Edinburgh Magazine,* vol. 28, p. 364. *The Iron Shroud,* by the author of *First and Last.* The story is signed M., and is by Mudford. Mudford's stories seemed well known to American readers of Poe's time. The *New York Mirror* says in noticing *Sharpe's London Magazine:* "There is also a tolerable article by Mudford, though somewhat coarse, as is usual with him, entitled 'Confessions of a Suicide'." *New York Mirror,* vol. 10, p. 299, 1832. Prof. Campbell has already pointed out that Griswold found the original of "The Pit and the Pendulum" to be "a tale in *Blackwood's,*" but he does not specify the tale.—*Nation,* vol. 90, p. 625.

side of the dungeon. The tall folding door, too, still seemed to stand beneath, in the center of those four, as it had at first stood in the center of the seven. But he could no longer doubt, what, on the preceding day, he fancied might be the effect of visual deception. The dungeon *was* smaller. The roof had lowered—and the opposite ends had contracted the intermediate distance by a space equal, he thought, to that over which the three windows had extended. . . . Some frightful purpose—some devilish torture of mind or body—some unheard of device for producing exquisite misery, lurked, he was sure, in what had taken place. . . . Another morning dawned upon the wretched captive, and the fatal index of his doom met his eyes. Two windows!—and *two* days— and all would be over! . . ."

"The Man in the Bell" details the sweeping from side to side of the ponderous bell within an inch of the face of the helpless victim. "Every moment I saw the bell sweep within an inch of my face;" . . . "To look at the object," he said, "was bitter as death"; but he could not prevent his eyes from following it instinctively as it swung. "The bell pealing above and opening its jaws with a hideous clamour," seemed at one time "a ravening monster raging to devour" him:—"In the vast cavern of the bell hideous faces appeared, and glared down on me with terrifying frowns, or with grinning mockery, still more appalling. At last the devil himself, accoutred, as in the common description of the evil spirit, with hoof, horn, and tail, and eyes of infernal lustre, made his appearance, ..."

Poe's story, "The Pit and the Pendulum," seems to embody points from both of the tales quoted above.—

"The vibration of the pendulum was at right angles to my length. To the right—to the left—far and wide—with a shriek of a damned spirit! to my heart, with the stealthy pace of the tiger!—I rolled my eyes nervously around on the barriers of iron that hemmed me in. Something unusual—some change which at first I could not appreciate distinctly—it was obvious, had taken place in the apartment. . . . although the outlines of the figures upon the walls were sufficiently distinct, yet the colors seemed blurred and indefinite. These colors had now assumed, and were momentarily assuming, a startling and most intense brilliancy, that gave to the spectral and fiendish portraitures an aspect that might have thrilled even firmer nerves than my own. Demon eyes of a wild and ghostly vivacity glared upon me in a thousand directions, where none had been visible before, and gleamed with the lurid lustre of a fire that I could not force my imagination to regard as unreal. . . . There had been a second change in the cell, and now the change was obviously in the form. As before, it was in vain that I at first endeavored to appreciate or understand what was taking place. But not long was I left in doubt. . . . The room had been square. I saw that two of its iron angles were not acute—two, consequently, obtuse. The fearful difference quickly increased with a low rumbling or moaning sound. In an instant the apartment had shifted its form into that of a lozenge and now flatter and flatter grew the lozenge with a rapidity that left me no time for contemplation—the closing walls pressed resistlessly onward.''

A suggestion for part of the plot of ''The Raven'' likewise seems to come from *Blackwood's Edinburgh Magazine.* Poe gave, according to the poem, his raven the eyes of a demon and made the ill-omened visitor, arriving in a storm at midnight, symbolize remorseless destiny. Moreover, it is known that he connected his raven with witches. Dr. Mathews, it seems, was discussing with Poe a play he had just written called ''Witch Craft,'' and Poe suggested to him the introduction of the raven flitting over the witch's head.[63] ''I seem to hear,'' Poe said during the conversation with Dr. Mathews, ''the melancholy of its croak as I used to hear it in my boyhood days at school in Stokenewington; I seem to hear the sordid flap of its wings in my ears.''

Poe's ''Raven,'' associated in his mind as we have seen with witch-craft, seems to echo the raven of a critical review in *Blackwood* of ''The Witch of Edmonton.'' The raven in the English review alights in a storm at midnight with the croak of a demon. And the reviewer says that the bird of ill-omen is no more distinct than are Shakespeare's witches. The review reads:

''Shakespeare's witches are in a class by themselves. They are neither sorceresses nor old women . . . Shakespeare has created our witches for us, . . . Neither their characters nor their forms are distinct, . . . No more does one see distinctly the raven that alights near his feet during some stormy midnight, and on some wild moor—with *sughing* wings and the croak of a demon.''[64]

What points in literary technique, as well as in subject-matter, did Poe learn from *Blackwood?* Barine, the French critic, is of the opinion, it will be remembered, that Poe owes at least a portion

---

[63]The information for this latter point is from an account published in the *Minneapolis Sunday Journal*, July 10, 1921, copied from a New York paper. Frances Aymar Mathews, niece of Dr. Cornelius Mathews, Journalist, sent to the New York University Archives, it seems, the story as told by her uncle of how Poe wrote *The Raven*.

[64]*Blackwood's Edinburgh Magazine,* vol. 6, p. 410. Review of *The Witch of Edmonton.*

of his technique to *"des romantiques allemands,"* and to Hoffmann in particular.[65]   Professor Gruener likewise considers Poe indebted to Hoffman for stylistic suggestions.[66]   Palmer Cobb, it will also be remembered, denies Poe's dependence on Hoffmann and other German story writers on any ground except the borrowing of subject-matter.[67]   I shall try to show, however, first, that Poe followed *Blackwood* tale writers as they applied critical opinions to their work, mainly those of A. W. von Schlegel; secondly, that Poe, on his own part, drew Schlegelian criticism from *Blackwood*; thirdly, that he derived the idea from *Blackwood* that the detailing of sensations arising from experience produces effective writing; fourthly, that the method of the sensation story among *Blackwood* writers, in all probability suggested to him a psychologic search for a further comprehension of the principle involved. In a later chapter I shall try to point out that he found a basis for effect proceeding from sensations in a study of Locke's psychology.

In order to demonstrate the first of the above points, namely, that Poe followed *Blackwood* tale writers as they were influenced by A. W. von Schlegel's critical opinions, it will be necessary to attempt to say to what extent Schlegel was known in Blackwood's magazine. According to Mrs. Oliphant, the author of "William Blackwood and his Sons," Lockhart was largely responsible for bringing German criticism to *Blackwood*.[68] Lockhart went to Germany, it appears, to complete his knowledge of the German language and literature, Mr. Blackwood furnishing the funds for the journey. In return payment, Lockhart translated Frederick Schlegel's "Lectures on the History of Literature."[69] A. W. von Schlegel was also known to Lockhart. An attack on British reviewers, intended chiefly it seems to arraign the method of Jeffrey of the *Edinburgh*, appeared in *Blackwood*[70] and was at first attributed to A. W. von Schlegel. Baron von Lauerwinkel, described as a famous German critic and a friend of Schlegel's, was afterwards

---

[65]Cf. note 28.

[66]*Publications of Modern Language Association*, vol. 19, p. 24. *Notes on the Influence of E. T. A. Hoffmann upon Edgar Allan Poe*, by Gustav Gruener.

[67]Cf. note 28.

[68]Oliphant, *op.cit.*, vol. 1, p. 184.

[69]A long review of Frederick Schlegel's *Lectures on the History of Literature, Ancient and Modern*, with copious extracts, appears in *Blackwood's Edinburgh Magazine*, vol. 3, p. 497.

[70]*Ibid.*, vol. 2, p. 670. *Remarks on the Periodical Criticism of England*.

credited with the piece; but Lockhart himself was finally, according to Mrs. Oliphant,[71] known to have been the author. A. W. von Schlegel was also known to Scott, since Scott in his "Essay on the Drama," had greatly depended on Schlegel's lectures on *Dramatic Art and Literature*.[72] Scott took an active interest in *Blackwood* and contributed to the magazine.[73]

In fact, indications point to Schlegel's being well known to *Blackwood* critics.[74] The following passages may be said to represent the general trend of English opinion concerning the German writer:

"They [the Schlegels] are the first aesthetic writers of our age; and they are in that comprehensive passionate sympathy with *everything* that is noble in antiquity, and *everything* that is beautiful in art—in all that marks them out as the genuine, universal, and unbigoted lovers of excellence—in the whole breadth and beauty of their theory."[75]

Again, another critic refers to A. W. von Schlegel as being, with his brother, the head of the literary sect in Germany known as the "Romantic";[76] and, in terms equally complimentary, another writer refers to him thus, showing his deference for his critical opinion:[77] " 'La Devocian de la Cruz' is not exactly the tragedy

[71]Mrs. Oliphant suggests that Carlyle may have derived his idea of Teufelsdrockh from Lauerwinkel, one of Lockhart's "apocryphal German Professors." *Op.cit.*, p. 195. Lauerwinkel's name frequently appears in the early numbers of *Blackwood*. One of his articles, *Remarks on the Poetry of Moore*, is found in vol. 4, p. 1. *Letters to Professor Laugner* from Lauerwinkel was printed in vol. 3, p. 689.

[72]Scott's *Essay on the Drama* appeared in the fourth through the eighth editions of the *Encyclopedia Britannica*, 8 ed., pp. 133-169. The following note appended to a long article entitled *On the Dramatic Powers of the Author of Waverly*, (*Blackwood*, vol. 19, p. 158), indicates how welcome Schlegelian criticism must have been to *Blackwood* critics: "I must beg to say, that Mr. North would confer a very great obligation on his readers, if he would insert in one of his Numbers, the latter part of Sir Walter Scott's brief but admirable Essay on the Drama, contained in the Supplement to the Encyclopedia Britannica."

[73]Oliphant, *op.cit.*, vol. 1, p. 156.

[74]*Blackwood* was by no means the only periodical feeling the influence of Schlegel. The *Edinburgh Review* had in vol. 26, published a long review by Hazlitt entitled *Schlegel on the Drama*. The *Quarterly Review* also has many references to Schlegel.

[75]*Blackwood's Edinburgh Magazine*, vol. 15, p. 620.

[76]*Ibid.*, vol. 17, p. 674.

[77]*Ibid.*, vol. 18, p. 83.

of Calderon's which our own unassisted taste might have selected, but it is one generally ranked among his best works. The highly-esteemed German critic, A. W. von Schlegel, has thought it deserving of the dedication of his time and talents to translating it into his own language." Another *Blackwood* critic, signing himself H. M., and writing on the "Early English Dramatists," also expresses the same feeling. He is referring to a criticism in the *Edinburgh Review* which, he says, displays on the part of the critic "all the philosophical eloquence of a Schlegel."[78] Other *Blackwood* reviewers, however, deplore what they term Schlegel's philosophical criticism. There are not always, one asserts, "deep predisposing causes for everything that occurs in the history of literature, and of all cants, the cant of philosophical criticism is the most contemptible. The Schlegels are the most critical canters of modern Europe. They account for everything."[79] Another reviewer maintains, likewise, in a contemptuous tone, that no matter what blunder may have been committed by an author, "Two or three hundred years hence, no question, some new Dr. William Augustus Schlegel will arise to justify them all in a course of lectures."[80]

Schlegel's principle of effect comes into *Blackwood*. Critics in the English magazine begin to take into account not only the idea of an effect or impression that a reader or spectator will feel from the printed page or the acted drama; they appear also to recognize a conscious method on the part of a writer to produce that impression.[81] Dramatic critics, in fact, make effect the standard of ex-

---

[78]*Ibid.*, vol. 2, p. 30. Cf. also vol. 30, p. 360.

[79]*Ibid.*, vol. 10, p. 731. Review of *Lyndsay's Dramas of the Ancient World.*

[80]*Ibid.*, vol. 13, p. 541. *Remarks on Mr. Barry Cornwall's New Poems.* There are also, dotted here and there, chance references showing how familiar a figure A. W. von Schlegel was in *Blackwood's Magazine*, e.g. "Madame de Stael's 'Germany' is in every hand; and Professor Schlegel's *Lectures on Dramatic Literature* are at least in many." *Blackwood*, vol. 14, p. 381. A passage that has apparently no particular reference, occurs in the *Noctes Ambrosianae*, No. IV. *Ibid.*, vol. 12, p. 108: "Odoherty: 'Would your lordship [Byron] wish to hear a Sanscrit ode I wrote to A. W. Schlegel?'"

[81]Schlegel had expressed very much the same idea: "The object proposed [the object of the drama] is to produce an impression on an assembled multitude, to rivet their attention, and to excite their interest and sympathy." Schlegel, Augustus Wilhelm. Bohn Ed., London, 1894, Black's translation. *Lectures on Dramatic Art and Literature*, p. 37. Schlegel carries the idea of effect throughout his volume.

cellence for a play. Certain reviewers speak with enthusiasm, in
a series of articles entitled the ''Acted Drama in London,'' of what
Schlegel calls ''stage effect,'' which apparently has the meaning
of some strong excitement, extraneous to the main thread of the
piece.[82] Miss Tree, in ''The Maid of the Mill,'' says the *Blackwood*
critic, introduces Moore's ballad of *Young Love,* and he is of the
opinion that he has never before heard it given with a more ''de-
licious effect.''[83] Mr. Kemble, according to the *Blackwood* reviewer, played the first scenes of ''Fazio'' with considerable spirit
and effect.[84] Another series of articles, entitled ''Modern British
Drama,'' discusses the same principle. The actress in ''The Fatal
Unction'' gives the mad scene, the critic says, with ''distracting
effect.''[85] And in still another instance a reviewer speaks in high
praise of the ''electrical effects of sympathy in the theatre.''[86]
Other dramatic critics deplore attempting to produce an impression by stage-effect alone; they contend that a drama is telling
in its effect only when the main idea of the piece is forced upon
the mind of the spectator from every part working together for
that end. One reviewer, in the series on the acted drama, considers that although Marlowe in ''The Jew of Malta'' may not have
given the variety of character and the moral purpose he did in his
''Edward II'' and in ''Faustus,'' yet he was able to engender and
sustain the same kind of effect throughout the piece. He also
states it to be his opinion that the oneness of effect he mentions is
due to ''that rare, and when judiciously applied, most important
quality, which we have called dramatic unity, . . .''[87] Another reviewer in discussing the drama ''Virginius,'' speaks of
the high state of interest produced on the spectator by all ''collateral circumstances'' of the play being so arranged as to ''bring
out and heighten the interest excited by the principal event.''[88]

---

[82]A. W. von Schlegel, *op.cit.,* p. 41.

[83]*Blackwood's Edinburgh Magazine,* vol. 6, p. 54. *Acted Drama in London.*

[84]*Ibid.,* vol. 2, p. 669.

[85]*Ibid.,* vol. 10, p. 60. *Modern British Drama.*

[86]*Ibid.,* vol. 1, p. 516. Review of *Modern Greece,* by Mrs. Hemans. Other
instances of stage effect are found in vol. 6, p. 386, *Acted Drama in London;*
vol. 4, p. 718, *The Opera;* vol. 3, p. 208, *Acted Drama;* vol. 7, p. 183; vol. 2,
p. 660; vol. 1, p. 392; vol. 4, p. 68.

[87]*Ibid.,* vol. 3, p. 209. *Acted Drama in London.*

[88]*Ibid.,* vol. 7, p. 308.

Still another critic warns against "writing carelessly forward."
Effect will not result, he contends, unless consistency is kept from
beginning to end:

"Shakespeare, certainly, . . . did not upon principle, always
take the easiest path to effect; and the consequence is, that there is
almost the same difference between his plays and those of his con-
temporaries, as there is between the poem "Don Juan" and the
novels of the Author of "Waverley," whose most singular attribute perhaps is, that he constantly contrives interest."[89]

Critics of the written drama, of poetry, and of the novel likewise,
judge of excellence in proportion to the effect or impression produced on the mind of a reader. In an article from a series entitled
"Horae Germanicae,"[90] one writer maintains that the faculty required for producing an effective novel or play is one of rare oc-
currence. It requires, he says, a "cool, cautious, artificial mood
of mind, akin to that of the mathematician or the algebraist." In
another article the critic considers in the piece that he is reviewing,[91] that the author has excelled in forcing horror into the reader's perceptions by weaving into a chain every direful incident, the
effect of which forms a spell that one can not escape. And the
inevitableness of this effect was ascribed, not to destiny alone, but
to other "principles which carry along with them all the force of
reason and conviction."

Not only was Schlegel's principle of effect known in *Blackwood*,
but English tale writers appear to be influenced by Schlegel's
criticism. An examination of literary reviews appearing in *Blackwood* through the first thirty-five volumes, reveals several points,
indicating it would seem, that the authors of "Buried Alive," "The
Involuntary Experimentalist," "The Man in the Bell," and of
other sensational stories, constructed their tales with effect in mind;
in other words, that they wrote "not carelessly forward," but with
a conscious intent to impress. In presenting these ideas, the following points may be seen: first, that a growth in the English
critic's appreciation of effect is plainly visible; second, that the
period when effect became an accepted principle marked too the
period when the sensation story was in greatest vogue in *Blackwood*.

Critics in the early reviews are silent on the question of effect.

[89]*Ibid.*, vol. 14, p. 560.
[90]*Ibid.*, vol. 21, p. 214. *Horae Germanicae*, No. XXII.
[91]*Ibid.*, vol. 21, p. 465. Werner's *Twenty-fourth of February*.

They evidently do not think of an author's writing with the intention of producing conviction in his readers' minds. Although they sometimes use the term effect, they appear to give it a loose, or indefinite meaning; occasionally they seem only to be quoting criticism, not applying it. Reviews of "Lalla Rookh" in volume I illustrate this point.[92] Passages in the same volume from a series of articles on Greek tragedy show the same critical spirit.[93] But it seems that from the third volume to about the thirteenth or fourteenth, many critics begin to take the principle into consideration. Some openly oppose effect in general; others lay an emphasis on stage effect alone; and still others take part in a controversy over the relative merits of a conscious method of criticism as against an uncritical attitude. One reviewer, in volume fourteen, opposes the whole idea of effect:

"To artists, the 'metaphysic' has been a down right Will-o'-the-wisp. . . . It has led them only into bogs. . . . The single word 'classical' has destroyed its thousands and ten thousands. How many acres of canvass have been barbarously ruined by 'effect!' How many poets have broken their backs in straining after 'dignity' and the 'heroic, according to Aristotle!' If Parliament were to pass a law to cause these terms to be proscribed and forgotten, . . . it would be a public benefit."[94]

Another reviewer in volume three, obviously hesitates between a conscious recognition of rules in criticism and a mere critical opinion, and seems, in that respect, to be in doubt as to the advantages of a writer's conscious intent to impress.—

"We have seen Mr. Elliston in the Duke Aranza, and in Archer.

---

[92]*Ibid.*, vol. 1, p. 509; vol. 1, p. 505. Vol. 1, p. 383. Review of *Fragment of a Literary Romance*.

[93]*Ibid.*, vol. 1, p. 40; vol. 1, p. 593.

[94]*Ibid.*, vol. 14, p. 249. *On the Sources of the Picturesque and Beautiful.* The passage refers to Aristotle. *Blackwood* critics may have had a first-hand knowledge of Aristotelian criticism. North refers to Pope's and Twining's translation of the *Poetica*. *Ibid.*, vol. 31, p. 156. Review of Sotheby's Homer. Other references to Aristotle are: vol. 13, p. 539; vol. 19, p. 220; vol. 20, p. 559; vol. 24, p. 885. Vol. 18, p. 238: "Banim has the power of managing his story very well. In his first tale, Crohoore of the Bill-book, it is impossible to anticipate the event; and yet when known, it is seen that the whole progress of the story tended to it. This in novel-writing is a great merit. We have the authority of Aristotle; and though Mr. Dugald Stewart and other learned people undervalue him, I should take his word in these matters for a thousand pounds—that the invention and ordering of incident is a higher and rarer power than even the delineation of character."

We were so much accustomed to receive unmixed pleasure from this gentleman's acting, before we were either capable or desirous of judging of its merits, [In the beginning of the article the writer calls himself no critic], that we are quite unable to think or even talk critically about it now. But we may yet be permitted to say that his return is truly delightful to us. It gives us back an image of the very springtime of our play going: a time that we thought nothing could have restored even the resemblance of. It is, indeed, *only* an image. . . . Criticism is a good thing enough in its way—but one hour of *that* time was worth a whole eternity of it. *Then,* what did we care how the magazines or newspapers thought or spoke of the last new play? What was it to us whether it was a good or a bad one? . . . It *was* a play—and that was enough for us. It made us happy—and what could we wish for more? . . . We have learned better since then; and we are heartily sorry for it. We have pryed into the arcana of nature and of art, and have paid dearly for our curiosity. We have acquired just skill enough to take the kaleidoscope to pieces, and find that its beautiful and ever-varying forms are composed of nothing but beads and bits of broken glass. But why should we complain? In learning to take the machine to pieces, we have also learned to put it together again: so that the delight we receive in looking through it is only changed in its kind,—not destroyed.''[95]

Instances of an emphasis on stage effect occur as we have seen, in vol. 3, p. 208; vol. 6, p. 386; vol. 4, p. 718; vol. 7, p. 183; vol. 4, p. 68.[96] After about the twelfth or thirteenth volume, as the term is used in the sense of dramatic unity, effect becomes an accepted principle. The volumes in which effect is thus treated are:

Volume 12, p. 35.
Volume 12, p. 39.
Volume 12, p. 78.
Volume 17, p. 728.
Volume 18, p. 119.
Volume 18, p. 238.
Volume 18, p. 240.
Volume 20, p. 559.
Volume 21, p. 214.
Volume 21, p. 465.

From the foregoing evidence it would seem to follow that the principle of effect had a gradual growth in the pages of *Blackwood.*

---

[95]*Ibid.*, vol. 3, p. 329. *Acted Drama in London.*

[96]Volumes 1 and 2 also contain references to stage effect, but the term is not used. Volume 2, p. 660.

It may now be observed that the period marking an interest in the sensation story coincides with the period when effect became a recognized part of a writer's method. From the list which I shall present, it will be seen that the sensation story does not appear in the early volumes of the magazine; that it does chiefly appear about the thirteenth volume:

Buried Alive, vol. 10.

Man in the Bell, vol. 10.

Confessions of An English Glutton, vol. 13.

Le Revenant, vol. 21.

First and Last Crime, vol. 25.

First and Last Sacrifice, vol. 26.

Diary of a Late Physician, vol. 28.

Involuntary Experimentalist, vol. 42.

In addition to what is apparently an unmistakable identity in time, there is, moreover, the fact that certain authors testify to their intention of creating an impression on the reader. Dr. Samuel Warren takes a great pleasure in knowing that his "The Man About Town" is exciting a sensation about the Clubs. He enumerates in a letter to William Blackwood the various effects the story is said to produce: "Horrible!" "ghastly," "frightful," he says are some of the expressions to which he has listened.[97]

Poe appears to have found in foreign magazines many suggestions both for theory and practice. During the course of his literary life, he formulated two statements of his method of effective writing. In 1842 he presented in his review of Hawthorne's "Twice-Told Tales" one of these statements. In 1846, in the "Philosophy of Composition," he further elaborates the explanation. He considers, he says, that an author should be able to point out step by step the processes by which any one of his compositions reached its completion. In fact, he asserts it to be his desire to have it thoroughly understood that no one part in any of his writings comes either from accident or from intuition; that (in this case he is speaking of the "Raven") the work proceeded step by step to its ending with "the precision and rigid consequence of a mathematical problem!" It will be interesting, therefore, at this point, the period of his early study, to attempt to say what English magazine writers suggested to him for his method as he later described it.

---

[97]Oliphant, *op.cit.,* vol. 2, p. 31.

Poe himself seems conscious of a connection between the method of the English writer of the sensation story and Schlegel's criticism as it was reflected by *Blackwood*. In favor of this supposition is, first, Poe's knowledge to which we have already referred, of the sensation stories, "Buried Alive," etc. Secondly, he knew the manner in which *Blackwood* critics discussed effect. We have already seen that he was familiar with the review of the "Devil's Elixir" and he could, therefore, have read the use that was made of the term. Hoffman, according to this review, owed the "unrivalled effect" which his work "as a whole produces on the imagination, to nothing so much as the admirable art" with which he has "married dreams to realities." It is then reasonable further to suppose that Poe would have known *effect* as we have noted it discussed throughout the magazine. Thirdly, he combines these two points just mentioned, in his statement that good examples of tales of effect were found in early numbers of *Blackwood*. Poe could likewise have observed the method of the *Blackwood* story writers. We have already seen that the type of terror dealing with the real experiences, as that type was analyzed in *Blackwood* criticism, appealed also to Poe. He could now have observed that *Blackwood* stories dealt, too, with a background of real experience. The physician in passages from the "Diary of a Late Physician," maintains that he has simply described what his eyes have witnessed.[98] The prisoner in "Le Revenant" asserts that he is "in a situation to speak from experience, upon that very interesting question—the sensations attendant upon a passage from life to death." He further assures the reader that one has little impression of the sadness of the reality of a criminal's last visits from his friends.[99]

He could have observed, too, that these real experiences were always those of terror. The *Blackwood* writer placed his character, usually a solitary figure, in some awful situation; he made him the victim in some terrible predicament. For example, the involuntary experimentalist, who it seems was a physician, finds himself, while attempting to be of help in a great fire in Dublin, trapped in a huge copper boiler which becomes like a fiery furnace. The "Man in the Bell" details the sensations of a man who, having

---

[98]*Blackwood's Edinburgh Magazine*, vol. 28, p. 921. *Passages from the Diary of a Late Physician: the Man About Town.*

[99]*Ibid.*, vol. 21, p. 409.

climbed up to a tiny loft to unmuffle the ponderous iron bell which
had been muffled for tolling at a burial, is caught under the bell
just as it is about to swing out from the sides of the small belfrey.
"It was a dreadful situation. Over me swung an immense mass of
metal, one touch of which could have crushed me to pieces." *Le
Revenant* tells of a miserable prisoner alone in his cell, who expects
to be hung in the morning. The "Iron Shroud" day by day closes
closer and closer on its unhappy victim.

Poe could doubtless have followed the *Blackwood* writer as he
described the growing sense of terror that overwhelms the unfortunate victim. In "Le Revenant" the steps of the increasing
horror can be definitely traced. "The shock of my first arrest was
very slight indeed; indeed, I almost question if it was not a relief,
rather than a shock, to me. . . . I do not believe I showed—
for I am sure I did not feel it—either surprise or alarm." In
the same dreamlike condition, the prisoner hears the charge of
guilty, and the Judge's voice saying that he should be hanged by
the neck until he was dead. The state of stupefaction, however,
gives way, later, to an insane fury. He jumped up and tore at his
iron bars with a force that bent them. Finally his terror became
so great that he sinks again into a benumbed condition, but in this
stupor his senses are keenly alive. Experience keeps on registering
sensations, and he notices the merest trifles as though they were
things of moment:

"I noticed the lamp which the turnkey had left on the floor, and
I thought to myself—even at that moment—that it had not been
trimmed since the night before. And I looked at the bare, naked,
iron bed-frame that I sat on; and at the heavy studs on the door
of the dungeon; and at the scrawls and writing upon the wall, that
had been drawn by former prisoners; and I put my hand to try my
own pulse, and it was so low that I could hardly count it:—I could
not feel—though I tried to make myself feel it—that I was going
to *die.*"

In "The Man in the Bell" the fears were first, as the sufferer
says, mere matters of fact:

"I was afraid the pulleys would give way, and let the bell plunge
on me. . . . but these soon gave way to fears not more un-
founded, but more visionary, and of course more tremendous."

Poe could also have been aware that the victim of the predicament
in the *Blackwood* stories records his sensations with a minuteness
of detail; that he appears to be desirous of relating his experience
with an almost scientific accuracy. We have already indicated the

morbid pleasures with which the physician in the "Diary of a Late Physician" seems to note the symptoms of his patient.[100] The same idea may now be viewed in the light of a technical method, as an effort to make the experience become again a real experience. The involuntary experimentalist who, it will also be remembered, belonged to the medical profession, even in the midst of his agony takes care to make records of his case:

"These tablets I have now before me; I have preserved them ever since, as a memorial to moments such as I trust have fallen to the lot of no other human being. I transfer the memoranda *verbatim*. It will be seen that many of the words are but half written, and that in some places entire words have been omitted; but if any one would try the experiment of writing in such a situation, I daresay his composition would be scarcely more correct. I began thus: 'I am Doctor ―――― of ―――― St. If anyone finds this, come to the copper in the new building, where I am burning to death for want of a ladder. Half-past 12 o'clock. Haste! Haste! (Two such memoranda as this I had already flung out by weights attached to my suspenders, but they seem to have fallen in the flames.) . . . I am wrapped in a cloud of steam from my wet clothes. The thermometer stands at 130°. It is now 26 minutes to 1 o'clock. The air is suffocatingly hot: I am drenched in perspiration. I will note all I can. 15 m. to 1 o'c. Therm. 137°. 13 m. 139°. 10 m. 153°! This is horrible. I can see the mercury mounting in the tube. The moisture from my clothes has all exhaled. They are now as dry as tinder, and hot and hard to the touch. 5 m. past 1 o'clock. Thermometer 170°. Have taken off both my coats and laid them over the hole—the rush of air from it agitated the hot atmos[phere] & made it intolerable.' "

In the tale *Le Revenant* the prisoner likewise makes a record of

―――――――――

[100]The *Edinburgh*, in various numbers, gives instances of diagnoses of diseased conditions which Poe may have resorted to for technical method. A review of the *Récherches et Expériences Médicales et Chimiques sur Diabéte Sucré*, by Nicholas and Guendeville, contains the critic's lament that specific facts are often lacking in a diagnosis. He says: "This rash mode of generalizing is too frequently adopted in medical inquiries. . . . It is worse than a false hypothesis, because it extends farther; and, by habituating the mind to mere terms, it may lead us to mistake new words for real knowledge." *Edinburgh Review*, vol. 3, p. 422. Another critical piece quotes a passage of some length from a work, *Traité du Goitre et du Crétinism*, by Fodéré, which presents the detailed method commented on by the former reviewer. *Edinburgh Review*, vol. 2, p. 169. A third article in the same periodical, again with the method under discussion, details observations on a surgical case, that relating to the growth and development of tumors. *Edinburgh Review*, vol. 5, p. 168.

his sensations, those arising from his present experience in his cell
and, as far as he can, those coming in anticipation from the death
he expects to die:—

"I sat down again on the bed, and tried seriously to commune
with myself, . . . : I recalled to my mind, that I had but a few
more [hours] to live. I tried to recollect all the tales I had ever
heard about death by hanging—that it was said to be the sensation
of a moment—to give no pain—to cause the extinction of life in-
stantaneously—and so on, to twenty other strange ideas. By de-
grees my head began to wander and grow unmanageable again. I
put my hands tightly to my throat, as though to try the sensation
of strangling. Then I felt my arms at the places where the cords
would be tied. I went through the fastening of the rope—the
tying of the hands together: The thing that I felt most averse to,
was the having the white cap muffled over my eyes and face. If
I could avoid that, the rest was not so very horrible!"

Poe finds in foreign periodicals further help for technique. He
gives it as his opinion that the proper length for a poem, stated in
figures, is about one hundred lines; stated in the time necessary
for perusual, about half an hour. Although there is no evidence
that from *Blackwood* he derived any philosophical basis for determining on the length given, a basis which it will be shown he
found both in the drama[101] and in a study of philosophy,[102] yet
the numerical limitations in the foreign magazines were doubtless
suggestive to him. A reviewer in *Blackwood* counsels poets to write
poems no longer than twenty to one hundred fifty lines. Most of
our living poets, he says, will be remembered after their death
either by their short poems or by particular passages from their
long ones. He thinks that Wordsworth has made a great mistake
in writing at the length he has.[103] Another writer discusses the
advantages of brevity in written and spoken language. He advises
limiting the length of a speech to something like forty minutes,
and he says that the most effective and accomplished orations are
always the briefest. He thinks that even the longest of the political speeches of Demosthenes were "spoken as they may now be
read, with sufficient slowness and distinctness, in less than one-half
hour."[104] The following bit from the "Noctes Ambrosianae,"
though given with the usual satire of the series, shows in all prob-

---

[101]Cf. Chapter III, Unity in the Drama and the Fine Arts.

[102]Cf. Chapter IV, Unity in Terms of Philosophy.

[103]*Blackwood's Edinburgh Magazine*, vol. 22, p. 376. Review of Moore's *The
Epicurean*.

[104]*Ibid.*, vol. 19, p. 582. *Prodigality of Words*, signed D.

ability that brevity in writing was a question for discussion with critics. The speaker is commenting on the Periodical Press:

Shepherd

". . . For my ain pairt, I never peruse what's ca'd the leadin' article in a newspaper—and to speak the truth, I'm gayen shy o' them in a magazine too—but I devoor the adverteesements, which beside lettin' you ken everything that's gaun on in a kintra respectin' the sellin' and nifferin' o' property, baith in hooses and lawns, are to my mind models o' composition, without ae single unnecessary word, for every word's pay'd for, and that gies the adverteeser a habit o' conceese thocht and expression, better than a Logic class.

Tickler

"Writing in Magazines, and speaking in Parliment, have an opposite effect—making the world wordy.

Shepherd

"An' preachin's warst of a' . . . .

North

"A sermon should never exceed twenty-five minutes."[105]

Evidence points strongly to the fact that from a British periodical Poe derived the idea that an epic may be considered a succession of brief poems. He maintains, in the "Philosophy of Composition," that the "Paradise Lost" is necessarily made up of short poetical effects, interspersed with parts essentially prose; he also announces it to be his belief that the *Iliad* was originally composed of a series of ballads. An article entitled the "Origin of the Homeric Poems," appearing in the *Quarterly Review* of 1831, advances the same theory.[106] The reviewer outlines three distinct points of view in which this collection may be placed; one of which is similar to that set forth by Poe.

Poe, on his own statement, admits that he expects (as did *Blackwood* critics, influenced as we have seen by Schlegel) to force an effect into the perception of his reader. The writer, he says in his review of Hawthorne,[107] chooses a unique or single effect which,

---

[105]*Ibid.*, vol. 22, p. 127. *Noctes Ambrosianae.* James Hogg was the Shepherd of the *Noctes;* and Robert Syme, the uncle of John Wilson, the North of the dialogues, was Timothy Tickler. (R. Shelton Mackenzie, *op.cit.*, vol. 1, p. xii.)

[106]*Quarterly Review*, vol. 44, p. 124.

[107]*Graham's Magazine*, 1842, vol. 20, p. 299.

when "wrought out," will leave its impress on the reader's mind. He obviously agrees with the criticism of the *Blackwood* reviewer and apparently with the practice of the English story writer that the best means by which this effect can be "wrought out" is by preserving consistency of tone and incident. The *Blackwood* critic had said, it will be remembered, ". . . every agonizing mood of mind, every direful incident, is forced on the reader's perception with all the vividness of reality, forming a spell from which he cannot escape." And the inevitableness of this effect was ascribed, it will also be remembered, not to destiny alone, but to other "principles which carry along with them all the force of reason and conviction." Such a passage, and others of a kindred nature, may have been in Poe's mind when he advised the inventing of just such incidents and the combining of just those events; the writing of just such words; and moreover, the combinations of just that tone which would aid in producing the effect he had chosen.[108]

It will now be seen that Poe, as well as the *Blackwood* writer, bases his method on experience. In Poe, especially in his early work, one meets again the solitary figure in some horrible situation; the growing terror; and the same method of analyzing and detailing with precision the flood of sensations that overwhelm the unhappy sufferer. As in the case of the physician, in the "Diary of a Late Physician," and of the medical man who was the involuntary experimentalist, Poe makes Egaeus in "Berenice" and the writer of the manuscript in the "MS. Found in a Bottle," record the sensations that arise. He gives the text, too, the form of a systematic record, separating by stars, groups of sensations that differ strikingly from each other.

From the evidence which this chapter has presented it seems reasonable to conclude that Poe has found in British periodicals, particularly in *Blackwood's Edinburgh Magazine*, the genesis of many principles governing his work. In the nature of the horror he wished to produce, and in suggestions for a technical method he seems to be particularly indebted to his British source. In matters pertaining to themes and plots, he likewise shows considerable dependence. He appears, however, to have considered the method, as a whole, inadequate for effective writing. In favor of this supposition, is first, the fact that he expresses himself aware of a

---

[108]*Ibid.*, *vol.* 20, p. 299. Review of *Hawthorne's Twice-Told Tales.*

certain absurdity in the over-use of sensations; in a footnote to a passage in "Loss of Breath" as the story is printed in the *Southern Literary Messenger*,[109] he says: "The general reader will, I dare say, recognize in these sensations of Mr. Lackobreath, much of the metaphysicianism of the redoubted Schelling." The passage in "Loss of Breath" to which he refers reads thus:

"I took delight in analyzing my sensations. Memory, which of all other faculties should have taken its departure, seemed, on the contrary, to have been endowed with quadrupled power. Each incident of my past life flitted before me like a shadow. Then . . . . **** Rapid changes were now taking place in my sensations. Confusion crowded upon confusion like a wave upon a wave. ***The night came, and with it a new set of horrors. The consciousness of my interment began to assume new distinctness."

In the second place, and intimately related with the above point, is the fact that he satirizes over-emphasis of experience in story writing. It is difficult not to believe ,that he is even directing satire against particular *Blackwood* stories. For example, the following passage from "Loss of Breath" is apparently a "takeoff" on "Le Revenant":

"I forbear to depict my sensations upon the gallows; although here, undoubtedly, I could speak to the point, and it is a topic upon which nothing has been well said. In fact, to write upon such a theme it is necessary to have been hanged. Every author should confine himself to matters of experience."

This passage seems to have reference to that part of the *Blackwood* story which reads thus:

"Now I am in a situation to speak from experience, upon that very interesting question—the sensations attendant upon a passage from life to death. I have been *Hanged,* and am *Alive.* . . . I read in the daily newspapers an account of my behavior at the scaffold—that I conducted myself decently, but with firmness . . . ."

The "Predicament," the sequel of "How to Write a Blackwood Story," may possibly be intended to satirize the "Man in the Bell." The belfry with the pendulum may be the belfry with the bell. Furthermore, although of course, one may be idly speculating, the city of Edina may be Edinburgh; Dinah may be the *Edinburgh*

---

[109]*S. L. M.*, vol. 1, p. 735. *Loss of Breath,* as well as others of the *Tales of the Folio Club,* was reprinted in the *Southern Literary Messenger.* As it first appeared, when presented in the manuscript form to compete for the *Baltimore Visitor* prize, and when printed as one of the *Tales of the Folio Club* in book form, it probably did not include this critical note.

Review; and Pompey, the small and grotesque negro servant, may be *Blackwood's Edinburgh Magazine,* or even, Mr. Blackwood, the Ebony of the critics.

Again, as a further indication Poe considered the *Blackwood* method inadequate for effective writing, is the fact that he revises his tales of effect and deletes many passages that relate sensations. He cuts from "Loss of Breath" the passage just given on sensations from the experience of hanging. He also removes from the version of "Berenice," as it was printed in the *Southern Literary Messenger,*[110] a long account of Egaeus' sensations, beginning, "With a heart full of grief, yet reluctantly and oppressed with awe, I made my way to the bed-chamber of the departed. The room was large, and very dark, and at every step within its gloomy precincts I encountered the paraphernalia of the grave. The coffin, so a menial told me, lay surrounded by the curtains of yonder bed, and in that coffin, he whisperingly assured me, was all that remained of Berenice." Poe had, it would seem, in this deleted passage, attempted to push the sensation method to the utmost limit. The deleted passage continues:—

". . . with a sense of suffocation I dragged myself to the side of the bed. Gently I uplifted the sable draperies of the curtains.

"As I let them fall, they descended upon my shoulders, and shutting me thus out from the living, enclosed me in the strictest communion with the deceased.

"The very atmosphere was redolent of death. The peculiar smell of the coffin sickened me; and I fancied a deleterious odor was already exhaling from the body."

And, finally, Poe's continued study to improve his own writing, a study which it will be the purpose of the following chapters to present, may be cited as further proof that he thought the *Blackwood* method, though worthy of imitation, as his early work attests, was yet not wholly adequate. It has already been intimated that an emphasis on sensations apparently led him to study Locke's psychology. That his study led him into other lines as well, is doubtless the case. One of these, and it would seem to have been one of the first, there is reason to believe, was a study of law methods for producing conviction. The following chapter will attempt to present Poe's legal interests.

---

[110] *Ibid.,* vol. 1, p. 333.

CHAPTER II
LAW

An examination of the *Southern Literary Messenger*, both before the time of Poe's editorship and during that period, leads one to entertain the probability of his having consciously studied law methods to increase his critical ability and to give him in his own writing the power of convincing others. The evidence favoring this supposition is contained in a mass of material which apparently shows Poe asking advice of lawyers in literary matters; perusing law books with more than the casual reviewer's care; and, in his critical comments, using a lawyer's phraseology.

Early in his career Poe seems to have found men in the legal profession a congenial and instructive company. It is known that to Mr. William Gwynn, a member of the Baltimore bar, Poe sent his MS. of "Al Aaraaf." William Gwynn was editor of a Baltimore paper, but it may have been the lawyer's opinion as well as the editor's that gave Poe so little encouragement for the light poetical vein of the early poem.[1] To Judge Beverly Tucker, to whom reference has already been made in a preceding chapter, Poe came to owe, as will later be shown, instruction in a method of literary criticism, and in principles of metrical theory. To John P. Kennedy, another Baltimore lawyer, Poe is known to have made a consistent and continual appeal for aid. Kennedy, it was, who first introduced him to the *Southern Literary Messenger;*[2] who charged himself with the first printing of the "Tales of the Folio Club";[3] who, on receipt of Poe's despairing letter, encouraged him to persevere in his literary work. Indeed, correspondence between Poe and Kennedy points to considerable intimacy between the two, in which Poe counts greatly on Kennedy's advice, and frequently on his financial support. It may have been Kennedy therefore that drew Poe's attention to Judge William Wirt[4] as a likely lit-

---

[1] *Works*, vol. 1, p. 73; 106.

[2] *Letters*, p. 17.

[3] *Ibid.*, p. 19.

[4] William Wirt, American statesman, gained great distinction by his forensic abilities. He was retained under the direction of President Jefferson as assistant counsel to the Attorney-General of the United States in the prose-

erary and legal figure well able to instruct an aspiring literary student. Certain evidence turns one toward this idea.

Kennedy, Poe's friend and counsellor, professed to understand the secrets of Wirt's preëminent success in his profession. Requested by the Baltimore bar, Kennedy delivered on the death of Wirt an address in which he dwelt on the qualities of the great lawyer's mind that made him a writer of distinction. He analyzed, too, the mental characteristics that gave him his power of impassioned eloquence. Wirt's influence may be said to pass over into the pages of the *Messenger,* for this Baltimore address was published in the first number of the magazine. In addition to this address was printed also a letter from Judge Wirt, purporting to be a reply to a law student who had asked, it seems, for help in methods of writing. According to the letter, the student was in residence at a university, although the name of the university was not given; and withheld, also, according to the remarks prefacing the letter, were the reasons relating to its insertion. And the jurist may even have spoken to Poe in particular. Indeed, it is interesting to think of Poe studying this letter; it is, moreover, a matter that holds the attention to speculate on the probability of his having been the law student who had sought instruction from Wirt. I shall now present, in part, Judge Wirt's letter.[5]

"You will find a rich mine of instruction in the splendid language of Burke. His diction is frequently magnificent; sometimes too gorgeous, I think, for a chaste and correct taste; but he will show you all the wealth of your language. . . . If you have access to Franklin's works, read them carefully, particularly his third volume, and you will know what I mean by *the habits of observing and thinking.* We cannot all be *Franklins,* it is true; but, by imitating his mental habits and unwearied industry, we may reach an eminence we should never otherwise attain . . . learn the simple, nervous language which is appropriate to that kind of thinking. Read the legal and political arguments of Chief Justice Marshall, and those of Alexander Hamilton, which are coming out. Read them, *study them;* and observe with what an omnipotent sweep of thought they range over the whole field of every subject

---

cution of Aaron Burr for high treason. He held the office himself of Attorney-General during the years 1817-1828. Among his literary productions were his *Letters of the British Spy.* Allibone's Dictionary of Authors.

[5] *S. L. M.,* vol. 1, p. 33. B. B. Minor, in his work, *The Southern Literary Messenger,* New York, 1905, p. 16, does not throw any light on the identity of the "Law Student."

they take in hand—and *that* with a scythe so ample, and so keen, that not a straw is left standing behind them. . . . Resolve to be the first lawyer of your age. . . . Master the science of pleading—master Coke upon Littleton—and Coke's and Plowden's Reports,—master Fearne on Contingent Remainders and Executory Devises, 'till you can sport and play familiarly with its most subtle distinctions. Lay your foundations deep, and broad, and strong, and you will find the superstructure comparatively light work. . . . You must be a master in every branch of the science that belongs to your profession—the law of nature and of nations . . . the outline of all which you will see in Blackstone's Commentaries. Thus covered with the panoply of professional learning, a master of the pleadings, practice and cases, and at the same time a *great constitutional and philosophic lawyer,* you must keep way, also, with the march of general science. . . . You must study the debates in Congress, and observe what have been the actual effects upon the country of the various measures that have been most strenuously contested in their origin. . . . You ask for instructions adapted to improvement in eloquence. This is a subject for a treatise, not for a letter. Cicero, however, has summed up the whole art in a few words! It is—*'apte—distincte—ornate dicere'*—to speak *to the purpose*—to speak *clearly and distinctly*—to speak *gracefully.* . . . In relation to this subject, I would strenuously advise you to two things: *Compose much, and often, and carefully, with reference to this same rule of apte, distincte, ornate;* . . . With regard to the style of eloquence that you shall adopt, that must depend very much on your own taste and genius. You are not disposed, I presume, to be a humble imitator of any man? If you are, you may bid farewell to the hope of eminence in this walk. None are mere imitators to whom nature has given original powers. . . . In what style of eloquence you are best fitted to excel, you, yourself, if destined to excellence, are the best judge. I can only tell you that the *florid and Asiatic style* is not the taste of the age. The *strong,* and even the *rugged and abrupt,* are far more successful. Bold propositions, boldly and briefly expressed—pithy sentences—nervous common sense—strong phrases . . . well compacted periods—sudden and strong masses of light—an apt adage in English or Latin—a keen sarcasm—a merciless personality—a mortal thrust—these are the beauties and deformities that now make a speaker the most interesting. . . . The florid and Asiatic was never a good style either for a European or an American taste. We require that a man should *speak to the purpose* and *come to the point*—that he should *instruct and convince.* To do this, his mind must move with great strength and power: reason should be manifestly his master faculty—argument should predominate throughout; . . ."

My reasons for thinking that Poe had studied the letter quoted above or that he may even have consulted Judge Wirt are:—

First, he testifies to a familiarity with Judge Wirt's writings.[6] He likewise points to the fact that he has corresponded with Judge Wirt. April, 1846, he writes to Duyckinck, "that some time ago, Wiley and Putnam advertised for autographs of distinguished Amer. statesmen. Is it so? I have well-preserved letters from John Randolph, Chief Justice Marshall . . . Wirt . . . and some others—and I would exchange them for books."[7] Granting Poe's well-known interest in autographs,[8] I think he may yet have had some other purpose that prompted him to write to so great a number of statesmen than that merely of collecting specimens of hand-writing. Is it reasonable to think that, since he addressed so many lawyers, he may have been seeking to know from the letters he would receive in reply, the style of lawyer's writing? Second, selections appear from time to time through the pages of the *Messenger*, during the period when Poe was purveyor[9] for the magazine and when he was editor, that follow the course of study prescribed by Judge Wirt. Poe having influence in shaping the contents of the *Messenger*, the choice of contributions would, in all probability, follow in a degree, at least, his interest. Many of these pieces, moreover, are, as we shall see, known to be from Poe's pen. Therefore, the text of the magazine dealing so conspicuously with Burke, Franklin, Chief Justice Marshall, and Blackstone, the chief names suggested in the letter—may possibly indicate on Poe's part that he was heeding the advice of the jurist. To ascertain how nearly Poe may be identified with this law-student, let us follow him in his legal interests.

Poe shows a marked interest in Chief Justice Marshall. He writes to White, who was at that time editor of the *Southern Literary Messenger* while Poe was purveyor: "I will do my best to please you in relation to Marshall's Washington if you will send it on. By what time would you wish the M. S. of the Review?"[10]

---

[6]*S. L. M.*, vol. 2, p. 66. Everything, Poe says in his review of *Memoir of Dr. Rice*, that emanates from the pen of William Wirt will be read with deep interest. *Ibid.*, p. 51.

[7]*Letters*, p. 231.

[8]*S. L. M.*, vol. 2, p. 205. *Autography.*

[9]Cf. Chapter I, *supra.*

[10]*Letters*, p. 7.

Mr. White, however, must have had little interest in Chief Justice Marshall as a subject for a contribution to the *Messenger,* for in a second letter Poe expresses his regret at White's refusal to publish the article, and writes again to Mr. White:—

"It gives me the greatest pain to hear that my Review will not appear in no. 11. I cannot imagine what circumstances you allude to as preventing you from publishing. The death of the Chief Justice, so far from rendering the Review useless, was the very thing to attract public notice to the Article. I really wish you would consider this matter more maturely and if *possible* insert it in No. 11."[11]

There is no evidence, however, that this review was ever printed, and the next time Poe speaks of Chief Justice Marshall is in welcoming, in a short critical piece,[12] an address on the famous jurist delivered by Mr. Binney at Philadelphia, and a discourse by Judge Story at Boston, both addresses occasioned by the death of the Chief Justice. "We have read them both," Poe says, "with an interest *created* by long admiration and love for the subject, but rendered more intense by the *manner,* in which the subject is displayed." He likewise chooses Marshall's words, extracted from a work under review, Francis Glass's "Washingtonii Vita," as a specimen of "Mr. G.'s Latinity." It is, he says, "Judge Marshall's announcement in Congress of the death of Washington."[13]

Again, Poe's interest in the Chief Justice was evidently so keen that it found expression in an original article on the jurist.[14] A long critique on Chief Justice Marshall's life and genius appears in the *Messenger* two months after the short notice that Poe wrote welcoming the addresses of Judge Story and Mr. Binney, and from the closing words of Poe's short notice, which I shall now quote, it seems only reasonable to conclude that Poe wrote the long critical article. Poe says in the short notice of December, 1835:—

"It is not our purpose now to review these two eulogies. A more extended notice of them, and of their great subject, we defer for our next number; in which we shall, perhaps, give also a few light personal reminiscences of Judge Marshall."[15]

---

[11]*Ibid.,* p. 12.

[12]*S. L. M.,* vol. 2, p. 66.

[13]*Ibid.,* vol. 2, p. 53. Review of *Life of George Washington, in Latin Prose:* By Francis Glass.

[14]The review is found in *S. L. M.,* vol. 2, p. 181. B. B. Minor thinks that Judge Beverly Tucker "was probably" the author of this article on Chief Justice Marshall. *Op.cit.* p. 39.

[15]*S. L. M.,* vol. 2, p. 66.

Several points seem of special significance in this long review on Marshall, which I feel from the above evidence fairly safe in thinking came from Poe's pen. Poe, it may be noted, in summing up Marshall's remarkable power of eloquence, his ability to produce conviction by logical sequence in the argument, presents in the main the opinions of Judge Wirt. Although on this point he quotes, too, from John Randolph, to whom he also testifies as a correspondent to the effect that Marshall's argument was "unshaken, and unanswerable," and "as strong as the fortress of Gibraltar," and, at the same time, gives copious extracts from the discourses he is reviewing; yet the long paragraphs he culls from "The British Spy," speak of deep interest in Marshall from Wirt's point of view. Poe praises Wirt's delineation of his great subject. It has "elegance and truth," he says, and "no extended account of Judge Marshall could hardly be deemed complete" without it. Of some significance, too, may be the fact that Poe, in choosing these selections from Wirt, chooses passages on eloquence similar to those contained in Wirt's letter to the law student. Indeed, Poe, in the following, seems to have mastered the contents of the letter.

" 'The . . . of the United States,' says Mr. Wirt, in *The British Spy*, 'is, in his person, tall, meager, emaciated . . . . This extraordinary man, without the aid of fancy, without the advantage of person, voice, attitude, gesture, or any of the ornaments of an orator, deserves to be considered as one of the most eloquent men in the world; if eloquence may be said to consist in the power of seizing the attention with irresistible force, and never permitting it to elude the grasp, until the hearer has received the conviction which the speaker intends. . . . How then, you will ask, how is it possible, that such a man can hold the attention of an audience enchained, through a speech of even ordinary length? I will tell you.

"He possesses one original, and almost supernatural faculty: the faculty of developing a subject by a single glance of his mind, and detecting at once, the very point on which every controversy depends. . . . I am persuaded, that his eyes do not fly over a landscape and take in its various objects with more promptitude and facility, than his mind embraces and analyzes the most complex subject.

". . . his premises once admitted, the demonstration, however distant, follows as certainly, as cogently, as inevitably, as any demonstration in Euclid.

"All his eloquence consists in the apparently deep self-conviction, and emphatic earnestness of his manner; the correspondent simplicity and energy of the style; the close and logical connection of

his thoughts; and the easy gradations by which he opens his lights
on the attentive minds of his hearers. The audiences are never permitted to pause for a moment. There is no stopping to weave gar-
lands of flowers, to hang in festoons, around a favorite argument.
On the contrary, every sentence is progressive; every idea sheds
new light on the subject; the listener is kept perpetually in that
sweetly pleasurable vibration, with which the mind of man always
receives new truths; the dawn advances with easy but unremitting
pace; the subject opens gradually on the view; until, rising, in
high relief, in all its native colors and proportions, the argument
is consummated, by the conviction of the delighted hearer.' ''

Of further significance may be the fact that Poe considers Wirt
and Marshall types of the same kind of genius. In the mentality
of both he sees a consistent working of reason with imagination.
Both illustrate, he says, the ''entire compatibility of such a love
for elegant literature with severe logic and closeness of thought.''
Thus it is with Marshall in mind, that he points to Wirt as an example of this duality of interest. And he launches forth in his
article on the Chief Justice in a characterization of William Wirt.
He has been told, he says, by one who knew Wirt well, of the
lawyer's great aptitude for work; of his habit of sitting for six
or seven hours at a time, intent on penetrating the meaning of
some one law question. Poe is of the opinion that it was Wirt's
imagination that guided him in ravelling the mysteries of knotty
legal problems. He was ''far more profoundly versed in the dry,
intricate lore of his profession, and by far more capable of thrid-
ding its nicest subtleties, than thousands, whose whole minds have
been occupied with its 'mystic, dark, discordant' tomes.'' To Poe,
such a man as Wirt was his highest conception of Marshall. We
may, at least, concede that Wirt was to Poe a compelling figure.

Poe's very evident interest in Franklin's method of writing may
be more or less significant in establishing him as the student who
had asked of Judge Wirt suggestions for literary composition.
It will be remembered that Mr. Wirt had said:—

''If you have access to Franklin's works, read them carefully,
particularly his third volume, and you will know what I mean by
the habits of observing and thinking. We cannot all be *Franklins,*
it is true; but, by imitating his mental habits and unwearied industry we may reach an eminence we should never otherwise attain. . . . learn the simple, nervous language which is appropriate to that kind of thinking.''[16]

---

[16]Cf. *supra.*

In the first place, Poe searches for unpublished essays of Franklin and sets them forth in the *Southern Literary Messenger,* thinking perhaps that the rarity of these articles will make them accept able to his readers. A friend in Philadelphia, he says, in a footnote, copied the essays for him from the original manuscript of Franklin.[17]   Rare letters of Franklin, Poe also publishes; letters for which, he says, he is also indebted to his friend in Philadelphia. He acknowledges that the letters from Anthony Afterwit and Celia Single were first printed in "the Doctor's *Weekly Pennsylvania Gazette,* which was commenced in 1727;" yet he is of the opinion that since they are not in the 1809 or the 1825 edition of the author's works, that he need make "no apology for publishing them in the *Messenger.*" In the second place, Poe chooses such passages from certain of Franklin's manuscripts that bear particularly on writing, and says in a footnote that his material comes from the same original manuscript that contained the letters and essays referred to above. He thus allows Franklin to speak for himself in methods of composition:—

"How shall we judge of the goodness of a writing? Or what qualities should a writing on any subject have, to be good and perfect in its kind?

"Answer 1. To be good it ought to have a tendency to benefit the reader by improving his virtue or his knowledge.

"The method should be just, that is, it should proceed regularly from things known to things unknown, distinctly and clearly, without confusion.

"The words used should be the most expressive that the language affords, provided they are the most generally understood.

"Nothing should be expressed in two words that can as well be expressed in one; i.e. no synonymes should be used or very rarely, but the whole be as short as possible, consistent with clearness.

"The words should be so placed as to be agreeable to the ear in reading.

"Summarily,—it should be smooth,

clear, and

short,

For the contrary qualities are displeasing.

But taking the query otherwise:

An ill man may write an ill thing well; that is, having an ill design he may use the properest style and arguments (considering who are to be his readers) to attain his ends.

---

[17] *S. L. M.,* vol. 2, p. 293. *Mss. of Benjamin Franklin,* Editor's note.

"In this sense, that is best wrote *(sic)* which is best adapted for attaining the end of the writer."[18]

Though there is not in the case of Burke, any more than in that of Chief Justice Marshall or Franklin, evidence definitely connecting Poe with Judge Wirt's recommendation to the law student, yet indications of Poe's more than ordinary familiarity with Burke's writings lead one to speculate on a possible connection. It will be remembered that Judge Wirt had said: "You will find a rich mine of instruction in the splendid language of Burke. His diction is frequently magnificent; sometimes too gorgeous, I think, for a chaste and correct taste; but he will show you all the wealth of your language."[19] Poe shows himself able to turn readily to particular passages in Burke. In August, 1836, he speaks of Judge Hopkinson's article on the "Right of Instruction," published that month in the *Messenger*, an article which refers to certain opinions of Edmund Burke; and he says he will supply one or two of the paragraphs to which he supposes Judge Hopkinson is alluding.

Accordingly, he publishes several selections from Burke's speech of 1780, at the Guild Hall in Bristol.[20] Again, in September, 1836, on solicitation, he shows himself able to present "another passage or two"[21] from the same speech of Burke at Bristol which will settle, he thinks, any misunderstanding of Burke's meaning in the selections he published the month preceding. Poe appears, moreover, to exhibit his knowledge of Burke with some little pride; with what seems to be an evident desire to make it apparent that it is Poe, the editor, who is familiar with legal matters. He appends a note to the answer of the above solicitation for further light on Burke's meaning, in which he says that, since some misapprehension has arisen, "it may be as well to state that *all after* this word 'Editorial' is strictly what it professes to be." Somewhat significant, too, may be the fact that several months previous to these references to Burke, Poe was commissioned by Judge Beverley Tucker to ask White of the *Messenger* to procure for him Burke's works

---

[18]*Ibid.*, vol. 2, p. 411. Other selections from Franklin appear in vol. 2, p. 445.

[19]Cf. *supra*.

[20]*S. L. M.*, vol. 2, p. 573. Editorial: *Right of Instruction*.

[21]*Ibid.*, vol. 2, p. 658. A correspondent, signing himself Q. V. Z., writes to the editor, asking him for more passages from Burke.

in three volumes, and to have them lettered on the back with the word Ardmore.[22]

An interest centers around Blackstone in the early numbers of the *Southern Literary Messenger*. Judge Beverley Tucker's law lecture delivered before the law class in the College of William and Mary is published in full in the issue of 1834.[23] Judge Tucker, it appears, had just been elected to fill the law chair of the college, and, in this, his opening lecture, he laid before the student body his plans for the course he intended to follow. Their study, he said, would be the municipal law of Virginia; their text book the American edition of Blackstone's Commentaries. During the exposition of his subject, in which he dwelt on the dignity of the profession and its exacting demands, he drew a distinction between the arrangement of subject-matter as Blackstone gave it, and the arrangement in the American edition, which, it appears, had been worked out by his father, St. George Tucker. He gave as his opinion that Blackstone's arrangement was philosophical; that it presented to the student the relation of each part of the "body politic" to the whole body. He recommended, however, taking up the study in "an inverted order." Individual rights should receive, he thought, the first attention. In the same way, he explained that Blackstone's Commentaries, being, as he thought, an example of "philosophical analysis," stressed too greatly the generalities of law with not sufficient regard for individual applications. Blackstone is further considered in a series of articles, two of which apparently intend to deal critically with the views of the English jurist. The title of the first reads, "Note to Blackstone's Commentaries, Being the Substance of Remarks on the Subject of Domestic Slavery, delivered to the Law Class of William and Mary College, December 2d, 1834."[24] The writer examines and exposes to his own satisfaction, at least, Blackstone's strictures on the system of slavery. A second article, bearing the title "Remarks on a Note to Blackstone's Commentaries," appears in February of the same year.[25] The writer of this article states that it is "with

---

[22]*Letters*, p. 24.

[23]*S. L. M.*, vol. 1, p. 145.

[24]*Ibid.*, vol. 1, p. 227. B. B. Minor assigns this article to Judge Beverly Tucker. *Op.cit.*, p. 22.

[25]*S. L. M.*, vol. 1, p. 266. For third article, mentioned below, see vol. 1, p. 388.

some surprise'' that he has read the note by the critic of Blackstone.   A third article, ''From the author of the 'Note to Blackstone's Commentaries','' attempts to answer the stand taken in the original cause of the controversy.

Blackstone is likewise cited, in the *Messenger,* as a standard for excellence in writing.   White, who was editor at this time, had, it seems, expressed dissatisfaction with many of the contributions sent to his paper; and, while not admitting an inability to cope with the difficulty, had yet announced no critical standards.   ''Taste,'' he said, ''is so subtle, variable, and uncertain a quality, that for an editor to establish his own, as a fixed and immutable standard— would seem invidious, if not absolutely odious.''   He decided, therefore, to admit into the[26] columns of the *Messenger* all literary composition in which he could detect a germ of genius, or even a desire to excel.   The result was that the contributions to the magazine were, many of them, of unquestionable mediocrity, and this weakness of critical spirit on the part of the editor provoked a vigorous protest from a certain correspondent publishing in the *Messenger.*

This contributor who signed himself X. Y., appeared in the *Messenger* the month following the editor's statement of dissatisfaction[27] with suggestions designed to meet this situation.   X. Y. advises Mr. White to be more selective in choosing material for insertion.   ''Print only for poets,'' he said, ''and poets will write for you.''   He censures the boldness of scribblers who rush into print.   ''A man who has sense enough to write a good book,'' he says, ''very often has too much sense to publish it.''   And he cites the example of Blackstone, who, a genius and a poet, yet forbore publishing his verses.   Not until his death when his unpublished manuscripts were examined was it known that the great English lawyer had written poetry.   And Blackstone's the ''Lawyer's Farewell to His Muse''[28] is printed in the *Messenger,* we may not be wrong in thinking, by the correspondent who was offering the editor suggestions for raising the standard of writing.

Poe's connection with this interest in Blackstone is, in some

---

[26]*Ibid.,* vol. 1, p. 191.

[27]*Ibid.,* vol. 1, p. 255, January, 1835.

[28]*Ibid.,* vol. 1, p. 316.   The poem appeared in the *Edinburgh Review,* vol. 11, p. 37, and was doubtless well known in America to magazine readers of the period.

cases, a matter for mere speculation. He could have been and
doubtless was an appreciative reader of any contribution in the
Messenger dealing with Blackstone. But, since in various places,
he claims a knowledge of Blackstone, the thread of his interest
may show even a closer acquaintance with the English lawyer.
Mr. Wirt had said, it will be remembered:—

"Master the science of pleading—master Coke upon Littleton—
and Coke's and Plowden's Reports—master Fearne on Contingent
Remainders and Executory Devises, 'till you can sport and play
familiarly with its most subtle distinctions. . . .You must be
a master in every branch of the science that belongs to your profession . . . the chart and outline of all which you will see
in Blackstone's Commentaries."

Poe testifies to what one might fancy, from his own words, a
somewhat intimate knowledge of the outline for study just now
referred to. In a critical notice of "Miscellanies of Literature,"
he says that the work he is reviewing reminds him of Coke upon
Littleton "with which whilom we were wont to be delighted."[29]
He likewise professes himself to be "especially taken" with "The
Most Important Parts of Blackstone's Commentaries Reduced to
Questions and Answers." The book is, in his estimation, of "unusual value" and he gladly recommends it to the jurist, the scholar,
and the general reader. Blackstone, thus edited, he says, is, to the
latter, "a convenient manual, not only of law, but of its origin,
and *principia*"; and he considers it for this reason, a better book
than the "Analysis" of Judge Field.[30]

To name Poe as the correspondent X. Y. who was endeavoring
with Blackstone in mind to raise the standard of writing in the
Messenger, is an assumption, at least, interesting. Poe as X. Y.
would have the same chance to be identified with Judge Wirt's
law student, as Poe in his interest in Chief Justice Marshall and
Franklin.

In the first place, X. Y. and Poe both call themselves purveyors
for the *Messenger.* It has already been noted that Poe, before he
came to Richmond, occupied that office. In evident sympathy with
X. Y., Poe also interested himself in combatting the ignorance of
pretentious writers. The same year in which X. Y. was writing,
he discussed with Judge Beverley Tucker the most efficient way of

[29]*Graham's Magazine,* vol. 19, p. 47.

[30]*Burton's Gentleman's Magazine,* vol. 5, p. 329. Hereafter this magazine
will be referred to as *B. G. M.*

demolishing scribblers.[31] Again, the same year, Poe discussed with
White the same question. From Baltimore, June 22, 1835, he
wrote to White expressing regret that he (White) had reprinted
the third number of the *Messenger*. He agrees that that number
is one of the very best issued, but he apparently feels that fact to
be little reason for either its republication, or for the insertion in
other papers of a critical notice in its regard. "Look zealously
to the future," he advises, and let "the past take care of itself."[32]
He is willing, however, to insert such notice if White is insistent.
White appears also to have employed Poe in occasionally stirring
up controversial contributions in the *Messenger*, with the intent,
no doubt, of not only increasing the subscription list of the new
magazine, but of eliciting thoughtful replies. In this regard, we
find Poe writing to White in May, 1835, that he sees no need of
replying to an attack in the *Compiler* on his critique on "Confessions of a Poet," published in the *Messenger*.[33] The book itself,
he thought, was too silly to warrant the controversy. Poe and
X. Y. both bitterly denounce the power of literary cabals to influence public opinion; X. Y. saying, "It is not fair to judge of
the poetical talents of our northern neighbors by the labored dull-
ness of a Barlow; or by the writings of a certain literary cabal,
which is trying to push its members into notice by mutual puffing
and quotation."

Poe and X. Y. both admit that they rarely dot an *i* or cross a *t*.
X. Y. writes to Mr. White, in a bitter tone, apparently following
a rebuke from the editor on the score of illegible writing: "I
shall do better in the future. While you continue to publish what
I send you, I shall continue to cater for you. In doing this, I shall
henceforth cross the t's and dot the i's in my copies, although this
should have been omitted in the original. 'I am wae to think'
indeed, as Burns says, what small critics would do for want of
such mistakes." Compare X. Y.'s admission with the following
from Poe, written to Mr. White the same year: "I will pay
special attention to what you suggested in relation to the punctuation, etc., of my future MSS." Poe further testifies, in a paragraph on the autograph of H. T. Tuckerman, of his contempt for

---

[31]*Letters,* p. 23.
[32]*Ibid.,* p. 8.
[33]*Ibid.,* p. 5.

too scrupulous care in punctuation, remembering, perhaps, his unpleasant experience with Mr. White on the subject:—

"He [Tuckerman] has contributed much of late days to the *Southern Literary Messenger,* with which journal, perhaps, the legibility of his Ms. has been an important, if not the principal recommendation."[34] B. B. Minor, a later editor of the *Messenger,* also testifies to Poe's failure to dot his *i's* and cross his *t's*. He writes to Professor James Harrison, Poe's biographer: "He never altered his final composition—he never dotted an *i* nor crossed a *t*."[35]

Poe appears to have been an appreciative reader of Judge Tucker's Law Lecture printed in the December number of the *Messenger,* for it will later be shown when considering Poe's tendency to criticize the arrangement of subject-matter in law books and some points in legal procedure, that he made use of Judge Tucker's contention in regard to Blackstone's philosophical arrangement. He may have had a more active interest in the case of the controversy over the "Note to Blackstone's Commentaries." This interesting bit in the early history of the *Messenger* presents the writer of the original cause of the controversy as a novice in the field he is occupying. In his reply to his adversary, he apparently feels he cannot defend himself against the attacks of an able jurist. He is "anonymous," he says; his antagonist is "an avowed author." "He (the antagonist) wears defensive armor. I am naked." Moreover, he does not wish to carry the controversy further. He says to White: "You judge rightly that I have no call to answer my censor." In the second place, the author of the "Note to Blackstone's Commentaries" disclaims any other purpose in writing his article than that of eliciting a response from an able writer. He is grateful, he says, to his antagonist, for helping him "to awaken the public mind." Although he thinks that his opponent has unfairly met his argument, he warmly praises "the style and matter of his essay." They both evince, he thinks, on the part of the writer a superior education. It is with evident satisfaction, too, that White, in an editorial remark, also commends this opponent's article. "The author has won many a trophy on the field of logic and eloquence."

From certain parts of the evidence already adduced, it might

---

[34]*Graham's Magazine,* vol. 19, p. 276.
[35]*Works,* vol. I, p. 221.

seem a fair conclusion that Poe had actively interested himself in a more or less attentive study of Blackstone's Commentaries, and that in the person of X. Y., in the stand he took against scribblers, he had fortified himself with the example of the English lawyer. Added testimony to his study of law is found in his knowledge of law books, of law doctrines, and in his apparent understanding of intricacies in questions pertaining to law.

Poe's review on "Robinson's Practice," a law book by Conway Robinson which appeared in 1836, indicates an acquaintance on his part with law books other than the one actually undergoing criticism. He speaks of the improved arrangement in the classification of the present volume over that of the former by the same author, issued three years before. On account of this improvement, he says, it is easier to find the doctrine desired on any given point. And in regard to subject-matter, he considers "Robinson's Practice" superior to the "Revised Code of Tate's Digest."[36]

A knowledge of law doctrines may, without doubt, be imputed to Poe from the ease with which he discusses decisions in the cases cited in the book he is reviewing. For example, observe in the following how warmly he praises the author on his ability to resolve cases into doctrines:—

"In his *abstracts of cases,* the author is, in the main, particularly successful . . . . he sometimes gathers from them doctrines, which the reporter has overlooked, and which a cursory reader would, therefore, be little apt to discover. For example, in pp. 20, 21, he states these two points, as decided in the case of *Blow vs. Maynard,* 2 Leigh, 21: 1st, that a fraudulent donee of personalty is accountable for it and its increase, and, also for hires, and profits, accruing since the donor's death, as executor *de son tort;* just as a rightful executor would be who has taken possession at the donor's death."

Of still more import in attributing to Poe a knowledge of law books is the fact that occasionally he ventures to criticize the author in some parts of his work. In one instance, he says, Robinson has failed to give general principles where they would be naturally expected, and it is with a certain petulance that he calls attention to this lack. "Some quarrel," Poe says, "we have with the *judicial* law, which principally fills the book. A head in the Table of Contents refers us to a page, where we expect to find a full elementary exposition of at least the leading doctrines that fall under that

[36]*S. L. M.,* vol. 2, p. 50. Review of *Robinson's Practice.*

head: but we see, perhaps, only a single *case,* or a judge's *dictum,* not at all realizing the promise of the reference, by unfolding all pertinent general principles. Thus, under the caption, 'WHEN STATEMENT OF A TRANSACTION MUST BE TAKEN ALTOGETHER,' instead of finding a general rule laid down on the point indicated, we find only a case briefly stated, from which we are left to deduce a rule *if we can.* (pp. 329-330.)'' Indeed, in one case, Poe even questions the validity of the lawyer's decision. He says the author ''has gainsayed'' a ''well settled doctrine''; and he explains his meaning in the following way:—

''Under the very next head, the well-established principle, that 'An Answer is no evidence for the defendant, as to anything it affirms, not responsive to the allegations of the Bill, but that it *is* evidence so far as it responds to those allegations'—is whittled away to the position that it is not evidence as to any affirmative matter, touching which the Bill *seeks no discovery.* Now, if the Bill positively alleges one thing (whether it calls for a *discovery* or not), and the answer as positively alleges the reverse; such denial stands for proof, and must be rebutted by testimony; and so, we conceive, do the cases clearly evince, which are cited by our author himself; *Beckwith* v. *Butler,* . . . and even *Taylor* v. *Moore,* whence he quotes (and quotes truly) in the form of a judge's *dictum,* the position in question—not to speak of 1 Call, 224, 390; the *dicta* of Roane and Carrington in the case of *Rowton* v. *Rowton,* 1 Hen. and Munf.; and many other authorities. The principle, in its true extent, is well illustrated by the case cited from 1 Johnson's Reports, 580, where an Answer alleging usury, of which the Bill had said nothing, was held *no evidence.* The case from 2 Leigh, 29, is infelicitously adduced. The *point* professedly quoted from it was there adjudged: it was only maintained by *one judge,* who (we say it with a deference heightened by affection, as well as by respect) seems to us to have therein gainsayed the well-settled doctrine we have referred to, and therefore to have erred.''

And, at the conclusion of his article on ''Robinson's Practice,'' as if to furnish unmistakable proof that he has criticized the decisions of the author aright, Poe mentions a decision that has evidently been overlooked.

He is also seen to criticize lawyers' practice. In his story, the ''Mystery of Marie Rogêt,'' it is interesting to note that he appears to base his criticism on a similar point already referred to in Judge Tucker's law lecture at the College of William and Mary. He seems to feel, as did Judge Tucker, that law considered only in its philosophical or general aspect may take little notice of the individual's right. Thus, he says, lawyers, in ''their small talk,'' are reprehensible in depending too entirely on "recognized and *booked* principles." This method, he grants, is philosophical, but it disregards the conflicting exception and thus may fail to render the individual justice. He quotes, as justification for his view, an extract signed "Landor," which he places as a footnote to the above contention in the text of his murder story.[37] The handling of material in Coke upon Littleton he likewise criticizes. Though, as we have seen, he declares himself to be delighted with the book; nevertheless he gives it as his opinion that the work is a mass of undigested writing.

A summary of the evidence already presented may be, perhaps, not unfairly stated in the following:—Since the foregoing course of study, that dealing with Chief Justice Marshall, Franklin, Burke, and Blackstone, may, as has been seen, be traced back to the outline sketched by Judge Wirt for the law student; and since these lines of work have been found to be those in which Poe was interested, and from which he appears to have drawn certain knowledge pertaining to legal doctrines, it seems reasonable to think that Poe may have followed the course prescribed by the jurist, or that he may even have been the law student with whom Judge Wirt corresponded.

Poe may be said to have learned a method and style of criticism from the legal profession. There is evidence leading to the supposition that, on the advice of Judge Beverley Tucker, he made his critical comments judicial. In the first place, it is known that he had weighed with Judge Tucker the value of critical methods employed in foreign quarterlies.[38] Possibly the distinction between mere opinion and the critical art as founded on principles drawn from the study of masters of criticism, a distinction which, as we have seen, grew up in British periodical literature, was in Poe's mind when he asked Judge Tucker to suggest means for combatting the ignorant writer. Whatever may be the truth of this supposition, he received in reply to his query: "I did not mean to deny the efficacy of a certain style of demolishing scribblers. I merely said it was not judicial."[39] In the second place, Poe frequently expresses Judge Tucker's contention, namely, that criticism should be judicial. He insists on method in critical analysis.

---

[37]*Works*, vol. 5, p. 33. *The Mystery of Marie Rogêt.*
[38]Cf. Chapter I.
[39]*Letters*, p. 23.

"The wildest and most erratic effusion of the Muse, not utterly worthless," he says, "will be found more or less indebted to *method* for whatever of value it embodies; and we shall discover, conversely, that in any analysis of even the wildest effusion, we labor without method only to labor without end."[40]   He likewise maintains that a literary critic can and should demonstrate his position.   "We make use of the word 'demonstrate'," he says in an editorial article in the *Broadway Journal,* "for it has always been a point with us to sustain as far as possible, by evidence or argument, whatever propositions we put forth.   But has the *Gazette* in the present instance, been equally careful?   Do we understand it as inclined to dispute the accuracy of any statement, or the validity of any deduction embodied in the critique to which it has referred?   If so, we are prepared to try the case upon its merits.   If, however, it is the simple *opinion* of the *Gazette* which is thus pitted against our own, we are by far too modest to say another word upon the subject—and must submit to the stern necessity of letting the whole matter remain precisely where it is."[41]   And, again, in one instance, he says it can be demonstrated that the mind of men cannot create;[42] in another, apparently recalling the language of Judge Tucker, that the critical position he assumes in asserting that only the simplest language should be used for subjects of grandeur, is a proposition "as susceptible of demonstration as any in Euclid."[43] The fact, too, that he was openly commended by Judge Tucker for the style of criticism he had adopted, might seem added proof that he had consciously tried to work out a lawyer-like method, and that, apparently from the jurist's approval, had succeeded.   Judge Tucker, it appears, wrote to White of the *Messenger,* January, 1836, in warm praise of Poe's Review of Mrs. Sigourney, Miss Gould, and Mrs. Ellett:—[44]

"Mr. P.'s review of the writings of a trio of these ladies (Mrs. Sigourney, Miss Gould, and Mrs. Ellet, January, 1836) in your

[40]*Graham's Magazine,* 1842, p. 216.   Review of *Poetry of Rufus Dawes.*
[41]*Broadway Journal,* vol. 2, p. 93.   *Editorial Miscellany.*   At the beginning of volume 2 of the *Broadway Journal,* Briggs has withdrawn from editorship, Watson was in charge of the music department, and Poe of the literary part.
[42]Cf. Chapter IV.
[43]*Graham's Magazine,* 1842, p. 121.   *A Few Words About Brainard.   Works,* vol. 11, p. 22.
[44]*Works,* vol. 8, Intro. p. xi.   Poe's review referred to is in *Works,* vol. 8, p. 122.

last number, is a specimen of criticism which for niceness of discrimination, delicacy of expression, and all that shows familiarity with the art, may well compare with any I have seen."

We shall next consider what further lesson Poe taught himself from his study of law. In other words, we shall try to discover the principles of literary technique that Poe deduced from his legal interests.

Certain principles of literary practice Poe appears to find in his investigation of a lawyer-like method. One of these concerned the relation which *clearness* bears to *brevity,* another, the advantages of a strictly logical structure, and a third, some little approach, though he seemed to feel it unsatisfactory, towards a rule whereby individual points are comprehended under a generalization. While it is true that, as we have seen, he had found these principles discussed with more or less frequency, in the pages of *Blackwood,* yet it was in law that Poe apparently found them, especially the first two, strikingly illustrated; for it was a writer's need of logical sequence and brevity that Judge Wirt had wished to convey in these words to the law student :—

"You ask," Judge Wirt said, "for instructions adapted to improvement in eloquence. This is a subject for a treatise, not for a letter. . . . In relation to this subject, I would strenuously advise you to two things: *Compose much, and often, and carefully, with reference to this same rule* [Judge Wirt had spoken before in the same letter of Cicero's rule] *of apte, distincte, ornate dicere.* Bold propositions, boldly and briefly expressed—pithy sentences—nervous common sense—strong phrases—well compacted periods—sudden and strong masses of light. . . . We require that a man should *speak to the purpose* and *come to the point*—that he should *instruct and convince.* To do this, his mind must move with great strength and power: reason should be manifestly his master faculty—argument must predominate throughout."

So clearly must Poe have recognized the value of the lawyer's principles of brevity and logical sequence that, in one of his own articles when he wished to ascribe these qualities to Chief Justice Marshall, we find him quoting from Judge Wirt, words which Judge Wirt had himself applied to Chief Justice Marshall:—

"Every sentence is progressive; every idea sheds new light on the subject; . . . the dawn advances with easy but unremitting pace; the subject opens gradually on the view; until, . . . the argument is consummated, by the conviction of the delighted hearer."

It is not surprising, therefore, that Poe began to use the same principles on his own independent effort, nor that in his endeavor he shows a tendency to translate into law terms the *Blackwood* method of producing effect by logical structure and brevity of expression. In his reviews of this period, the period of his connection with the *Southern Literary Messenger,* when his law interests are most noticeable, we find such criticisms as the following from his review of "Robinson's Practice":—

"There is *not enough compression* in some parts. In this volume, it is true, not a tithe of the statute law is quoted, that over-burthens the former one; but when he does cite a statute, the author still gives it to us in all the exuberance of legislative verbosity. Thus, he fills the third part of a page with the law of *lapsing legacies;* (p. 91) when, considering that only the *substance* was essential, . . . it might more clearly, and as satisfactorily, have been couched in five lines. . . . And he takes *three-quarters of a page* (copied from the Revised Code) to say that 'a surety may in writing notify the creditor to sue upon the bond, a bill, or note, which binds the surety; and unless the creditor sue in reasonable time, and proceed with due diligence to recover the sum due, the surety shall be exonerated.' (pp. 132, 133). In the name of all that is reasonable, why should not a writer disencumber his pages of the rubbish of *howbeit, provided, notwithstanding, nevertheless,* and *aforesaid,* when, by doing so he might save himself and his readers so much time and toil?"

He likewise sees that an important step in the simplification, or as he says, the *"unquacking"* of a legal style may be found in the edition of "Blackstone's Commentaries Reduced to Questions and Answers," to which reference has already been made. Law need not, he is convinced, be so complex or its expression so shrouded in mysterious numbers as its devotees are wont to think.[45]

And the same point is made in the following review;[46] namely, that brevity produces clearness:—

"The authors of the works here reviewed have attempted to unfold, and to show the worthlessness of, those technical mysteries which have so long enveloped the science of Law. 'The Forms of Deeds, etc.' is from the pen of Mr. Okey. He gives several examples of English and French deeds—printing them on opposite pages. The difference in conciseness is said to be four to one in favor of the French, while in clearness they admit of no comparison. The greater brevity of the French documents is attributed to the existence of a Code. 'The Mechanics of Law Making' in-

---

[45] *B. G. M.,* vol. 5, p. 329.
[46] *S. L. M.,* vol. 2, p. 59. Review of *Mechanics of Law-Making.* Critical notice of *Westminster Review.*

sists upon the necessity of reform in the arrangement, language, classification, and contents of the British Acts of Parliament, and in the agency by which the laws are 'prepared, made, promulgated, superintended, enforced, and amended.' The Review is brief, but concurs heartily in the necessity alluded to.''

In the review of Bland's *Chancery Reports*, Poe likewise complains of the lack of brevity. He says:—''Many of its cases are inordinately voluminous. . . . They might all, we are full sure, have been shortened by two-thirds. with great advantage to their perspicuity as well as to the reader's time, patience and money.''[47]

But perhaps there are no better instances that show how plainly Poe was drawing on his study of law than his criticisms that distinctly transfer to literary technique a lawyer-like method. He says, in reviewing ''Nick of the Woods'':—

''But Dr. Bird's great excellence is in the ingenuity and contrivance of his story. This could not be so told as not to be interesting. State the leading facts of the case with the formality of a lawyer; let the parties be A. B. and C.; let no spoken word, no incidental circumstance be introduced to enliven the narrative or to illustrate character, and we shall still listen eagerly to hear the event, and in the end sit down in quiet satisfaction, under a result in strict conformity to poetical justice, and brought about by *natural means*. . . . The reader easily works the equation by extinguishing these superfluous opposing quantities, and feels that all that is essential to the story has happened just as it ought.''[48]

And again,[49] in reviewing ''Conjectures and Researches Concerning Tasso'' the critic demands a lawyer-like method:—

''We must . . . declare our regret that Mr. Wilde did not more clearly express his own opinion, and that he did not start by stating briefly what he wished to prove, and go on step by step to prove it. This would, we think, have rendered the book more popular with general readers, and perhaps more clear and satis-factory to all.''

Likewise from the same review:—

''The patient industry with which Mr. Wilde has collected his materials cannot be too highly commended, and is surpassed only by the clear and luminous manner in which he lays the whole evidence before the eye of the reader, and by the ingenuity with

[47]*Ibid.*, vol. 2, p. 731. Review of *Bland's Chancery Reports*.

[48]*Ibid.*, vol. 3, p. 254. Review of Dr. Bird's *Nick of the Woods*. Prof. Campbell suggests that this review may, with propriety, be ascribed to Poe. *Nation*, vol. 89, p. 10.

[49]*Graham's Magazine*, 1843, p. 203. This review is not listed in *Works*.

which he makes his deductions. Nothing, indeed, can be more lawyer-like than the conduct of the whole case; not, we would be understood to say, that there is anything technical in the style; still less that there is anything of wire-drawn argument or forced construction; but simply that the arrangement of facts is evidently the result of practice in the art of collecting and exhibiting evidence in the most direct and intelligible form, and that the method of arriving at the end is as distinctly that which could be applied only by a clear reasoning mind not unaccustomed to such pursuits.''

Continued suggestions pointing to Poe's legal interest appear from time to time during the course of his literary work. One of these is his use of technical law expressions. In one instance he says that *"cui bono"* is a legal phrase, meaning ''for whose advantage,'' and that the term is mistranslated in ''all the crack novels.''[50] He arraigns the author of ''Norman Leslie'' quite after the manner of a prosecuting attorney.

''We will dismiss the 'Editor of the Mirror' with a few questions. When did you ever know, Mr. Fay, of any prosecuting attorney behaving so much like a bear as *your* prosecuting attorney in the novel of ''Norman Leslie''? When did you ever hear of an American Court of Justice objecting to the testimony of a witness on the ground that the said witness had an interest in the cause at issue?''[51]

We may doubtless at this point conclude that Poe had found in a study of law certain suggestions that helped him in his work as a writer. In the main, these suggestions have been seen to center around the advantages of legal argument, for, presumably in the person of a student who had asked advice from lawyers, he considered that convincing writing must be brief, to the point, and strictly logical.

But, as further evidence shows, he later came to feel that a lawyer-like method, though effective, was not all of the writer's art. He testifies to the need of an understanding of unity. The next chapter will attempt to present Poe's study of unity in the drama and fine arts.

---

[50] *Works*, vol. 5, p. 299. *Thou Art the Man.*
[51] *S. L. M.*, vol. 2, p. 54. Review of *Norman Leslie.*

CHAPTER III
UNITY IN THE DRAMA AND THE FINE ARTS

Unity of effect, Poe maintains, is the artist's governing principle. The drama may be said to have led him to a deeper consideration of the means a writer may employ to produce an effect on his reader's mind deeper than the means he apparently found in *Blackwood,* or testifies to having gained in his study of law. However strange it may seem, law had not revealed to him more than a suggestion of unity. For, it will be remembered with what dissatisfaction, in a review of a legal document, he had bewailed the lack of a generality governing a mass of particulars. But in the drama, the idea seems to have invested itself with a new and a fuller meaning. Indeed, evidence points to the fact that after a study of dramatic principles, he is convinced that the brief article in prose and verse is, in its nature, allied to a dramatic composition, and depends for its effect on the same rules that govern the drama. He is even of the opinion that the unities, especially those of time and action, find their most perfect manifestation in the writing of a brief article. And so intimate does he appear to think is the connection between the short story and the drama, that his ideas, when composing his short pieces or when commenting on what he presents as the proper method in their production, seem often tinged with notions of dramatic representation. The fine arts appear also to have been a field for his study of unity. There is reason to believe that he studied paintings of eminent artists, and, moreover, that he assumed the rôle of art critic with a seriousness born no doubt of the conviction that he was establishing a well-known standard of criticism.

Much of Poe's understanding of the essential features of the drama came from A. W. von Schlegel's "Lectures on Dramatic Art and Literature."[1] Although Poe had met with Schlegel in the pages of *Blackwood,* it is safe to assume that he went beyond *Black-*

---

[1]Professor Prescott is of the opinion that Poe probably read Schlegel as early as 1831; he bases his assumption on the fact that Poe's expression, *the bee Sophocles,* doubtless drawn, he says, from Schlegel's calling Sophocles the *Attic Bee,* appears in his *Letter to B——*. (Prescott, F. C., *Poe's Critical Essays.* Henry Holt and Company, p. 325.)

wood criticism for a knowledge of the German critic. Professor Prescott points out Poe's indebtedness to Schlegel, but he seems not to have gone further than mentioning certain general grounds of dependence. He speaks of Poe's borrowing from Schlegel the principle of unity or totality of interest; of gleaning from the Lectures certain notions and curiosities for *Pinakidia;* of having obtained from that source most of his knowledge of Greek and Latin literature and important notions in regard to poetry. But more specific dependence can doubtless be established. It is highly probable, for example, that it was due to a study of Schlegel that Poe turned from the method of producing effect by logical sequence or a strict following of causal relations in the argument to a consideration of effect through unity. Poe appears to agree with Schlegel in the points that follow.

Unity in the drama, Schlegel says, cannot be taken in the sense in which Aristotle has attempted to represent it, that of a beginning, middle, and end. Such a "plurality of connected events" or "concatenation of causes and effects,"[2] virtually reaches no necessary completeness. Corneille, in Schlegel's opinion,[3] also errs in his definition of unity, placing it as he does in the idea of connection between cause and effect. It is true, Schlegel admits, that logical coherence, or the causal connection is essential to the drama; yet he feels that if this is the fundamental principle of drama, then *effect* is diminished and true excellence is impossible. But, on the other hand, effect is greatly increased, according to Schlegel, if all the events are gathered under one point of view and denoted by a single name. This conception of unity involves, he says, the idea of *One* and *Whole* and is properly sought in a "system of metaphysics."[4]

Poe, as has just been said, is apparently following Schlegel in his change from a strictly logical procedure for producing effect to that of a comprehension of ideas under a single point of view. In his review of Macaulay's "Critical and Miscellaneous Essays"[5] he sums up what he feels to be the weakness of the rigidly logical style. Macaulay has erred, he says, in depending too entirely upon logical sequence in his argument. In fact, this *closeness*

[2]Schlegel, *op. cit.*, p. 242.
[3]*Ibid.*, p. 243.
[4]*Ibid.*, p. 244.
[5]*Works*, vol. 10, p. 156.

of logic is the trait for which, in his opinion, Macaulay is especially remarkable. The English writer leaves *"no minute gap which the reader might have to fill up with thought."*[6] He thus preserves the "entire chain of his argument" at the expense of his subject as a whole. But, Poe says, " 'Truth for truth's sake' is seldom so enforced." It is scarcely too much to say that the style of the profound thinker is never too closely logical. And he cites the instance of George Combe "than whom a more candid reasoner never, perhaps, wrote or spoke—than whom a [more] complete antipode to Babington Macaulay there certainly never existed." Poe then analyzes Macaulay's argument and tries to show that in its close reasoning the author has forgotten "the very gist of his subject," the one main point about which all details in the argument turned.[7]

The source of this mistaken method of producing effect (for Poe is evidently putting it forth as an error), he feels lies in a tendency of the public mind towards logic for logic's sake. People are apt, he says, to be caught by the closeness of the logic, and they comprehend the points and the sequence of the argument, but in yielding assent to this progress, the one great truth, the purpose of the chain of reasoning, is often lost. And Poe, in another place, expresses the same idea:—

"Few minds can immediately perceive the distinction between the comprehension of a proposition and an agreement of the reason with the thing proposed. Pleased at comprehending, we often are so excited as to take it for granted that we assent."[8]

It can doubtless be seen from what Poe has just said that he believed, with Schlegel, that while logical coherence in an argument is essential to forcing conviction, it is still not the main point of the writer's art. The *oneness* of the argument, the comprehending of all the details under one head, the connecting of all parts into a whole, in short, the unity of the piece, is the sole and rightful means of producing effect.[9]

Not only was Poe indebted to Schlegel for this changed understanding of producing effect, but we find indications that he was also using Schlegel's explanations of the necessary means for at-

[6]*Ibid.*, p. 157.
[7]*Ibid.*, p. 160.
[8]*Ibid.*, vol. 14, p. 191. *A Chapter of Suggestions.*
[9]*S. L. M.*, vol. 2, p. 667. Review of *Hazlitt's Remains.*

taining a unified whole. Through this advance in the study of
unity, he seems to be considering the fundamental principles of
dramatic writing. Accordingly, the mechanism of the drama, the
unities of time and action and what he believed to be attendant
considerations—namely, the object of the dramatic author, the
means of attaining that object, the beginning and the dramatic
aspect of the length of a piece—begin to appear in Poe's work.

The dramatic writer according to Schlegel, and the writer of
the brief article as Poe explains it, agree in the object they propose for their undertaking. Poe may not for this point have followed the text of Schlegel's "Lectures on Dramatic Art and Literature" to any greater degree than he followed *Blackwood* criticism; yet, it is highly probable that the definite statement Schlegel
gives to the object of the dramatic writer caught his attention.
Schlegel thus expresses the idea:—

"But how does a dramatic work become theatrical, or fitted to
appear with advantage on the stage? . . . In general, the
answer to this question is by no means so difficult. The object
proposed is to produce an impression on an assembled multitude, to
rivet their attention, and to excite their interest and sympathy.
In this respect the poet's occupation coincides with that of the
orator."[10]

Poe's statement, to which reference has been made,[11] emphasizes,
in a similar way, it will be seen, the object of the dramatic writer.
"A skillful literary artist," says Poe in his review on Hawthorne,
must in constructing a tale conceive "with deliberate care, a certain unique or single *effect* to be wrought out." In addition to
this statement of the object of the literary artist, Poe gives,
throughout his work as a critic, a constant reiteration of the same
dramatic principle.

The drama and the short story or short poem likewise coincide in
the nature of the impression to be produced. In both cases the impression must be a unique and single effect. Schlegel's discussion
of this essential of dramatic writing has already been referred
to in considering the influence he brought to bear in turning Poe
from a strictly logical method to a further understanding of unity.
Reviewing for a moment what the German critic has said in this
connection, we recall that he considered the three unities not to

[10]Schlegel, *op. cit.*, p. 37.
[11]Cf. Chapter I.

have been rightly defined. In general, his main criticism was that Aristotle's "beginning, middle, and end" make no provision for direction towards a single end; that Aristotle's understanding of action is something that merely takes place, or in other words, is something that is entirely external. Therefore, says Schlegel, "completeness" would be "altogether impossible."[12] But his view explained in greater detail shows him to follow De la Motte in substituting for Aristotle's unity of action, unity or totality of interest.[13] He now offers the opinion[14] that unity of action must be founded in a higher sphere of ideas; that it must take into account not simply external order of events, but a "more mysterious unity than that with which most critics are satisfied." It is best explained, he thinks, by the unity which "exists only for the understanding, and is neither visible to the eye nor palpable to the touch." As an example of this type of unity, he cites the organic unity of a plant or of an animal which consists in the idea of life. This unity, he contends, while itself is "incorporeal, nevertheless manifests itself through the medium of the corporeal world." Then he transfers this conception of unity to a dramatic piece and says:—

"The separate parts of a work of art, and (to return to the question before us) the separate parts, consequently, of a tragedy, must not be taken in by the eye and ear alone, but also comprehended by the understanding. Collectively, however, they are all subservient to one common aim, namely, to produce a joint impression on the mind."

Poe obviously follows Schlegel in this conception of unity, for, in the first place, he seems to be aware of the German critic's dissatisfaction with Aristotle's treatment of the unities. In the early days of his connection with the *Southern Literary Messenger,* a short passage in that magazine summarizes the points that Schlegel had presented as Aristotle's inadequate view.

---

[12]Schlegel, p. 242. It is of course to be understood that Schlegel himself, as well as other writers of his time, did not fully comprehend Aristotle's meaning and his point of view. This is evident from Professor S. H. Butcher's Aristotle's *Theory of Poetry and Fine Art,* London, 1898. We are here, however, concerned only with Schlegel's and Poe's understanding of Aristotle.

[13]*Ibid., op.cit.,* p. 243.

[14]*Ibid.,* p. 244.

Schlegel, p. 237	*Southern Literary Messenger*
"It is amusing enough to see Aristotle driven perforce to lend his name to those three Unities, whereas the only one of which he speaks with any degree of fullness is the first, the Unity of Action. With respect to the Unity of Time he merely throws out a vague hint; while of the Unity of Place he says not a syllable."	Vol. 1, p. 698 The Unities "Aristotle's name is supposed to be authority for the three unities. The only one of which he speaks decisively is the unity of action. With regard to the unity of time he merely throws out an indefinite hint. Of the unity of place not one word does he say."

It is impossible not to consider Poe as responsible for the insertion of this bit in the *Messenger,* for, although he was not editor at the time, he was an active purveyor for the magazine and he was, as we know, studying Schlegel's "Lectures on Dramatic Art and Literature." Furthermore, Poe in a critical review gives Schlegel credit for the principle, and he thus shows that, in the nature of the effect to be produced, he is in full accord with dramatic criticism. "In pieces of less extent," he says in writing of Mrs. Sigourney's "Zinzendorff, and Other Poems," "the pleasure is *unique,* in the proper acceptation of that term . . . and thus its effect will depend upon what is rightly termed by Schlegel the *unity or totality of interest.*"[15] Unquestionably, Poe feels, with Schlegel, that Aristotle has not been clear on the subject of the unities.

The beginning of a drama and the beginning of a short story or poem also appear to have points in common. Schlegel thus explains that the dramatic writer must begin at once to produce the effect he intends: . . . "The dramatic poet, as well as the orator, must from the very commencement, by strong impressions, transport his hearers out of themselves, and, as it were, take bodily possession of their attention."[16] And Poe on his part is of the opinion that the skillful literary artist must, from his "very initial sentence," start to bring out the effect he intends to produce. If he fails to begin at once, Poe says, then he has failed in his first step.[17]

Unity of time in the drama seems to have given Poe further light

---

[15]*S. L. M.,* vol. 2, p. 113. Review of *Zinzendorff and Other Poems* by Mrs. Sigourney.

[16]Schlegel, *op. cit.,* p. 38.

[17]*Graham's Magazine,* vol. 20, p. 299. Review of Hawthorne's *Twice Told Tales.*

on the question of the length of a composition. From *Blackwood*
we have already noted, Poe found notions for numerical length
and for length expressed in time limitations.[18] From law, we
have also observed,[19] he derived the idea that clearness and brevity
bear a certain relation to each other. The drama appears to add
to these former suggestions a physical and psychological point of
view. While it is true that the length of a composition in its
psychological bearings was evidently a common topic among certain critics, e.g. Kames and Blair, and doubtless Poe was aware
of their comments,[20] yet it is obvious that Poe found Schlegel's
discussion helpful. The writer must "diligently avoid," said
Schlegel, "whatever exceeds the ordinary measure of patience or
comprehension."[21] Poe expresses the same idea in demand-

---

[18]Cf. Chapter I.

[19]Cf. Chapter II.

[20]Poe refers to Kames and Blair as though familiar with the method they
pursue in their criticism. He likens the *"magnificent critiques raisonnées"*
of Augustus Wilhelm Schlegel and of Frederick Schlegel, to those of Kames,
of Johnson, and of Blair.—*Graham's Magazine*, 1842. The *New York Mirror*
notices in 1832 the reprinting in America of Kames' *Elements of Criticism*
and Blair's *Rhetoric*. Kames, the notice says, has translations affixed to quotations in foreign languages.—The *New York Mirror*, vol. 10, p. 395, 1832.
Kames thus discusses the point referred to in the text: "I am ready to
show, that a . . . representation, with proper pauses, is better calculated
for . . . making the deepest impressions. This will be evident from the
following considerations. Representations cannot very long support an impression of reality; for when the spirits are exhausted by close attention, and
by the agitation of passion, an uneasiness ensues, which never fails to banish
the waking dream. Now supposing an act to employ as much time as can
easily be given with strict attention to any incident, a supposition that cannot
be far from the truth; it follows, that . . . a continued representation
of longer endurance than an act, must have a bad effect, by overstraining
the attention and producing a total absence of mind." Kames, Lord, *Elements of Criticism*. Edinburgh: Printed for A. Millar, London, and A.
Kincaid and J. Bell, Edinburgh, 1765, vol. 2, p. 414. Locke, as quoted by
Kames, may also have been suggestive to Poe: "The . . . mind is so
constituted that it can by no effort . . . keep its attention long fixt
upon the same object." *Ibid.*, vol. 1, p. 291. Blair likewise speaks to the
same point. "The sublime . . . is an emotion which can never be long
protracted." Blair, Hugh, *Lectures on Rhetoric and Belles Lettres*. London:
1823, p. 48.

[21]Schlegel, *op. cit.*, p. 37. It is interesting to note that Aristotle does not
affix any time limit to a dramatic composition. It is true that he draws a
comparison between the necessity for the magnitude of a living organism

ing[22] for the tale only that length which will not result in the reader's weariness. And in the following he appears especially to emphasize length in the light of unity of time: "Without excessive and fatiguing exertion, inconsistent with legitimate interest, the mind cannot comprehend at one time . . . the numerous individual items which go to establish the whole."[23]

Unity of action, as Poe applied it to the composition of a brief article, appears to be the outgrowth of a combined study of Schlegel and Aristotle.[24] The question seems to resolve itself into a consideration of the dramatic plot. It has been pointed out that Poe was doubtless aware of Schlegel's dissatisfaction with Aristotle's definition of unity of action; and, moreover, that he considered Schlegel to have "rightly" termed it the unity or totality of interest. While there is not evidence sufficient to prove that Poe later came to feel that Schlegel had misunderstood Aristotle's definition of unity of action, yet certain indications point to that probability. In the first place, he advances the opinion that Schlegel errs in regarding the dramatic plot in the light of intrigue. "The somewhat over-profound criticisms of Augustus Wilhelm Schlegel," he says, "have discussed the plot in bearings of complication, mystification, in short, of intrigue, to the utter avoidance of the simple and direct."[25] Such a conception which is, he thinks, the conception of N. P. Willis in his drama "Tortesa," is after the manner

---

being such that it may be embraced in one view, and the length of a plot being such that it can easily be embraced by the memory; but he uses no principle in determining the length. He only requires, he says, that the length shall admit of the whole being perspicuous; and again, that in tragedy the length should confine itself, as far as possible, to a single revolution of the sun. Indeed, he distinctly states that "the limit of length in relation to dramatic competition and sensuous presentment, is no part of artistic theory." Aristotle, *The Poetics of Aristotle*. London and New York, Macmillan and Co., 1895; Translated by S. H. Butcher, p. 31.

[22]*Graham's Magazine*, vol. 20, p. 290. Review of Hawthorne's *Twice-Told Tales*.

[23]*Works*, vol. 10, p. 122. Review of Bulwer's *Night and Morning*.

[24]Professor Prescott comments on Poe's reference to Aristotle. He asserts that Poe in *The Letter to B——* in maintaining poetry to be "the most philosophical of all writings" misunderstands and misquotes *The Poetica*. He is of the opinion that in this regard Poe's reference to Aristotle is "casual and second-hand."—Prescott, *op cit.*, p. 324.

[25]*Works*, vol. 13, p. 43. *The American Drama;* vol. 10, p. 116. Bulwer's *Night and Morning*.

of many pieces of the Spanish drama and is, he further says, nothing short of folly.[26] In the second place, he announces it as his conviction that Schlegel's unity or totality of interest, or in other words, Schlegel's understanding of unity of action, has in reality the same meaning as the dramatic plot.

Before permitting Poe to explain himself on this question, it may be well first to examine what grounds he had for thus reasoning on it. Schlegel, it will be remembered, had demanded for unity of action the meaning of a "mysterious unity," a unity that exists only for the understanding; and had denied to Aristotle's beginning, middle, and end any such interpretation. It comprised the idea, he said, of a living organism, in which each part does a peculiar work, with all parts functioning for the good of the whole. If we compare this conception of unity of action, or totality of interest, as Schlegel had agreed to call it, we shall find that it re-states in idea, at least, Aristotle's explanation of the dramatic plot, though the German critic does not admit that for it Aristotle was helpful to him. For, in the passage from "Lectures on Dramatic Art and Literature," which I shall cite below, does not the "inward necessity" Schlegel speaks of as existing between each scene in "Romeo and Juliet" with reference to the whole play, have much the same meaning as the "mysterious unity" he had demanded when reviewing unity of action? And, on his own wording, does not the outcome of this "inward necessity" re-state Aristotle's plot in the drama? From the parallel columns which follow, the agreement will, I think, become apparent.

The Poetics pp. 33 and 83	Schlegel p. 361
"The plot being an imitation of an action, must imitate one action and that a whole, the structural union of the parts being such that, if any one of them is displaced or removed, the whole will be disjointed and disturbed. For that which may be present or absent without being perceived, is not an organic part of the whole."	"In an essay on *Romeo and Juliet,* I went through all the scenes in their order, and demonstrated the inward necessity of each with reference to the whole; . . . From all this it seemed to follow unquestionably, that . . . nothing could be taken away, nothing added, nothing otherwise arranged, without mutilating the perfect work."

[26]Schlegel's discussion of plot as intrigue, partaking of the nature of the Spanish comedy, is found in his *Lectures on Dramatic Art and Literature,* p. 182. Cf. also, Poe's remarks in the *New Comedy, Broadway Journal,* vol. 1, p. 205.

"The plot manifestly ought to be constructed on dramatic principles. It ought to have for its subject a single action, whole and complete. It will thus resemble a living organism and produce its proper pleasure."

Allowing Poe now to present his idea of plot, we find him, as has been said, to be following a combination of Aristotelian and Schlegelian precepts, a dependence which shows, it would seem, that he had critically compared his two masters. At one time, plot is to him a unity, a totality, of interest; at another, an organic whole in which, for the good of the whole, each part has performed its peculiar function; and again, he identifies it with unity of action. For example, in his review of Bulwer's "Night and Morning," with evident delight he dwells on the totality of beauty which, he says, arises from the plot structure. And the plot, in terms of an organism, is clearly worded from Aristotle, as the following passages testify:

The Poetics of Aristotle p. 33	The American Drama Works, vol. 6, p. 45
"The plot, being an imitation of an action, must imitate one action and that a whole, the structural union of the parts being such that, if any one of them is displaced or removed, the whole will be disjointed and disturbed. For that which may be present or absent without being perceived, is not an organic part of the whole."	"We may consider a plot as of high excellence, when no one of its component parts shall be susceptible of *removal* without *detriment* to the whole."[27]
p. 83	
"The plot manifestly ought to be constructed on dramatic principles. It ought to have for its subject a single action, whole and complete. It will then resemble a living organism, and produce its proper pleasure."	

[27] It is true that in various reviews in British periodical literature one encounters paraphrases of Aristotle's wording of plot structure, yet I have found no instance of a wording so nearly resembling Aristotle's as does Poe's. The following from *Blackwood* is a statement of plot structure that is simi-

In some instances Poe comes even nearer Aristotle's wording, than in his passage just cited. In his review of Bulwer's "Night and Morning" he uses Aristotle's term *disjointed* to designate the effect produced by a faulty plot. Bulwer, he thinks, has executed his plot in error with the result that the pleasure derived from it is "disjointed . . . and evanescent."[28] And Lowell, he contends, has produced in his prose efforts mainly rambling plots, in which "a certain *disjointedness* may be observed."[29]

Poe is evidently convinced of the applicability, even the necessity, of the dramatic unities of time and action to the effective brief article. Unity of time, as we have seen, he considered to be destroyed by length; and, on this score, he considers that the novel cannot be a dramatic composition. "Without becoming fatigued, the mind," he says, "cannot comprehend *at one time*—the numerous individual parts which make up the whole." Unity of action, confounded as we have seen in Poe's mind with unity of effect, and, again, with the dramatic plot, he thinks is denied by a constant shifting of scenes and a continued effort to "bring up" events to a certain moment of time. On this score, he advances the opinion that Bulwer's theory of dramatic composition is altogether erroneous; that the effort the English novelist makes in his prefaces to "pre-coax" one to believe he has attained plot perfection and dramatic excellence, is at least questionable art.[30] Indeed, Poe states as his belief that, although Bulwer, could he see these comments, would doubtless loftily maintain for his "Night and Morning" dramatic qualities, the novel yet contains only the deficiencies and not the essential features of the drama. Thus, unity of time and unity of place, in Poe's estimation, may only properly be applied to the brief article. If a writer's intention is to be dramatic, why can he not, Poe asks, content himself with the brief tale? That is a species of composition, he says, which admits of the highest development of artistical power.

Poe's application of dramatic criticism in his own critical work

---

lar to Aristotle's: "It [the tragedy] is a chain so curiously wrought, . . . that, by leaving out a link, or thread, the whole is irreparably injured." *Blackwood's Edinburgh Magazine*, vol. 21, p. 469.

[28]*Works*, vol. 10, p. 120. Review of Bulwer's *Night and Morning*.

[29]*Ibid.*, vol. 13, p. 168. Review of Lowell's *Fable for Critics*.

It will later be shown that Poe worked out the idea of plot structure in scientific terms.

[30]*Works*, vol. 10, p. 124. Review of Bulwer's *Night and Morning*.

has already been noted. In theory he has constructed both tale and poem on fundamental principles of the drama. In practice, what did Schlegel and Aristotle mean to Poe? In the first place, the drama obviously caused him as he advanced in the art of story writing to begin more directly to make the impression. The long prologue in the "MS. Found in the Bottle," one of his earliest stories, does not appear in following tales. It might seem, therefore, that this story represented the period preceding any dramatic influence; it may represent the time when that of *Blackwood* predominated. In fact it appears to agree with the tale of effect, as *Blackwood* writers gave it, in possessing the long prologue, which in both cases seems to be used to establish a ground-work of reality. Compare the following opening paragraphs of the "MS. Found in a Bottle" and several of those from sensation stories in *Blackwood*, with those of "Berenice."

In the "MS. Found in a Bottle" the long prologue reads:

"Of my country and of my family, I have little to say. Ill usage and length of years have driven me from the one, and estranged me from the other. Hereditary wealth afforded me an education of no common order, and a contemplative turn of mind enabled me to methodize the stores which early study diligently garnered up. Beyond all things, the works of the German moralists gave me great delight; not from my ill-advised admiration of their eloquent madness, but from the ease with which my habits of rigid thought enabled me to detect their falsities. . . . After many years spent in foreign travel, I sailed in the year 18—, from the port of Batavia, in the rich and populous island of Java, on a voyage to the Archipelago Islands. . . . Our vessel was a beautiful ship of about four hundred tons, copper-fastened, and built at Bombay of Malabar teak."

As will be seen, the beginning of the "MS." is quite similar to the beginnings of the *Blackwood* sensation stories. In the "Involuntary Experimentalist" the setting of the story is given in a prologue of considerable length:—

"The destruction by fire of the distillery of Mr. B. in Dublin, some time since, will be in the recollection of many of our Irish readers. . . . I am a medical man, residing, etc."

And in the "Man in the Bell" the prologue is also used:—

"In my younger days, bell-ringing was more in fashion among the young men of ———— than it is now. Nobody, I believe, practices it there at present except the servants of the church, and the melody has been injured in consequence. Some fifty years ago, about twenty of us who dwelt in the vicinity of the cathedral. . . ."

In "Berenice," however, the impression to be made appears to be in the writer's mind from the start:—

"Misery is manifold. The wretchedness of man is multiform. Over-reaching the wide horizon as the rainbow, its hues are as various as the hues of that arch—as distinct, too, yet as intimately blended. Over-reaching the wide horizon as the rainbow! How is it that from beauty I have derived a type of unloveliness?—from the covenant of peace, a smile of sorrow? But, as in ethics, evil is a consequence of good, so, in fact, out of joy is sorrow born."

While a semblance of a prologue thus appears in "Berenice," yet it may be noted that only such points as are necessary to enable one to grasp the thread of the story are given, and, that moreover, these facts are so permeated with the impression to be made, that they do not detract from the oneness of effect. As the story advances Egaeus explains certain details relating to his family and ancestral home, yet he so interweaves into these facts misery and madness that they enhance rather than diminish the effect of the misery and madness that starts from the very beginning. For example, the towers of his ancestral halls were gloomy and gray; his family was a race of visionaries; the books in his library were of a peculiar nature. He relates facts of his birth, and recollections of his earliest years, yet with the same oppressive sense of misery and overhanging madness. He continues with his boyhood and education and the same gloomy madness hangs over his head. In "Shadow" there is apparently no semblance of a prologue. The shadow of death overhangs the tale from the very initial word.

In the second place, the influence of the drama is seen in the change from a solitary figure overwhelmed with sensation crowding on sensation, to what may perhaps be said to be an imitation of an action. Although the sensation method is never completely abandoned, yet the solitary figure gives way to several acting characters. "Metzengerstein" marks an advance in plot interest; the "Cask of Amontillado" may be said to be a little drama.

It remains now to show that Poe, in working out his stories, held dramatic representation in mind. In this regard, one has only to note how he intermingles dramatic terms with the writer's efforts at perfection. "Most writers," he says, ". . . would positively shudder at letting the public take a peep behind the scenes at the elaborate and vacillating crudities of thought, . . . at the careful selections and rejections—at the painful erasures and interpolations—in a word, at the wheels and pinions—the tackle for scene shifting—the step-ladders and demon-traps—the cock's feathers, the red paint and the black patches which, in ninety-nine cases out of the hundred, constitute the properties of the literary histrio.''[31]

Not only did Poe study unity in the drama, but there are indications to show that he found the same principle extending throughout the Fine Arts as well. In favor of this conclusion is the testimony offered by his criticism. In the first place, he speaks of unity in literature and unity in the plastic arts as being contro-vertible terms in criticism. All the rules of the plastic arts, he says in his review of "Peter Snook," founded as they are in a true perception of the beautiful, "will apply in their fullest force to every species of literary composition."[32] And, again, in the same article, he considered the satisfaction a literary critic receives from a narrative in which an unusual fact is developed, analogous to the "unalloyed pleasure" that the artist derives from meaningful strokes of the brush. Moreover, it is to be noted that throughout his critical work, Poe continued to use the painter's conception of unity as a standard for literary excellence. A striking example of this use of art criticism appears in his comments on Dickens' "Watkins Tottle, and Other Sketches" written in 1836. The "Pawnbroker's Shop," one of the sketches, will illustrate, Poe thought, the artist's idea of unity of effect, and to make his point plain, he contrasted it with a passage also on a pawnbroker's shop in a novel by William Leete Stone, "Ups and Downs in the Life of a Distressed Gentleman."[33] In the one, the reader is conscious, Poe said, that the anecdotes introduced by the author bear only a "shadowy relation" to their subject; while in the other, the work of Dickens, the effect is one of a "gradually perfecting picture," in which the pawnbroker's shop, in its wretchedness and extortion, is the main idea. To this idea, the reader feels, all the groupings and fillings-in are subservient. And Poe adds:—"So perfect, and never-to-be-forgotten a picture cannot be brought about by any such trumpery exertion, or still more, trumpery talent, as we find employed in the ineffective daubing of Colonel Stone. The scratchings of a school-boy with a slate pencil on a slate might as well be compared to the groupings of Buonarotti.''

[31]*Ibid., Philosophy of Composition.*

[32]*S. L. M.*, vol. 2, p. 730. Review of *Peter Snook*, October, 1835.

[33]*Ibid.*, vol. 2, p. 458. Review of *Watkins Tottle, and Other Sketches, by Boz.* Poe's review of Stone's book, *ibid.*, p. 457.

Of quite as much interest in revealing Poe as an art critic, is his further point about "Peter Snook."[34] Conscious of unity in this composition, he expressed himself in painter's terms. "The merit," he said, "lies in the *chiaro'scuro*—in that blending of light and shadow where nothing is *too distinct*, yet where the idea is fully conveyed." And, again, in his review in 1836 of the "American in England"[35] he uses the technical language of the artist. The author was right, Poe said, in not putting upon his canvass all the actual lines which he might have discovered in his subject. He comprehended that only by toning down or even totally neglecting certain portions of his object, could he bring out the portions by whose sole instrumentality the idea of the whole composition could be conveyed. In Poe's opinion, the author of the "American in England" was well aware that "the apparent, not the real, is the province of a painter." Likewise, in 1839, in reviewing "Tortesa,"[36] a drama by N. P. Willis, he warmly compliments the author on the fine ideal elevation of his work, a point which, according to Poe, is "forgotten or avoided by those who with true Flemish perception of truth wish to copy her peculiarities in disarray." And, he quotes, with approbation, a passage chosen from Hazlitt, in which the English writer explains what he means by the ideal in art. Hazlitt had said, it seems, that a painter's art lies not "in rejecting the peculiarities of form, but in rejecting all those which are not consistent with the character intended to be given, and in following up the same *general idea* of softness, voluptuousness, strength, activity, or any combination of these, through every ramification of the frame."[37] Finally, in the statement of his critical theory given in 1842, as a summary of preceding lines of investigation, art terms are found to have their place. "A picture is at length painted which leaves in the mind of him who contemplates it, with a kindred art, a sense of the fullest satisfaction."[38]

More decisive, however, than the testimony of literary reviews which show Poe to be working with the painter's technique, was

---

[34]*Ibid.*, vol. 2, p. 730.

[35]*Ibid.*, vol. 2, p. 192. Review of the *American in England* by the author of *A Year in Spain*.

[36]*B. G. M.*, vol. 5, p. 117.

[37]*S. L. M.*, vol. 2, p. 668. Review of *Literary Remains of the Late William Hazlitt*.

[38]*Works*, vol. 11, p. 108. Review of Hawthorne's *Twice-Told Tales*.

his criticism on art itself.   He undoubtedly wrote some of the
articles on the Fine Arts in the *Broadway Journal*.   Professor Harrison lists "La Sortie du Bain," though he does not publish the
piece.   Professor Campbell thinks that Poe wrote most of the
articles on art in the second volume of the *Broadway Journal*.[39]
Although it will be seen that Poe could not have written all the
articles that Professor Campbell suggests, it can yet be shown that
he was responsible for a certain number in both volumes.

An inquiry into the arrangements made for differing work in the
magazine may help in assigning Poe his proper art contributions.

Briggs, the originator of the *Broadway Journal*, withdrew from
his editorship at the end of the first volume.   Several reasons point
to the fact that it was doubtless he who was principally concerned
with the Fine Arts department during the time he was editor.   In
the first place, he names no one as the head of the art department.
In his announcement of his plans for the conduct of his magazine,
he mentions, as a special editor, only the one in charge of the music
section, Henry C. Watson.[40]   Of the three, Briggs, Poe, and Watson,
Watson could not have been the one chosen for the work on art.
Briggs, moreover, is known to have been himself an art critic, Poe
saying of him in the compilation of papers known as the *Literati*:
"Among the principal papers contributed by Mr. B., [Briggs]
were those discussing the paintings at the last exhibition of the
Academy of Fine Arts in New York."[41]   A further reason assigns
to Briggs the Art Department of the first volume.[42]   In the second
number of that volume, four weeks[43] before the selection of assistant editors, appeared an article on the "Art Union Pictures"
which was presumably from Briggs' pen, for the author speaks of
filling a "vacant department of editorial labor."[44]   Briggs also

---

[39]*The Nation*, vol. 89, p. 624.   *Bibliographical Notes on Poe.*

[40]Briggs says, February 22, 1845, in Notices to Readers: "We have the
pleasure of announcing to our readers that hereafter Edgar A. Poe and Henry
C. Watson will be associated with the Editorial Department of our Journal.
Mr. Watson will have the entire control of the Music Department of the paper,
and will give it the full benefit of his well-known abilities."   The *Broadway
Journal*, vol. 1, p. 127.

[41]Godey's *Lady Book*, 1846, p. 199.

[42]The *Broadway Journal* started January 4, 1845.

[43]Cf. *supra*, note 42.

[44]*Broadway Journal*, vol. 1, p. 36.

prided himself, according to Poe,[45] on his "personal acquaintance with artists and his general connoisseurship,"[46] and was, it seems, a member of the Art Union. We may safely assume then that Briggs interested himself in the Fine Arts Department of the first volume of the *Broadway Journal.*

Poe, however, seems to have written certain of the articles on art in the second volume. A controversy arose between Briggs and Poe, in which the two disagreed concerning principles of art. It will be remembered that Poe had expressed his disapproval of the methods of Flemish painters, saying that they erred in their attention to detail. That they failed to conceive of their art as governed by the principle of unity, seemed to be his main contention. He now applied this same criticism to Briggs, both as writer and art critic:—

"If Mr. Briggs has a *forte*, it is a Flemish fidelity that omits nothing, whether agreeable or disagreeable; but I cannot call this *forte* a virtue. . . . I may be permitted to say that there was scarcely a point in his whole series of criticisms on this subject, at which I did not radically disagree with him. Whatever taste he has in art, is, like his taste in letters, Flemish.''[47]

Briggs on his part attacked Poe.[48] The trouble grew and the magazine was temporarily suspended,[49] but reorganized with Poe as chief editor. Watson remained, however, presumably in his capacity of head of the music section. Poe and Watson, therefore, could alone be responsible for the editorial articles on art in the second volume. Evidence suggests that they collaborated in the department of Fine Arts, for, in one number, the department presents two articles; one signed P. and the other W. On this testimony, Poe was undoubtedly author of the criticism on the "Ivory Christ," the sculpture brought, as the article states, from Italy by C. Edwards Lester, American consul at Genoa.[50] Later,

---

[45]Godey's *Lady Book,* 1846, p. 199. *Literati.*

[46]Doubtless Briggs in his office as editor, and owing to his fondness for artists, may have been responsible for Page's articles on the *Use of Color* which appeared in the early numbers of volume 1 of the *Broadway Journal. Works,* vol. 15, p. 265.

[47]Godey's *Lady Book,* 1846, p. 199. *Literati.*

[48]*Works, Biography,* p. 211.

[49]*Ibid.,* p. 212.

[50]*Broadway Journal,* vol. 2, p. 214. Watson's article is entitled *National Gallery at the Rotunda.*

October 25, 1845, Poe became the sole editor of the *Broadway Journal*.[51] It is much more to be supposed then, that after obtaining full control of the magazine, his efforts would be at least as great to insure its success. Before this time when he had secured only a third pecuniary interest in the paper, Poe writes in a letter to Thomas[52] that he is working fourteen or fifteen hours a day, and that his hopes are high for the final success of the *Journal*. He writes to Griswold:[53] "It will be a fortune if I can hold it." One may then assume that he would take advantage of his full control to allow only the expression of his own views to enter the magazine. With this assumption we may be safe in assigning to Poe, after the date of his full editorship,[54] not only "La Sortie du Bain,"[55] but also some remarks[56] concerning Titian's "Venus." Other articles on art in the *Broadway Journal* may also be attributed to Poe. In his few remarks on Titian's "Venus" he mentions having written a former article on the same subject. He says in the columns of the Fine Arts Department: "Under this head we have very little to observe. Titian's "Venus," concerning which we had some remarks in a previous number, is again being exhibited in Broadway."[57] The first article on the same subject is in the first volume of the *Broadway Journal*. This fact is significant since it shows Poe to be writing on art during the time of Brigg's editorship. Another contribution on art may possibly be ascribed to Poe. In the series of comments on the paintings at the American Art Union,[58] published in the *Broadway Journal* of September 13, 1845, is an announcement of a future critical account

---

[51]*Ibid.*, vol. 2, p. 248. In the *Editorial Miscellany* is a note to this effect: "With this number it will be seen that we assume the sole control (proprietary as well as editorial) of the *Broadway Journal*. May we hope for the support of our friends?" See also *Letters*, pp. 216 and 217.

[52]*Letters*, p. 203.

[53]*Ibid.*, p. 216.

[54]The last number of the *Broadway Journal*, however, Poe says was entirely the work of Thomas Dunn English. *Works, Biography*, p. 248. "The last number of the *Broadway Journal*—the work having been turned over by me to another publisher—was edited by Mr. English. The editorial portion was wholly his and was one interminable Paean of his own praises. The truth of all this will no doubt be corroborated by Mr. Jennings, the printer."

[55]*Broadway Journal*, vol. 2, p. 260.

[56]*Ibid*, vol. 2, p. 276.

[57]*Ibid.*, vol. 2, p. 276.

[58]*Ibid.*, vol. 2, p. 155; also vol. 2, p. 214.

of the "Ivory Christ," and it is to be noted that these remarks
are identical with Poe's introduction to his criticism on the "Ivory
Christ." This part of the series of comments must, then, be Poe's.
It is difficult to say whether the remaining pieces in the series are
by Poe, or whether Watson is their author. The "Death Struggle,"
one of these pieces, however, contains a critical point that is characteristic of Poe. The picture has unity, the critic says. In fact,
this principle characterizes all the art criticism that I have attributed to his pen.

Unity as a literary criterion, in 1845, the date of Poe's articles
on art in the *Broadway Journal,* was not the unity of his early
criticism. From the purely dramatic criticism that he found in
Schlegel and Aristotle, the principle passed, as I shall show in the
next chapter, through a philosophic stage, and later through a
period characterized more particularly by scientific investigation.

It is this last stage in an understanding of unity that is used for
the criticism of art products in the *Broadway Journal.* The "Ivory
Christ," Poe thought, was an expression of truth. The figure depended from the cross, he said, *precisely* as the human form would
depend in the circumstances. The contraction of muscles, more
particularly, in Poe's opinion, about the calves and toes, were absolute in the truth of their expression. In short, the whole figure
was perfect. And of "La Sortie du Bain" he speaks of the per
fection of proportion. In like manner is unity discussed in the
"Death Struggle." He says in this instance, that the "anatomy
is well made out."

What did Poe study to acquire his knowledge of art? It can be
shown, in the first place, that he read art magazines, for he speaks
in his essay, "Anastatic Printing,"[59] of having a leaf of the *London
Art Union* before him. He also appears to have studied paintings
with the evident intention of applying to them what he believed
to be standard measures in criticism. In favor of this assumption
is the testimony found in a long article written in 1839[60] entitled,
"Half an Hour in the Academy of Fine Arts at Philadelphia,"
and signed, "By a Philadelphian." The identity of the critical
points contained in this article and those of both Poe's literary and
art criticism before and after the date of its publication, leads one
to suggest Poe as its author. In the first place, both the Fine Arts

[59]*Ibid.,* vol. 1, p. 230.
[60]*B. G. M.,* vol. 5, p. 78.

article and Poe agree that talent is not to be praised simply because
it is native talent. The article reads:—

"The first thing that engages our attention is Alston's huge
painting of the dead man restored to life by touching the corpse of
Elisha. (Catalogue No. 46). The painter is what the cant of the
times denominates a 'native artist', and it is therefore a high of-
fense against patriotism, honor, good feeling and the seven cardinal
virtues in a lump, to bestow on the performance anything else than
'honied words of praise'. Phew! The delineator of such a mon-
strosity aught [sic] to be rolled up in his canvas, and both of them
burnt together on the altar of beauty."[61]
And Poe gives expression to the same idea. In 1836 he wrote:—
"We get up a hue and cry about the necessity of encouraging native writers of merit. . . . In a word, so far from being ashamed
of the many disgraceful literary failures to which our own inordi-
nate vanities and misapplied patriotism have lately given birth,
and so far from deeply lamenting that these daily puerilities are
of home manufacture, we adhere pertinaciously to our original
blindly conceived idea, and thus often find ourselves involved in
the gross paradox of liking a stupid book the better, because, sure
enough, its stupidity is American."[62]

Beauty, in the opinion of the author of "Half an Hour in the
Academy of Fine Arts," is the most fitting subject for art. He
is criticizing Alston's picture of the dead man restored to life:—

"The taste which selected this subject for the pencil was un-
acquainted with that strict boundary line within which the graces
have encircled this art. Pleasure is the sole end of painting; beauty
is the sole source of unqualified pleasure: beauty then is the supreme law of this, and all the other, arts of design. The Greeks
I take to be the despotic law-givers for the world in all that concerns art: they painted, not to display their skill or exhibit a
resemblance, but to produce an object whose loveliness should
gratify the spectator. *Impression*, which most modern artists seek,
was not their aim; beauty was their constant Latium; and if they
ever selected subjects of a tragical nature, they softened down the
terror under the control of beauty."[63]
Poe, likewise, makes the same contention. The sense of the beautiful, he says, is an important condition of man's immortal nature.
On this score he criticizes Longfellow for the choice of his themes.[64]

---

[61]*Ibid.*, vol. 5, p. 78. *Half an Hour in the Academy of Fine Arts.*
[62]*S. L. M.*, vol. 2, p. 326. Review of Drake's *Culprit Fay.*
[63]*B. G. M.*, vol. 5, p. 78. *Half an Hour in the Academy of Fine Arts.*
[64]*Graham's Magazine*, vol. 20, pp. 190; 248.

In a following chapter we shall find that he makes beauty the foundation of his definition of poetry.

Unity in the composition is necessary to the painter's art. "Death on the Pale Horse" the writer condemns since it lacks this principle:—

"Let us give one glance to 'Death on the Pale Horse,' which stands in the next room. I have always had a profound contempt for West, as the most commonplace and wooden of painters; but this figure compels admiration. . . . Yet the picture is a leap, not a flight of genius; in the filling up of the canvas,— in the unworthy idea of a particular death in the midst of a general wasting of the world, . . . we detest the essential meanness of West's imagination,—that innate groveling temper from which he never long escaped. Almighty heaven! when the incarnate spirit of destruction was galloping on his pallid courser over the earth robed in night, and his extended fists flashing hell-fires, and universal life was fainting beneath his deadly breath, was it a time to think of lions snapping at horses' noses or bulls tossing boys? Faugh! I could kick the unworthy corner out of the picture. . . .'"[65]

With Poe, unity was, as we know, the basis of his study of the critical art.

The student of the pictures discusses *indefinitiveness*, making it a standard by which to judge the "Dead Man Restored to Life" by Alston:—

"The artist can exhibit but a single moment of time and a single point of view, and his production, moreover, is to be often examined, and long dwelt on. The portrait painter should therefore seize that expression of the face which is the most strictly *natural*, which is the center and hinge of every other phase of the countenance, to which every phase can be referred and from which all can be derived: the historical painter should select the moment of the story which is the most pregnant with future meaning, and leads on to higher and higher interest; the most elevated point of excitement should not be chosen, but the prelude to it. A common artist in Greece painted Medea slaying her children: Timomachus more wisely showed her meditating their death. Something must be left to the fancy, or else pictures become lifeless, and the art ceases to be poetic, and becomes merely mimetick. The sculptor of "Laocoon" chisels a sigh; imagination superadds a shriek; had he exhibited a shriek, imagination could do nothing. The business of art is to stimulate interest, not to satisfy it. Now Mr. Alston has seized a passion and a state of it which admitted of no progression of wonder; the next moment and a second glance will destroy it.

---

[65]*B. G. M.*, vol. 5, p. 78.

There is no climax of emotion, no aggrandizement of interest: there is no future to the story; the present comprises and includes all: the drama is fairly over, and the excitement ended. Had he shown us a fiend or giant thus rising on his astonished enemies, we should have been chained in expectant interest; *now* there is nothing to follow; the next instant will unknit the corrugated brows of the bystanders, and turn surprise to simple joy. The subject in fact is poetical and not pictorial; but as the painter did select it, he should have shown us the dead man rising before the company were aware of it, so that we might be arrested in wonder as to what they would think when they perceived the miracle.''[66]

Poe's remarks on *indefinitiveness* are strikingly similar. Music, he says, demands a certain ''wild license and *indefinitiveness*—an *indefinitiveness* required by every musician who is not a mere fiddler, as an important point in the philosophy of his science. Give to music any undue decision, imbue it with any very *determinate* tone, and you deprive it at once of its ethereal, its ideal, and I sincerely believe, of its intrinsic and essential character.''[67] Identity of critical views is also seen in the connection between *music* and *proportion*. The author of the article on the Fine Arts discusses music in its metaphysical bearings. He seems to feel that, in this sense, it has the power of presenting to the mind a series of images that form of themselves a picture. He says:—

''This picture, [''Holy Family'' after Raphael D'Urbino] calls to mind the notion of Byron, or Browne, of the *music* of a beautiful face. The forms are disposed in commingling curves with such liquid grace,—the dark and manly face of Joseph and the age-brown and care-withered, yet pleasing, countenance of Elizabeth relieve so harmoniously the young and glowing cheeks of all the rest,—that *musical*, is the epithet that at once occurs to every spectator. The expression has been charged with a false license of metaphor, but it is strictly true to the laws of mind, and if metaphysics ever come to be written by a man who knows how to think, it will be stated that all sensations and impressions—thoughts, sounds, odors, and all others—present themselves to the mind as images; and, being *homogeneous*, may of course be compared. Go over an overture in your mind, and you will find that it is a picture.''[68]

Poe also expresses his conviction that there lies between *music* and *proportion*, a connection the philosopher, the scientist, the painter, and the poet can both detect and appreciate. In the chap-

---

[66]*Ibid.*, vol. 5, p. 79.

[67]*Ibid.*, vol. 5, p. 332. Review of *George P. Morris*.

[68]*Ibid.*, vol. 5, p. 80.

ter on science, I shall present evidence to show how the idea grew up in his mind. We shall see there his correspondence on the subject with Judge Tucker, who appears to have been the one who first brought the matter to his attention. Judge Tucker did not offer any explanation of this connection; he claimed to be conscious of it, he said, only from the "accuracy" of his ear.[69] As was the case with the writer of the Fine Arts article, Poe appeared to find a reasonable solution in a study of metaphysics. And he engages in what he appears to consider illuminating discussions of the principles of equality and of proportion, deriving from them what he states to be a satisfactory interpretation of the music of the spheres. In natural science he meets with the physical law on which he considers the connection between music and proportion rests. In short, Poe, on the basis of this connection, defines and illustrates, it will be seen, his whole theory of metrical art.

A point other than identity of criticism to establish Poe as the author of "Half an Hour in the Academy of Fine Arts" is the evident fact that the writer is a literary critic who is studying art from a standpoint of literary technique. In the main he argues for the superiority in power of producing effect of the poet over the painter. In the first place, the poet is more universal in his appeal.—

"When the poet tells us of the *impression* which his Genevieve produces on his heart, every reader can appropriate the emotion to himself; each calls to mind the particular lady whom he most admires, and the poem seems to him precisely and exclusively applicable to her; because the same passion has been felt by all, though produced by qualities as various as the nature of each. But of all these causes, the painter is limited to a single set; and what he places on his canvas can affect only that fraction of beholders who may happen to agree with him in definite notions of the highest beauty—a number in any case small, and farther narrowed by the power of moral qualities in warping the natural conceptions of ideal fairness. His most beautiful woman *must* be an individual."

The poet is again placed over the painter, since he is permitted to describe persons by impressions rather than by delineations.—

"Look . . . at old Homer; what do we know from the poet of the face or form of her who 'for nine long years has set the world in arms'? Not a bit. 'She was the most beautiful woman in the world,' says Homer, and there's an end of it. But when

---

[69]*Letters*, p. 23.

we see the cold and hoary sages of the council rising to look after her as she leaves the room—when we reflect that she was all that Venus could contrive, all that Paris could demand, all that Menelaus wished for—when we remember that for her Achilles struck, for her great Hector died—then we feel how wise was the forebearance of the poet, and how superior is poetry when rightly managed, to the best performances of the painter. We see Helen as we see the wind; only by the commotion which her presence occasions. Ah! those old fellows knew what they were about.''

Moreover, the writer of the Fine Arts article was not only a literary critic, but his literary interests led him into a field in which Poe, at the time the article was published, was known to be actively engaged. The interest in both cases centers around Pope. In the first place, the writer of the article considers Pope's work of demolishing scribblers. He says ''Poetry never won richer laurels than when Sandy Pope fought her battles.'' He disagreed with Lessing, who, he said quoted ''with triumph'' from Warburton to the effect that Pope disapproved of the pictorial essays of his youthful muse. But the writer of the piece on the Fine Arts contends that Pope, in calling description a ''heavy feast of sauces,'' was only satirizing the manner usually practiced. Indeed, in his opinion, Pope was a master of the art of pictorial description. He cites as a striking instance the moonlight scene in the book of Pope's translation of Homer.

Poe, as has just been said, was also interested in Pope's work of elevating the standard of literature. That he followed Pope for the betterment of American letters, I shall now try to show. Poe was familiar with the ''Dunciad,'' for, in discussing versification, he quoted nine couplets from the first book of the satire.[70] He stresses the importance of Pope as a satirical critic. The critical art in America, he says, should no more neglect its duty than in the days of the ''Dunciad''.[71] The forms of Pope's satires are also known to Poe. In his review of Wilmer's ''Quacks of Helicon,'' he accuses Wilmer of imitating the ''sarcastic epistles of the times of Dryden and Pope.''[72] Poe even sees in Wilmer a following of ''the most trivial points''—''the old forms of punctuation, the turns of phraseology, the tricks of rhythm, the arrangement of the paragraphs.'' It is probable also that he knew the ''Art of Sinking

---

[70] *S. L. M.*, 1837, vol. 3, p. 42. Review of *Bryant's Poems*.

[71] *Graham's Magazine*, 1842, vol. 20, p. 69. *Exordium*.

[72] *Ibid.*, 1841, vol. 19, p. 90. Review of *The Quacks of Helicon: a Satire*.

in Poetry,''[73] and that he learned from it that the use of magnifying and diminishing figures would produce an effect of bathos. Poe applied this idea of the bathetic to Drake's poem "To a Friend": "Stanza the fourth, although beginning nobly, concludes with that very common exemplification of the bathos, the illustrating natural objects of beauty or grandeur by reference to the tinsel of artificiality.''[74] He also uses the same principle in his criticism of "The Fall of Niagara,''[75] by John C. Brainard. That poet, it seems, had compared the majestic fall of the cataract to water poured from the hand of the Deity.

"The third line embodies an absurd and impossible, not to say, a contemptible image. We are called upon to conceive a similarity between the *continuous downward* sweep of Niagara and the momentary splashing of some definite and of course trifling quantity of water *from a hand;* for, although it is the hand of the Deity himself which is referred to, the mind is irresistibly led by the word 'poured from his hollow hand' to that idea which has been *customarily* attached to such a phrase. . . . Thus bathos is inevitable.''[76]

Poe also knew Pope's art of versification, and there is reason to suppose that the writer of the Fine Arts article had the same knowledge. Two years before the publication of the article on Fine Arts, Poe had spoken of Pope's understanding of counterbalancing fluctuations that have been used for the relief of monotone.[77] On that occasion he gave several examples from the "Dunciad" to show that Pope freely used this method to produce the metrical effect of equalization. It will be remembered that this connection of music with proportion was noted as an identity of critical views between Poe and the author of the Fine Arts article. It is therefore conceivable that the student in the Philadelphia art gallery, having already shown himself a student of Pope, may have derived some part of his idea of the connection between music and proportion from Pope also.

Quite as convincing, however, as the identity of criticism in the field of both art and literature, in establishing Poe's authorship to

---

[73]The satire in which Pope, Swift, and Arbuthnot collaborated.

[74]*S. L. M.*, vol. 2, p. 333. Review of Drake.

[75]*Graham's Magazine*, 1842, vol. 20, p. 120. *A Few Words About Brainard.*

[76]Other references to *Bathos, Works*, vol. 2, p. 95; vol. 1, p. 306.

[77]*S. L. M.*, vol. 3, p. 42. Review of *Bryant's Poems*. This point will be more fully treated in Chapter V.

the "Half Hour in the Academy of Fine Arts," is his account of
his contributions to the magazine in which it was published. Burton, the chief editor, had accused him, it seems, of supplying only
two or three pages of manuscript a month. Poe replied by tabu-
lating month by month the number of pages that he wrote, his
computation showing that he supplied by the month, on an average,
no less than eleven pages. If Poe's figures are accepted, then, as
Prof. Campbell suggests, more material must be assigned to his
pen than has hitherto been done.[78] That part of this extra material
was the article on the Fine Arts might be inferred from what Poe
himself adds in his letter to Burton, to the effect that "at first"
he wrote long articles for the *Gentleman's Magazine*. The publishing of the Fine Arts article agrees in time with this early period
which Poe mentions, since it appeared one month after Poe's connection with Burton began. These points are contained in what
Poe writes to Burton:—

"Upon the whole, I am not willing to admit that you have greatly
overpaid me. That I did not do four times as much for the magazine as I did was your own fault. At first I wrote long articles
which you deemed inadmissible, and never did I suggest any to
which you had not some immediate and decided objection."[79]
The fact that Burton deemed the long articles "inadmissible" need
not, it would seem, preclude some of them from having been published, since the article in question was signed with a pseudonym.

A reasonable conclusion following this consideration of the
article on the Fine Arts, may possibly be that, owing to the identity
of criticism existing between Poe and the writer of the article, the
fact that the art student was also a literary critic, the evidence that
Pope was a common interest, and the necessity of giving Poe added
material to make the extent of his contributions to Burton's magazine reach his own figures, the art student and Poe were the same
person. It may further be concluded that Poe was finding principles in the drama and in the fine arts to improve his standard of
literary criticism, and his practice in constructing his tale of effect. In fact, it may properly be said that his understanding of
the dramatic principles of unity of action and unity of time had
much to do with the form he gave the short story.

---

[78]*Works, Biography*, p. 165. Poe's letter to Burton. Cf. *Nation*, vol. 89, p
623.

[79]*Works, Biography*, pp. 166; 148.

A principle so congenial to the needs of a writer did Poe find in the drama that he appears to contemplate it abstractly. The following chapter will endeavor to present Poe as he philosophized upon unity.

CHAPTER IV
UNITY IN TERMS OF PHILOSOPHY

Poe's interest in philosophy was an added influence on his literary art. By this study he enlarged and strengthened his power of thinking, and, as a consequence his comprehension of the principle of unity—the principle which, as has been shown, he had found explained to a certain extent in *Blackwood,* and further elaborated in various writings on the drama.

Current literary criticism was doubtless one source from which Poe drew the idea that philosophy was an important factor in attaining excellence in writing. He may have been familiar with A. W. von Schlegel's[1] suggestion that the principle of unity as applied to literature was best sought for in a system of metaphysics.[2] A fuller development of the idea there is reason to believe he found in his readings of both Wordsworth and Coleridge. It becomes, then, a matter of moment to conjecture to how great an extent Poe knew the critical opinions of writers of his time. First of all, is the testimony of his own references to Wordsworth and Coleridge. Professor Prescott has pointed out that Poe had an early knowledge of Wordsworth's "Prefaces to the Lyrical Ballads."[3] He shows that Poe, evidently in a spirit of hostility, quoted in the "Letter to B—"[4] certain passages from the "Prefaces." A further investigation, however, reveals instances of Poe's early indebtedness to Wordsworth that are of a more sympathetic nature. His early announcement that popularity is no test of literary merit bears a striking resemblance to Wordsworth's long discussion of the subject in his essay "Poetry as a Study,"[5] for he took Wordsworth's standpoint that the sale of a book was no proof of its value as a literary production. In his answer to Theodore Fay, the author of "Norman Leslie,"[6] the popularity of whose book he had ridiculed, Poe thus states Wordsworth's argument:—

---

[1] Cf. Chapter III for evidence of Poe's knowledge of Schlegel.

[2] Schlegel, *Lectures on Dramatic Art and Literature,* p. 244.

[3] Prescott, F. C., *op.cit.,* Introduction, p. xxxii.

[4] *S. L. M.,* vol. 2, p. 501.

[5] Wordsworth, William. *The Prose Works of William Wordsworth.* Grosart ed. London, 1876, vol. 2, p. 129. The date of this essay is 1815.

[6] Theodore Fay was one of the editors of the *New York Mirror.* Poe con-

"Mr. Fay wishes us to believe that the sale of a book is the proper test of its merit. To save time and trouble we *will* believe it, and are prepared to acknowledge, as a consequence of the theory, that the novel of 'Norman Leslie' is not at all comparable to the 'Memoirs of Davy Crockett,' or the popular lyric of Jim Crow.''[7]

Poe also appears to have found helpful a passage from Wordsworth's "Of Poetry as Observation and Description." This passage deals with Wordsworth's distinction between fancy and imagination. Wordsworth, praising the advantages of the imaginative or indefinite element in poetry over those of the fanciful, considers it a poetic excellence not to limit the range of thought by any definite imagery.—

"Having to speak of stature, she [Imagination] does not tell you that her gigantic Angel was as tall as Pompey's Pillar; much less that he was twelve cubits, or twelve hundred cubits high; or that his dimensions equalled those of Teneriffe or Atlas;—because these, if they were a million times as high . . . are bounded.''[8]

Poe also sees the advantages of the indefinite element in poetry. Although at this time he does not, as does Wordsworth, free the imagination from any numerical bound, yet he so stresses its flight that one feels at least a note of Wordsworthian influence. For example,[9] in attempting to show that fancy and not imagination has prompted Drake in his "Culprit Fay" to employ definite imagery and that the poet has sacrificed much beauty by his choice, he says:—

"Their mistake [meaning the mistake of those who had admired the poem chiefly on the grounds of what they thought to be its imaginative quality] would be precisely analogous to that of many a schoolboy who admires the imagination displayed in *Jack the Giant-Killer*, and is finally rejoiced at discovering his own imagination to surpass that of the author, since the monsters destroyed

sidered Fay's book, as he says, the very worst book ever published, and he doubtless thought its popularity confirming testimony of the truth of Wordsworth's point. *S. L. M.*, vol. 2, p. 54.

[7] *S. L. M.*, vol. 2, p. 340. Other references to Poe's idea that popularity was no test of excellence: Review of *Charles O'Malley*. (*Works*, vol. 4, p. 86). Review of Dickens' *Barnaby Rudge*. (*Works*, vol. 4, p. 40.)

[8] If Poe is granted to be the writer of the article on the Fine Arts, signed by a Philadelphian, discussed in Chapter III, he, probably, for this principle, is indebted to Lessing's *Laocoon*. But he is apparently also indebted to Wordsworth's Essay, *Of Poetry as Observation and Description*. (Cf. Wordsworth's *Prose Works*, vol. 2, p. 141.)

[9] *S. L. M.*, vol. 2, p. 332. Review of Drake's *Culprit Fay*.

by Jack are only about forty feet in height, and he himself has
no trouble in imagining some of one hundred and forty."

Poe's very evident acquaintance with Wordsworth's Essays,
makes it not surprising, then, that we find him considering, with
Wordsworth, their main thesis; namely, the connection between
philosophy and literature. Indeed, nowhere is his attentive study
of the "Prefaces" so manifest as in his agreements and disagree-
ments with this point. His growing belief that poetry, in a sense,
rises from a ground-work of metaphysics, a sense which this chapter will endeavor to explain, has at its start a positive denial of the
connection. In 1831, in the spirit of hostility referred to above,
he bitterly protests against Wordsworth's doctrine that poetry is a
study. He says:—

"As for Wordsworth, I have no faith in him. . . . He was
to blame in wearing away his youth in contemplation with the end
of poetizing in his manhood. With the increase of his judgment
the light which should have made it apparent has faded away.
. . . Against the subtleties which would make poetry a study
—not a passion—it becomes the metaphysician to reason—but the
poet to protest."[10]
"Learning," he adds, "has little to do with the imagination—in-
tellect with the passions—or age with poetry." At this time he
expresses his conviction that poetic fervor cannot be understood by
the cool judgment of a critic. But in 1836 he appears to reverse
his opinion, and in an article entitled "Genius"[11] he appears to

---

[10]*Ibid.*, vol. 2, p. 502. Prescott explains that the *Letter to B——* was first
prefixed to Poe's poems issued in 1831. The letter is dated, "West Point,
1831." Prescott considers the *Letter to B——* a protest against Wordsworth's contention that poetry is a study. Cf. notes to Prescott's work,
p. 324.

[11]*S. L. M.*, vol. 2, p. 297, *Genius*. Dr. John W. Robertson, in his bibliographical study of Poe, suggests the probability of Poe's authorship of the
article entitled *Genius*. He points out that the Editor's note appended to
Genius is similar to that which follows *The Letter to B——*, which Poe had
published in the *S. L. M.* In both these notes, the editor apologizes for
the opinions expressed, saying that of course he cannot be held responsible
for them. Had the similarity ended with these notes, Dr. Robertson adds,
it would be impossible to assign to Poe the authorship of *Genius*. But he
thinks that he can see in it marks characteristic of Poe; the article dealing,
he says, with the definition of poetry and containing "equally pronounced
ideas as to its true object."—Robertson, *Edgar A. Poe, A Study*. San Francisco, 1921, p. 251. But additional proof of Poe's authorship can certainly
be presented. In the first place, the article appears to mark a turning point
in Poe's attitude toward study. Poe's work of 1831 maintained that a poet

agree with Wordsworth, first, that poetry is a study, and secondly, as a necessary corollary, that philosophy and poetry are indissolubly connected.

Genius, Poe says in 1836, is not wholly a question of natural talent or of strong inclination.[12] It is rather a "decided preference for any study or pursuit, which enables its possessor to give the close and unwearied attention necessary to insure success. When this constancy of purpose is wanting, the brightest natural talents will give little aid in acquiring literary or scientific eminence; and where it exists in any considerable degree, it is rare to find one so ill endowed with common sense as not to gain a respectable standing." He quotes the words of many master writers that testify to their dissatisfaction with their first literary efforts and to their arduous attempts to attain greater perfection. Molière, he thinks, gives testimony that speaks for the need of a writer's painstaking effort.—

"Voila, s'écria Molière, en interrompant son ami á cet endroit, voilà la plus belle vérité que vous ayez jamais dite. Je ne suis pas du nombre de ces esprits sublimes dont vous parlez; mais tel que je suis, je n'ai rien fait en ma vie dont je sois veritablement content."

Pascal, too, he describes as spending much time in "revising and correcting what to others appeared from the first almost too perfect for amendment." And Gray was "never content with the polish which repeated revisions were able to give his works." He cites the conclusion of Boileau's *Second Satire*, saying it is appropriate to his purpose. "Un sot, en écrivant, fait tout avec plaisir: . . ."

Thus Poe is apparently satisfied that writing is a matter of studied effort; that, to borrow in part the testimony of those whose words he was quoting, it needs "close and unwearied attention." He, therefore, concludes that successful writing must be viewed

---

wrote only through inspiration; his reviews, beginning 1836, assert that a poet owed his excellence to arduous toil.—*S. L. M.*, vol. 2, p. 330. *Culprit Fay*. It shows, too, an attitude toward Coleridge differing from that in 1831 and similar to that in 1836.—*S. L. M.*, vol. 2, p. 330. Corroborating evidence is likewise found in Poe's definition of the word *industria*. It has, he says, a more variable meaning than is usually given it, a mental rather than a physical exertion, and really signifies what moderns attach to the term *genius*. —*S. L. M.*, vol. 2, p. 392. Review of *Anthon's Sallust*.

[12]*Ibid.*, vol. 2, p. 297. *Genius*. Poe gives Pope credit for the idea that genius is synonymous with strong inclination.

with philosophic bearings, and to this end, it can be shown he sought help from various sources.

Not only from opinions of literary critics did Poe learn to connect philosophy with literature, but there is reason to believe that he was also indebted to his study of the writings of philosophers of his own time and of periods preceding. Twice in his article "Genius" he shows that he is familiar with Dugald Stewart. "The following quotation," he says, in the article referred to, "is from the seventh chapter, sixth section of Stewart's 'Elements of the Philosophy of the Human Mind',"[13] and in characterizing the composition of Robert Hall, he again has reference to Stewart. " 'I am tormented with a desire to write better than I can,' said Robert Hall in a letter to a friend; and yet his works are said by Stewart (himself an admirable writer in points of style) to combine the beauties of Addison, Johnson, and Burke, without their defects, and to contain the purest specimens of English language.'"[14] In an editorial note Poe also quotes from Stewart:—

"Dugald Stewart justly observes, that by confining our ambition to pursue the truth with modesty and candor, and learning to value our acquisitions only so far as they contribute to make us wiser and happier, we may perhaps be obliged to sacrifice the temporary admiration of the common dispensers of literary fame; but, we may rest assured, it is thus only we can hope to make real progress in knowledge or to enrich the world with useful inventions.''[15]

In another note to the same editorial article, Poe gives the "Philosophy of the Human Mind" as the source of the following quotation: " 'It requires courage indeed,' (as Helvetius has remarked) 'to remain ignorant of those useless subjects which are generally valued:' but it is a courage necessary to men who love the truth, and who aspire to establish a permanent reputation.''

Poe, likewise, was familiar with Locke.[17] It has been already noted that he may have been guided to Locke from acquaintance with the *Blackwood* sensation story based on experience. Though a second-hand knowledge of Locke may have come to him through

---

[13]*Ibid.*, vol. 2, p. 298.

[14]*Ibid.*, vol. 2, p. 299.

[15]This passage coincides with Wordsworth's suggestion. Cf. note 6. *Ibid.*, p. 141.

[17]It is an interesting fact that Locke's *Essay on the Human Understanding* was the first book published by Harper Brothers. The book, says the *S. L. M.* of September, 1839, vol. 5, p. 629, was eminently successful and thus afforded a happy prognostic of the future career of the publishing firm.

the pages of Dugald Stewart, whose work is filled with Lockian philosophy, there are indications that point to Poe's first-hand knowledge of that philosopher. He says himself that he has read Locke's "Essay on Education";[18] and inklings here and there suggest a familiarity with Locke's "Essay on the Human Understanding." For example, in one instance he speaks confidently of Hazlitt's being a just criticism of that work;[19] in another,[20] he claims a knowledge of Locke's treatment of the Memory. A further indication that he knew Locke from a first-hand reading, is the fact that he gives Locke credit for the principle of personal identity which he makes the thesis of "Morella," one of the tales of the Folio Club. In fact, he clearly copies from the pages of the Essay, the outstanding points in Locke's presentation of the subject. "That *Identity*," he says, quoting from Locke's chapter, Of Identity and Diversity, "which is not improperly termed *Personal*, I think Mr. Locke truly defines to consist in the sameness of a rational being. And since by person we understand an intelligent essence having reason, and since there is a consciousness which always accompanies thinking, it is this which makes us all to be that which we call *ourselves*—thereby distinguishing us from other beings that think, and giving us our personal identity."[21] He appears, moreover, in his article "Genius," to summarize other passages from Locke's "Essay on the Human Understanding," and he definitely states that Locke has been the source of this material. The following parallel columns will show how clearly Poe gathers together the main points in Locke's treatment of the origin of our ideas, and how obviously he is trying to see argument in its philosophic bearings.

---

[18]*S. L. M.*, vol. 2, p. 388. This passage appeared during Poe's editorship and since it forms a part of *Verbal Criticisms* and is unsigned, it seems only reasonable to conclude that Poe was its author.

[19]*Ibid.*, vol. 2, p. 668. Review of *Hazlitt's Remains*.

[20]*Ibid.*, vol. 2, p. 505. Review of *Letters to Young Ladies*. By Mrs. L. H. Sigourney.

[21]*Ibid.*, vol. 1, p. 448. *Morella*. This was one of The Tales of the Folio Club presented to *The Baltimore Visitor* in competition for the prize. What Poe says on personal identity is apparently drawn from vol. 2, p. 52 of Locke's works. London, 1801.

Essay on the Human Under-
standing—Locke
vol. 1, p. 78

". . . Our senses . . . do convey into the mind several distinct perceptions of things, according to those various ways wherein those objects do affect them: . . . This great source of most of the ideas we have, depending wholly upon our senses, and derived by them to the understanding, I call SENSATION.

"Secondly, The other fountain, from which experience furnisheth the understanding with ideas, is the perception of the operation of our own mind within us, as it is employed about the ideas it has got; which operations when the soul comes to reflect on and consider, do furnish the understanding with another set of ideas, which could not be had from things without; and such are Perception, Thinking, Doubting, Believing, Reasoning, Knowing, Willing, and all the different actings of our own minds; which we being conscious of and observing in ourselves, do from these receive into our understandings as distinct ideas, as we do from bodies affecting our senses. . . . But as I call the other sensation, so I call this REFLECTION, the ideas it affords being such only as the mind gets by reflecting on its own operations within itself. By reflection then, . . . I would be understood to mean that notice which the mind takes of its own operations, and the manner of them; by reason whereof there come to be ideas of these operations in the understanding. These two, I say, viz. external

Genius—Poe
S. L. M., vol. 2, p. 300

"Locke has sufficiently proved that all our ideas are originally derived from the senses. These first impressions form the basis of all human knowledge.

"General conclusions drawn from comparisons of such sensations are abstract thought. Reasoning and reflection on these abstract ideas thus obtained, constitute speculations of still greater refinement.

material things, as the objects of sensation; and the operations of our own minds within, as the objects of reflection; are to me the only originals from whence all our ideas take their beginnings. The term operations here I use in a large sense, as comprehending not barely the actions of the mind about its ideas, but some sort of passions arising sometimes from them, such as is the satisfaction or uneasiness arising from any thought.

"Would you have a man reason well, you must use him to it betimes, exercise his mind in observing the connection of ideas, and following them in train. Nothing does this better than mathematics. . . . For, in all sorts of reasoning, every single argument should be managed as a mathematical demonstration; the connection and dependence of ideas should be followed till the mind is brought to the source on which it bottoms. . . ."

"Comparing and combining ideas in the mind, for the purpose of discovering relations as they exist in nature, is argument."

Beyond question, Poe scanned the pages of Dugald Stewart and Locke.

This study which Poe made of philosophy apparently led him to consider not only the presence of the philosophic element in poetry, but also the relation which the two bear to each other. In other words, his study of philosophy appears to resolve itself into a consideration of the distinction between subject-matter and technique.

In the early days of his study, Poe disagrees with Wordsworth's view of connecting philosophy with subject-matter. He understands Wordsworth to think that metaphysics in its connection with poetry means instruction.[22] Working from this basis, he began in 1831, an attack on didacticism—an attack which, it will later be shown, he kept up consistently throughout his literary career.[23]

---

[22]*S. L. M.*, vol. 2, p. 501, *Letter to B——*.
[23]Cf. Chapter V.

He likewise disagreed with Wordsworth in the view that technique springs from subject-matter. He did not comprehend, in this early period, the philosophical import of Wordsworth's subject-matter chosen from "real Life."[24] He says, in direct contradiction to the validity of Wordsworth's experiment :—

"The dull scenes of real life can never be suffered to chill the ardor of a romantic imagination. And as the poet finds truth too plain and unadorned to satisfy his enthusiastic fancy, he is compelled to seek subjects and scenery of a more faultless nature and brighter hues than this world affords."[25]

Though, as has been shown, he agreed with Locke that argument, or the combination and comparison of abstract ideas, is originally derived from the senses, he yet does not in this early period of philosophic study connect the point with subject-matter.[26] Instead, he stresses philosophy chiefly in its bearing on technique. Coleridge doubtless was one of the influences that led him to this view.

In favor of the supposition that from Coleridge came the suggestion of connecting philosophy mainly with the technical side of writing, is the evidence of Poe's critical work of 1836. He speaks in his review of Drake's "Culprit Fay" of the value in the production of a fine poem of the "powers of Causality," and he is strongly of the opinion that Coleridge possessed these powers in abundance, this "metaphysical acumen." Since he could not in any way have considered the subject-matter of "The Ancient Mariner" or of "Christabel" to be philosophical, he must have meant that Coleridge was metaphysical from the standpoint of technique.

---

[24]It is suggested that a study might be made of Wordsworth's indebtedness to Locke's philosophy for the "experiment" in poetry. The language arising from experience, from a state of vivid sensation, seems to be Wordsworth's meaning of a "philosophical language," and seems, therefore, to explain his choice of incidents and situations from common life.

At the time of writing the first paragraph of this note Professor Arthur Beatty's study of Wordsworth had not been read. Professor Beatty's work treats of Wordsworth's literary theory as arising from a basis of English philosophy, emphasis being laid chiefly on the philosophic ideas of Hartley. But the study of Wordsworth as a student of philosophy may, I think, be extended further than Professor Beatty has carried it, especially as it may be found to explain and develop a method of writing that follows natural processes of mental growth. Such a system might, from its genesis in scientific methods of observation and experimentation, be called a scientific system.

[25]S. L. M., vol. 2, p. 297. Genius.

[26]In a later chapter it will be shown that Poe came to feel that forceful and effective writing has no greater ally than the intent to depict real life.

In the review of the "Book of Gems"[27] he again reveals himself a student of Coleridge's attitude toward philosophy and literary technique. In this instance, he professes to see a distinction between the sense in which Donne and Cowley are metaphysical and that in which Coleridge is. With them, he said, ethics were the end; with Coleridge, ethics are the means. This distinction he explains in the following way:—

"The poet of the "Creation" wished, by highly artificial verse to inculcate what he considered moral truth—he of the "Auncient Mariner" to infuse the *Poetic Sentiment* through channels suggested by mental analysis. The one finished by complete failure what he commenced in the grossest misconception—the other, by a path which could not possibly lead him astray, arrived at a certainty and intensity of triumph which is not the less brilliant and glorious because concentrated among the very few who have the power to perceive it."

And, further, with an apparent effort to comprehend more fully the bearing of philosophy on technique in writing, he launches forth into a study of the question from the pages of the "Biographia Literaria."

In the first place, Poe's reading can be traced to the place in the "Biographia Literaria" where Coleridge explains the idea of unity in variety. It has already been noted by Professor Prescott[28] that Poe's definition of the imagination may, perhaps, be an "echo" of Coleridge's definition of the same faculty. In idea, at least, as the following parallel columns indicate, the two appear to be strikingly similar.

Biographia Literaria—Coleridge p. 144	Review of *Culprit Fay*—Poe S. L. M., vol. 2, p. 328
"The primary imagination I hold to be the living power and prime agent of all human perception, and as a repetition in the finite mind of the eternal act of creation in the infinite I AM."	"Imagination is, possibly, in man, a lesser degree of the creative power in God."

Coleridge gave his definition, which we may grant Poe knew, to summarize[29] his previous explanation of a principle back of the

---

[27]*S. L. M.*, vol. 2, p. 585.

[28]Prescott's Notes to Poe's Review of Drake's *Culprit Fay*. Critical Essays, Prescott, *op. cit.*, p. 326.

[29]Coleridge, *Biog. Lit.*, p. 144. Coleridge prefaces his definition of the imagination with the following: "I shall content myself for the present with stating the main result of the chapter."

working of this mental faculty.[30]   It is reasonable to think that
Poe, knowing the summary, would in all probability read the preceding pages leading up to the summary, and would, therefore,
have been familiar with this discussion of unity.   Another fact
points to the supposition that Poe had an early knowledge of these
pages in the "Biographia Literaria."   In his "Letter to B—" he
quotes a passage that occurs in Coleridge's discussion of the question.[31]   Poe would, therefore, have been familiar with the principle
of unity in variety as it was explained by Coleridge.   Granting
this knowledge on Poe's part, one may with reason believe that he
could consider with Coleridge the principle back of the imaginative faculty.   He would have found it explained to be the working
of two contrary counteracting forces; first, as an abstract idea suggested as Coleridge says from astronomical law, and secondly, as a
fact in our mental life.[32]   The significance of this knowledge that
we are doubtless justified in attributing to Poe, will appear in the
chapter[33] on science.

The application of this philosophical understanding of unity in
variety to literary technique was, doubtless, a further point in Poe's
study of Coleridge.   In the first place, he could well have found,
during his study of the pages in question, Coleridge's promise to
explain the bearing of the principle on criticism in the fine arts.[34]
He could, also, have read the fulfillment of this promise as it occurs in the chapter following these pages.[35]   In the second place,

---

[30]*Ibid.*, pp. 114-144.

[31]*Ibid.*, p. 121.   *"J'ai trouvé que la plupart des sectes ont raison dans une
bonne partie de ce qu'elles avancent, mais non pas tant en ce qu'elles nient."*

[32]*Ibid.*, pp. 134; 141.

[33]See Chapter V.

[34]Coleridge, *op.cit.*, p. 128.

[35]Coleridge clearly expresses in the following passage the action of the two
counteracting forces in terms of literary technique: "The office of philosophical disquisition consists in just distinction; while it is the privilege of
the philosopher to preserve himself constantly aware that distinction is not
division.   In order to obtain adequate notions of any truth, we must intel-
lectually separate its distinguishable parts; and this is the technical process
of philosophy.   But having so done, we must then restore them in our conceptions to the unity in which they actually co-exist; and this is the result
of Philosophy.   A poem contains the same elements as a prose composition; the
difference, therefore, must consist in a different combination of them, in consequence of a different object proposed.   According to the difference of the
object will be the difference of the combination."—*Ibid.*, p. 147.

certain indications point to the fact that Poe made original research for the purpose of enlarging his understanding of the relation of philosophy to the art of writing. There is, first, the testimony of his very probable knowledge of Coleridge's incomplete explanation of this relationship.[36] Poe may, therefore, have wished to supplement Coleridge's study. Another indication is the fact that a large body of material in the *Southern Literary Messenger* appears during the time of Poe's editorship which bears evidence that a more or less systematic research had been made into philosophy. That the student conducting this research may have been Poe is a likely supposition, since the articles in general follow the line of interest which I have just shown to be Poe's; namely, that of the relation of philosophy to technique. In addition to this reason is the fact that some of these articles are signed P., and one in particular has the editorial tone.

This original research shows itself in an evident effort, on the part of a student, to extend his knowledge of classical writers. A list of Greek authors,[37] chronologically arranged, appears in the *Southern Literary Messenger* in 1836. It is signed, "P." and gives information concerning the titles and numbers of works extant of Greek writers, beginning with Homer. A second list, citing editions of the classics "fittest to enter a literary collection of the Roman and Greek authors"[38] also appears in the *Southern Literary Messenger* of the same year. Poe had, without a doubt, called for the compiling of this list, since a letter indicating that it was in answer to the editor's request prefaces the article.[39] The student

---

[36]At the end of Chapter XII, *Biographia Literaria*, Coleridge announces that he intends, in his explanation of the imagination, "to go back much further than Mr. Wordsworth's subject required or permitted." At the end of Chapter XIII, he says he has been deterred by a very "judicious letter" (which he publishes in full) from giving all the explanation he had intended. He gives, he says, the "main result" of the chapter which he reserves "for that future publication, a detailed prospectus of which the reader will find at the close of the second volume." The editor adds in a footnote: "Mr. Coleridge did not issue this prospectus."—*Biographia Literaria*, p. 144.

[37]*S. L. M.*, vol. 2, p. 301. B. B. Minor definitely assigns this article to Poe. *Op. cit.*, p. 42.

[38]*Ibid.*, vol. 2, p. 677. *Classical Bibliography*.

[39]Poe was Editor. The letter is signed, "E. W. J., South Carolina College." The information contained in the list appears to be drawn largely from Brunet's Manual, which is one of the sources mentioned in the article.

advances in his effort to acquire a knowledge of classical literature as is shown by a number of short contributions all bearing on
the subject. One short piece, entitled "Greek Song," bears the sig-
nature, "P.",[40] and reveals an interest in versification which, as the
following chapter will show, was preëminently an engrossing subject with Poe. Another piece, "Palaestine,"[41] signed "P.", contains references to Tacitus. "Pinakidia,"[42] reveals Poe in his interest in classical literature. At least thirty-three of the selections
in this compilation deal with classical subjects. Even the name
of the collection indicates a leaning toward the classics, for Poe
says: "We have chosen the heading 'Pinakidia' or 'Tablets'. It
was used for a somewhat similar purpose by Dionysius . . ."
In addition to these pieces which from their signatures are unmistakably Poe's, there are six other pieces[43] unsigned that, owing to
their connection with the classics, might be considered as either
revealing the Editor's choice in contributed matter, or even as proceeding from his pen. We are in either case, it might seem, justified in naming Poe as the student who was investigating classical literature.

Poe's interest in classical learning appears in this original investigation to limit itself to philosophy of the ancients. There
is reason to believe that he wrote three articles entitled "Philosophy
of Antiquity."[44] In favor of this supposition may be cited Poe's
known tendency to philosophize on any and all subjects.[45] Of

---

[40]*S. L. M.*, vol. 2, p. 38.

[41]Professor Harrison has admitted this piece into his edition of Poe's *Works*,
vol. 14, p. 1, saying in a note that the *S. L. M.*, 1836, enters it in the index
as one of Poe's compositions.

[42]*S. L. M.*, vol. 2, p. 573.

[43]*Ibid.*, vol. 2, p. 737. *Character of Coriolanus.*

Ibid., vol. 2, p. 466. Story entitled *Erostratus*. B. B. Minor hints that
Poe may have been the author of this piece. *Op. cit.*, p. 49.

S. L. M., vol. 2, p. 93. Article on a translation of one of Horace's *Odes*.

Ibid., vol. 2, p. 154. The *New Testament*.

Ibid., vol. 2, p. 159. *Statius.*

Ibid., vol. 2, p. 221. *The Classics.* B. B. Minor does not suggest the
authorship of this last piece. *Op. cit.*, p. 41.

[44]*S. L. M.*, vol. 2, p. 739. *Philosophy of Antiquity.*

Ibid., vol. 3, p. 33. *Philosophy of Antiquity.*

Ibid., vol. 3, p. 158. *Philosophy of Antiquity.*

[45]*Graham's Magazine.* 1848, February-May, p. 130. *Philosophy of Furni-
ture. Works: Philosophy of Composition, Rationale of Verse, Philosophy of
Point.* Also *Works*, vol. 5, p. 27. *The Mystery of Marie Rogêt.*

some importance, too, may be the fact that after Poe withdrew from the editorship of the *Messenger*, the last number of the series of "Philosophy of Antiquity" was made to occupy an insignificant place in the magazine. At this point a few words regarding Poe and White as they worked together may furnish a background that explains this disposal of the piece. Poe and White, it seems, disagreed in the nature of suitable contributions to the *Messenger*. White appears not to have been sympathetic with material Poe proposed. Half-heartedly White promises in a letter to Poe to "get more than the first portion of Pym in," although he much fears that "that will be impossible." If he had read "ten lines of Magruder's manuscript," he would never have had the type set for a line of it. And, with an especially vicious turn he adds: "It is all . . . bombast. He will have to live a little longer before he can write well enough to please the readers of the *M*." Recalling this division of opinion between White and Poe, one may not be greatly in error if he thinks some connection exists between Poe's withdrawal from the magazine and the extremely insignificant position that the third number of "Philosophy of Antiquity" is made to occupy; for Poe's resignation from the *Messenger* and the uncomplimentary position of the piece referred to, occur the same month. Moreover, further points connect Poe with these articles. Their thesis is identical with that of Poe's known work of the same period. In 1836, the year of their publication,[46] his critical reviews were largely occupied, it will be remembered, with the literary principle of unity. He had used Schlegel's unity of effect and unity of interest as criteria for praising or condemning the work that came under his notice. The author of "Philosophy of Antiquity" also dwells on unity. It will be shown that he considers unity as a principle of the universe in the way that Pythagoras, Xenophanes, Zeno, and other ancient philosophers explain it. While he gives Schlegel, Tennemann, Tiedmann, and Lemprière as his sources, it appears from comparing the articles in question with Tennemann's "Manual of the History of Philosophy,"[47] that that philosopher furnished him with practically all the

---

[46] The last of the series was published at the beginning of 1837.

[47] Tennemann, *A Manual of the History of Philosophy*. Translated from the German of Tennemann, by the Rev. Arthur Johnson, M.A., London, Bohn Ed., 1852. The preface to the edition 1852, which is stated to be the second, says that its basis was "the Reverend Arthur Johnson's translation, printed at Oxford in 1832."

material he needed. While verbal similarities extend throughout pages, I shall only indicate by short passages what the nature of the dependence is.

A Manual of the History of Philosophy	Philosophy of Antiquity
Tennemann—p. 55	S. L. M., vol. 2, p. 739

A Manual of the History of Philosophy
Tennemann—p. 55

"The starting-point of philosophy was the question concerning the origin and the elementary principle of the world."

"*Thales* . . . was the first Grecian who discussed, on principles of reason, the origin of the world. *Water* . . . was in his opinion (formed in consequence of some empirical observations very partial in their nature) the original element, . . ."

Philosophy of Antiquity
S. L. M., vol. 2, p. 739

"The *point de depart* of philosophy was the origin of the world and its elementary principle."

"According to Thales the principle of the world is water. He is said to have been induced to adopt this, in consequence of some partial experiments."

The writer of the articles in the *Southern Literary Messenger* concludes that the point which these philosophers have in common is that of unity. However widely these systems varied, he says, whether they belonged to the empirical school or whether they came under the head of the idealists, they still saw unity as the elementary principle of existence,[48] a point which brings the writer and Poe, as has already been said, into sympathetic relations.

The thesis of "The Philosophy of Antiquity" agrees, too, with "The Classics" which we felt justified in connecting with Poe's name; the latter article containing a long discussion of unity, philosophically considered. "The eternal spirit of the universe," says the author in this article, "is a beauty and unity of design."[49]

Another feature binds together the various parts of this research into philosophy and, it would seem, unmistakably presents them as the work of one person. This outstanding note is the need expressed for philosophic study. Indeed, such an argument runs consistently throughout the body of material under consideration. The general agreement seems to be that many advantages attend the concentration on the pursuit of philosophic truth. In the first place, several of the articles cite the need from the point of view of the limited time allotted to human life. The editorial article

---

[48]*S. L. M.*, vol. 3, p. 158. *Philosophy of Antiquity.*
[49]*Ibid.*, vol. 2, p. 221. *The Classics.*

entitled "Selection in Reading" warns the reader that, owing to
the brief space of his existence, he should "confine his ambitions
to pursue the truth with modesty and candor."[50] "The Classics"[51]
discusses the same point at length. The ancient philosophers, says
this article, understood that philosophic truth was the "most important and natural inquiry which would present itself to a being of limited powers of knowledge and enjoyment, and whose
existence at most is brief." In the second place, the pursuit of
philosophic truth is said to develop the spiritual life. The value
of our acquisitions in knowledge, says the editorial article "Selection in Reading," is in proportion to their power to make us wiser
and happier.[52] An elaboration of the same subject is in "The
Classics," the article asserting that ancient philosophies furnish
the best means of attaining happiness. These means are rules of
virtue, "cold, cautious inductions of philosophy," but, the eloquence of Plato breathed into them, they become radiant and impressive arguments to exalt our spiritual being.[53] The opening
words of the first article on the "Philosophy of Antiquity" may
also have a similar import. Philosophy is there spoken of as a boon
for which modern times have every cause to be grateful.[54] From
the foregoing evidence, it may not be unreasonable to suppose that
Poe was the author of the articles, the "Philosophy of Antiquity,"
and that he was the student who was interesting himself in ancient
philosophies.

I shall now try to show that Poe's interest in classical learning
was again narrowed, this time into what would seem a profound
and concentrated understanding of unity; not unity in the general sense one might have inferred during the course of the proof
brought forward to establish him as a student of ancient philosophy
and the author of the articles mentioned; but unity in the sense
of unvarying law, a law that governs the universe, by what may be
called an approach to a scientific method.

It is of special interest to observe how Poe works out in this early
period of study what seemed to him a reasonable understanding of
unvarying law in the universe; for, at this beginning of philosophic

---

[50]*Ibid.*, vol. 2, p. 141.   Editorial Note *Selection in Reading.*
[51]*Ibid.*, vol. 2, p. 230.   *The Classics.*
[52]*Ibid.*, vol. 2, p. 141.
[52]*Ibid.*, vol. 2, p. 232.   *The Classics.*
[54]*Ibid.*, vol. 2, p. 739.   *Philosophy of Antiquity.*

research, he shows himself laying the ground-work for his later disposal of the matter in "Eureka." In the next chapter it will be
seen that the doctrine he now encounters among ancient philosophers he uses as, in his belief, did Laplace, for an hypothesis on which
to build with as much scientific certainty as he was able.[55]

It will be remembered that Poe had already met Coleridge's
transcendent interpretation of unity in variety. He had found
Coleridge placing most emphasis on these forces as they exist in
the human intelligence; Coleridge asserting that they lie back
of and explain the creative imagination, likening them, with terms
borrowed from astronomy, to centrifugal and centripetal forces
in nature. He had found, moreover, that Coleridge had declared
his system came from that of Plato, but from Plato purified "from
impure mixtures."

Poe now transfers his study from Coleridge's explanation, which
as was said at a former point in this chapter he doubtless found
unfinished, and considers the question, as we have seen his study
of Tennemann shows, at first hand with Pythagoras, Plato, Leucippus, and other ancient philosophers. He is evidently impressed
with Pythagoras' doctrine that the world is an harmonious whole
—that its very name means *kosmos* or order. This unified whole,
however, he finds Pythagoras saying, is subdivided into imperfect
parts, each revolving around a common centre and following harmonious laws. And the unvarying law displayed in this working
of variety in uniformity is, he agrees with the ancient philosopher,
fittingly described as the music of the spheres. He is likewise interested, he says, in the doctrine of Zeno. He quotes Tennemann
to the effect that Zeno, the apologist for the Eleatic system, provides for the opposing forces of unity and variety, in that all entities
are said to possess similarity and its opposite; unity and plurality;
motion and repose. He considers also that the school of Leucippus
is deserving of special notice, since its doctrine so nearly corres-
ponds with the atomic theory of his own day. It will be seen in
the following chapter that Leucippus had perhaps been strikingly
suggestive to him in the idea of all atoms in the universe tending
toward an ultimate indivisibility; for in "Eureka" he seems to
think, apparently following Leucippus's doctrine, that this final
indivisibility of atoms is a physical example of unity; and that the
combination and separation of atoms in the course of their return

---

[55] Cf. next chapter.

to oneness, accounts for creation and destruction of worlds. But he speaks of Plato with most enthusiasm. "Plato was the philosopher," he says, in "The Classics," "whose beautiful conception of the spirit of the universe" was "at once so poetical and sublime."[57] He dwells with apparent delight on the order and system that Plato sees in the universe; quoting from the "Republic," in his story of the *Coloquy of Monos and Una,* several passages on music as a method of Athenian education, and following the quotation by an explanation that, in his opinion, Plato meant by *music* not only its ordinary meaning, but creation in its widest sense; or, as he says in "Marginalia," proportion and adaptation generally.[58] He is convinced that by giving the Platonic word the translation of *proportion* and not its usual meaning of *music,* the real sense of music of the spheres comes to light, and with it the Platonic sense of unvarying law that is working in the astronomical world. In the latter part of this chapter, it will be seen that Plato's doctrine of the *Many* in *One,* a principle than which in Poe's opinion no better example of unity could be found, was suggestive to Poe as a literary principle. As a summary of Poe's appreciation of Plato, it may be well to quote his words from the "Classics." Plato was "the author whose psychologic system presaged the Christian revelation as the morning twilight betokens the coming sun."[59]

CHRISTIAN PHILOSOPHY

There is evidence pointing to the fact that the work of the so-called Christian philosophy also had an influence on Poe's literary art. In the article on "The Classics" Poe strongly advises the study of Christian philosophy.[60] In another instance[61] he refers to Christian philosophy as the "truest of all philosophies." There is some indication that he was familiar with the Cambridge Platonists. From Dr. Henry More he quotes an argument on "true miracles."[62] Of Thomas Burnet, the author of "Theoria Sacra," he appears to have some knowledge. He thinks with the critic in the *Edinburgh Review* that the continued misspelling of that philosopher's name by the editor of the book in which it appeared, betrayed an ignor-

---

[57]*S. L. M.,* vol. 2, p. 232. *The Classics.*
[58]*Ibid.,* 1849, *Marginalia.*
[59]*S. L. M.,* vol. 2, p. 232. *The Classics.*
[60]*Ibid.,* vol. 2, p. 232. *The Classics.*
[61]*Ibid.,* vol. 2, p. 66. Review of *Reverend D. L. Carroll's Address.*
[62]*Democratic Review,* April, 1846. *Marginalia.*

ance of the seventeenth century writer.[63]   Of Burnet, Poe doubtless
had a better acquaintance than one might infer from the point just
brought forth.   He could have read in the *Southern Literary Messenger* of 1836, in a series of articles on fanciful theories of the
universe, Burnet's theory rather fully explained.[64]   To Cambridge
commentators, who have opened up the field of Platonist writers,
especially to Porson and Parr, he acknowledges a debt of grati-
tude.[65]

Modern Christian philosophers were also known to Poe.   Of
Abraham Tucker, a Christian philosopher of the nineteenth century, he speaks with enthusiasm.   Tucker is, he says, the one who
of all modern philosophers best understands the meaning of Plato.[66]
Of Dr. Thomas Dick he appears to have considerable knowledge.
Referring the reader, as he does in one instance, to the "excellent observation of Dr. Dick, in his *Christian Philosopher*," he testifies, it would seem, to a more than casual acquaintance with that
philosopher's work.[67]   The *Bridgewater Treatises* likewise appear
to have engrossed Poe's attention.   He outlines the plan[68] and con-

---

[63]*Works*, vol. 8, p. 83. *Review of the Edinburgh Review of July, 1836.* The
book reviewed by the Edinburgh critic which contained the misspelled word of
Burnet, was the *History of the Revolution in England in 1638*, by Sir James
Mackintosh.

[64]The articles referred to in the *Southern Literary Messenger* are entitled
Hints to Students of Geology, by Peter A. Browne, Esq. *S. L. M.*, pp. 162,
300.

[65]*S. L. M.*, vol. 2, p. 223. *The Classics.* The commentators are the same
as those mentioned in the Classical Bibliography for the compiling of which
it has been noted Poe evidently called. Cf. note 38.

[66]*Ibid.*, vol. 2, p. 232. Abraham Tucker's book, *The Light of Nature Pursued.*

[67]The preface of Dick's *Christian Philosopher* reads (Preface to second edition, 1824): "This work in its original form, has had an extensive sale, not
only in Great Britain but also in the United States of America." (Dick,
Thomas, LL.D., *Complete Works, The Christian Philosopher*, vol. 2, p. vi,
Cincinnati, 1855.) Poe's remarks are from his review of *Sacred Philosophy
of the Seasons*, by Reverend Henry Duncan.—*B. G. M.*, vol. 6, p. 151.

[68]*S. L. M.*, vol. 1, p. 716. Poe gives the *London Quarterly* as the source of
his information, referring particularly to the article *The Universe and its
Author.* This article is in volume 50 of the *Quarterly Review.* Poe's remarks, however, as he outlines the plan, run almost parallel with the explanation of the plan as it is given in the *Edinburgh Review*, vol. 58, p. 423, in an
article entitled *Astronomy and General Physics Considered with Reference to
Natural Theology*, by the Reverend William Whewell.

ditions under which the Treatises were written. Paraphrasing Poe's account of the plan, we find him saying in his review of "Roget's Physiology," that Francis Henry, earl of Bridgewater, who died sometime in the beginning of the year 1829, directed certain trustees mentioned in his Will to arrange for the publication of one thousand copies of a work *On the Power, Wisdom, and Goodness of God as Manifested in the Creation*. Eight thousand pounds were to be invested in public funds to be paid by the President of the Royal Society of London to such a person or persons as he, the President, should appoint to write, print, and publish the work. This work was to be illustrated by such reasonable arguments as, for instance, the variety and formation of God's creatures, the construction of the hand of man, discoveries ancient and modern, in arts, sciences, and the whole extent of literature.

Apparently Poe followed with interest the series of articles[69] which this plan executed. On one occasion he speaks of the appearance of the "seventh Bridgewater Treatise," in two volumes. It is by the Reverend William Kirby, the naturalist, he says, and

---

[69]The *Edinburgh Review*, vol. 58, p. 423, thus explains the issuing of a series of articles: " 'The late President of the Royal Society, Davies Gilbert, Esq., requested the assistance of his Grace the Archbishop of Canterbury, and of the Bishop of London, in determining upon the best mode of carrying into effect the intention of the testator. Acting with their advice, . . . Mr. Davies Gilbert appointed the following eight gentlemen to write separate treatises on the different branches of the subject as here stated.

On the Adaptation of External Nature to the Moral and Intellectual Constitution of Man—The Rev. Thomas Chalmers, D.D., Professor of Divinity in the University of Edinburgh.

On the Adaptation of External Nature to the Physical Condition of Man— John Kidd, M.D., F.R.S., Regius Professor of Medicine in the University of Oxford.

On Astronomy and General Physics—The Rev. William Whewell, M.A., F.R.S., Fellow of Trinity College, Cambridge.

The Hand: Its Mechanism and Vital Endowments, as Evincing Design— Sir Charles Bell, K.H., F.R.S.

On Animal and Vegetable Physiology—Peter Mark Roget, M.D., Fellow of, and Secretary to, the Royal Society.

On Geology and Mineralogy—The Rev. William Buckland, D.D., F.R.S., Canon of Christ Church, and Professor of Geology in the University of Oxford.

On the History, Habits and Instincts of Animals—The Rev. William Kirby, M.A., F.R.S.

On Chemistry, Meteorology and the Function of Digestion—William Prout, M.D., F.R.S.' "

treats of the history, habits and instincts of animals.[70]   In the
same review he considers the treatise entitled "The Universe and
Its Author," "one of the most admirable essays ever penned." He
speaks critically of Dr. Roget's book on Animal and Vegetable
Physiology, giving as his opinion that he does not think it "the
best of the Bridgewater series," though he has "heard it so
called."[71] He also criticizes the Bridgewater Treatises on the score
of one of their fundamental tenets.   They have failed to perceive,
he says, that the divine system of adaptation is mutual.[72]

As ancient philosophy explained to Poe the principle of unity
in the sense of unchanging law, so Christian philosophy came to
have for him the same meaning.   Let us examine this law as Christian philosophers conceived it, noting only the writings with which
we have found Poe to be acquainted, and then pass on to the manner in which it entered Poe's theory and practice.

Christian philosophers agree that God is the only creating power
in existence.   They conceive of the Supreme Being as governing
the universe according to unchanging law, an idea which they explain with more or less elaboration in discussions on the intention
of the Deity, on His premeditated design, on divine law seen in terrestrial and astronomical adaptations, and on reciprocity between
cause and effect.   In their opinion, the more one increases his
scientific knowledge of the universe, the greater will be his comprehension of its Maker's marvellous plan, and the deeper will
be his appreciation of the Deity's power and intelligence.

Amongst other sources, the *Quarterly Review* gives a definition
of the term Christian philosophy.   The writer of the essay on the
"Universe and Its Author" there defines it to be information regarding the universe that proceeds from the researches of scientists
as well as from the revelations of enlightened faith.[73]   He says
further:—

"The re-examined and accumulated results of the researches of
geologists, and of the combined labors of astronomers and mathematicians, cannot have been intended for the mere entertainment of
those who have devoted themselves to such pursuits.   They point
to a higher destiny.   The more successfully the sciences have been

---

[70]*S. L. M.*, vol. 1, p. 716.

[71]*Ibid.*, vol. 2, p. 202.   Review of *Roget's Physiology*.

[72]*Democratic Review*, 1844.   *Marginalia.*   On this point see chapter on
Science.

[73]*Quarterly Review*, vol. 50, pp. 6, 7.   *The Universe and Its Author.*

cultivated, the brighter and more numerous have become the signs, and we may add, the demonstrations of the existence of an Omnipotent Intelligence by whom all things are made.''

Terrestrial adaptations are explained in an article in the *Edinburgh Review* on William Whewell's ''Astronomy and General Physics.''[74] The reviewer comments on the point thus:—

''The first *Terrestrial Adaptations* which Mr. Whewell considers are those in which the structure of plants is adjusted to the length of the year, or the time of the earth's revolution around the sun; and he maintains that these are so indicative of design that any change in the length of the year would throw the botanical world into utter disorder.''

And astronomical adaptations are likewise considered:—

''The invariable regularity with which the earth accomplishes its orbit is in itself a striking proof of the divine perfection with which that orbit was traced out. A difference of ten days at one time, or three weeks or a month at another, in the length of our year, would disappoint the labors of the husbandman, and render every attempt at chronology abortive. The dexterity, if we may use such a phrase, with which the earth preserves its path in space, without encountering any of the numerous comets which are perpetually wandering in all sorts of orbits through all the firmament, is the result of a provision that must have been made before one of those enormous masses was launched upon its course.''[75]

But perhaps the most concise statement of this doctrine of adaptation is in Dr. Dick's work.[76] The section on the Wisdom and Intelligence of the Deity reads:—

''In surveying the system of nature with a Christian and a philosophic eye, it may be considered in different points of view. It may be viewed either as displaying power and magnificence of the Deity in the immense quantity of materials of which it is composed, and in the august machinery and movements by which its economy is directed;—or, as manifesting His wisdom in the nice adaptation of every minute circumstance to the end it was intended to accomplish.''[77]

Dr. Dick further brings out the idea that the more one studies physical law as it manifests itself in nature, the greater will be the understanding of God's unvarying law. In order to understand

---

[74]*Edinburgh Review*, vol. 58, p. 422. Whewell, William, *Astronomy and General Physics*. The *New York Mirror* of 1832, vol. 10, p. 378, announces the publishing of William Whewell's book in America.

[75]*Quarterly Review*, vol. 50, p. 24. *The Universe and Its Author.*

[76]Cf. *ante*, note 67.

[77]Dick, *Works*, vol. 2, p. 27. *The Christian Philosopher.*

"Almighty power," he says in "The Christian Philosopher," a definite train of thought must be pursued. One should commence with those magnitudes which the mind can easily grasp, and proceed through all the higher gradations of magnitude. One should fix his attention on every portion of the chain until he arrives at the object or magnitude of which he wishes to form a conception. By the "light of science"[78] one must endeavor to form a conception of the "bulk of the world in which we dwell." He must contemplate "those magnificent globes which float around us in the concave of the sky." From the solar system he must extend his view to the starry heavens, "those trackless regions of immensity."

The idea of mutuality of adaptations is discussed in one of the reviews of the Bridgewater Treatises. The fitting of means to the end, the reciprocal adaptation of part to part, is explained by the article in question in the following way: Either our vegetables are suited to our year, or our year to them. "In either case we see a law of mutual adaptation which demonstrates the necessity of previous design."[79]

What gleanings, one may ask, did Poe make from his readings in Christian philosophy, and in what way did he manage his source material?

It is not difficult to detect Poe's indebtedness to his sources. In some instances, he preserves only the idea; in others, he practically reproduces the wording of his model; while in still other cases, especially when he is following Dr. Dick, he appears to carry over into his own writing a certain reverence of tone that is strongly apparent in that philosopher.

Let us now allow Poe to speak on the subject of God as the only creator. In this regard, he criticizes Coleridge for attributing to man's imaginative faculty the power to create.[80] He was familiar with Coleridge's assumption that the imagination in man was "the repetition in the finite mind of the eternal act of creation in the

---

[78]*Ibid.*, p. 18.

[79]Poe may have encountered this idea of mutuality of adaptation in Kant's *Criticism of the Judgment*, for he may have been led to an investigation of Kant by the very warm praise that Schlegel bestows on him. Cf. Schlegel, *op. cit.*, p. 69. If Poe read Kant's work, he could have found in it the subject of reciprocity of action explained. Kant, Emanuel, *Criticism of the Judgment*, p. 277.

[80]*B. G. M.*, vol. 6, p. 53. Review of *Alciphron*.

infinite I AM."[81] But he considers, in opposition to Coleridge's
"dogmatism"[82] that it is the Deity alone who creates.[83] In 1836,
however, he admits the possibility of man's possessing this power
in a "lesser degree." In 1840, he decisively denies to man's mind
the power of creating. The fancy, he says, as nearly creates as the
imagination; and neither creates in any respect, all novel conceptions being merely unusual combinations. He summarizes the point
thus: "What the Deity imagines *is*, but was not before. What man
imagines *is*, but *was* also. The mind of man cannot imagine what
is not."[84] In another instance he states that he adopts the God-
head as the starting-point in the scheme of creation;[85] and in
"The Classics,"[86] he dwells upon the creative mind of God.

Poe is next of the opinion that God, the creating principle, manifests His power in the universe through unvarying law. Accordingly, as did the Christian philosopher, he explains his meaning in
discussions on the design and intention of the Deity. "To look
upwards," he says in his review of Drake's "Culprit Fay" "from
any existence, material or immaterial, to its *design*, is, perhaps,
the most direct and the most unerring method of attaining a just
notion of the nature of the existence itself. Nor is the principle at
fault when we turn our eyes from Nature even to Nature's God."[87]
And anyone, he says, in his article, "The Classics," who has trained
his mind in Christian philosophy can understand how nature manifests God's unvarying law; such a man "looks out upon the stars,
'those isles of light' which repose in the liquid blue of the vaulted
heavens, and they speak to him of wisdom and love, of beauty and
peace. He walks abroad amid the works of nature, and traces in
all her hidden harmonies a beauty and unity of design which speak
but of one spirit, and that the infinite and eternal spirit of the
universe."[88] Contrasting the perfect adjustment according to the
divine plan, with that adjustment governed by human intelligence,
he sees on the side of the human a receding from perfection—the

---

[81]*Biographia Literaria*, p. 144. For the probability that Poe knew this particular passage in the *Biographia Literaria*, cf. *ante.* note 29.

[82]*B. G. M.*, vol. 6, p. 53. Review of Moore's *Alciphron.*

[83]*S. L. M.*, vol. 2, p. 328. Review of Drake's *Culprit Fay.*

[84]*Ibid.*, vol. 2, p. 328. Review of Drake's *Culprit Fay.*

[85]*Works*, vol. 16, p. 205. *Eureka.*

[86]*S. L. M.*, vol. 2, p. 230. *The Classics.*

[87]*Ibid.*, vol. 2, p. 327. Review of Drake's *Culprit Fay.*

[88]*Ibid.*, vol. 2, p. 231. *The Classics.*

presence of chance relations, and he says: "He [the Christian philosopher] compares the order and beauty of the physical universe, which submits all its motions to the divine will, with the moral government of man—at once the sport and victim of his own caprices."

Poe affirms that scientific study of the universe will reveal to one the power of the unchanging Creator. He speaks, in his article on "The Classics," of the need of studying "the great chain of truth."[89] Each link which is discovered seems, he says, "in the enthusiasm of the vision, another step on that ladder by which man mounts from earth to heaven." Each hidden harmony which is discovered in nature "is another thought of the divine mind," for the knowledge thus discovered serves to bind one "still more closely in that communion into which the Creator permits" one to enter with Him. It serves to bring one closer to Him who is pure, perfect, and unnchangeable. On another occasion, he asserts that the love of scientific truth is a human instinct. From the contemplation of the wonders and beauties of the universe, man becomes possessed with the "unconquerable desire—*to know.*"[90]

Again, increase of this scientific knowledge of the universe, he thinks will result in increase of man's reverence and veneration for the Creator's power. In the first place, putting Poe and his source together, we find them both to agree that man's disposition to regard the superiority of the Divine Being with veneration is a human instinct.

Chapter on the "Omnipotence of the Deity," pp. 24-27—Dick

"[Man] is every moment dependent on a Superior Being for every pulse that beats.

"Profound veneration of the Divine Being lies at the foundation of all religious worship and obedience."

Review of Drake's *Culprit Fay, S. L. M.*, vol. 2, p. 328, Poe

". . . we discover in all men a disposition to look with reverence upon superiority, whether real or supposititious It has been . . . justly considered a primitive sentiment . . . . It is, indeed, the instinct given to man by God as security for his own worship."

In the second place, according to further parallel columns, both are seen to agree that this reverence for the Deity concerns itself with the wonders and glories of His work.

---

[89]*Ibid.*, vol. 2, p. 231. *The Classics.*
[90]*Ibid.*, vol. 2, p. 328. Review of Drake's *Culprit Fay.*

Christian Philosopher, p. 25	*S. L. M.*, vol. 2, p. 328
". . . we must contemplate him through the medium of those works . . . by which he displays the glories of his nature to the inhabitants of our world. I have already exhibited a few specimens of the stupendous operations of his power, . . . and there is, surely, no mind in which the least spark of piety exists, but must feel strong emotions of reverence and awe, at the thought of that Almighty and Incomprehensible Being, who impels the high masses of the planetary globes with so amazing a rapidity through the sky. . . . Even these manifestations of Deity which are confined to the globe we inhabit, when attentively considered, are calculated to rouse, even the unthinking mind, to astonishment and awe. The lofty mountains, and expansive plains, the mass of waters in the mighty ocean . . . ."	"Thence [from this sentiment] spring immediately admiration of the fair flowers, the fairer forests, the bright valleys and rivers and mountains of the Earth—and love of the gleaming stars and other burning glories of Heaven."

Poe and the Christian philosopher are likewise of the opinion that reverence for these wonders and glories increases as knowledge of the Creator's work increases.

pp. 25, 26	
"But in order to reverence God aright, we must know him; . . . . in proportion as we enlarge the sphere of our contemplations, in a similar proportion will our views of God himself be extended, and a corresponding sentiment of veneration impressed upon the mind."	"Mingled up inextricably with this love and admiration of Heaven and of Earth [is] the u n c o n q u e r a b l e desire—*to know.*"

There are some indications that Poe also made an original research into the doctrines of Christian philosophy. He appears to be endeavoring to find the same unity in the God of the Old and New Testament that he found in the God of the ancient philosopher.

In "Pinakidia"[91] are over thirty passages which deal with the Hebrew Jehovah, or the Christian's God. Several of these passages merely show an interest in subjects allied to Jewish history. Others seem to be attempts to ascertain an idea of the degree of acquaintanceship that existed between the Greeks and Jews in Biblical times. In Lucian, he says, is given the account of the Deluge that most nearly resembles the one given by Moses. "The heathen poets are mentioned three times in the New Testament. Aratus in the seventh chapter of Acts—Menander in the fifteenth chapter of I Corinthians—also Epimenides."[92] Dionysius, he says, mentions in a letter dated Heliopolis, in the fourth year of the 202d Olympiad (the year of Christ's crucifixion), a total eclipse of the sun at noon. " 'Either,' according to Dionysius, 'the author of nature suffers, or he sympathizes with some who do'." Josephus agrees with St. Paul in supposing man to be compounded of body, soul, and spirit. The distinction, Poe says, between soul and spirit, is an essential point in ancient philosophy. There are passages also which indicate that Poe was endeavoring to understand the Jewish conception of God as a unity. The full meaning of Jehovah, he says, is "the self-existing essence of all things."

Thus Poe may be said to be gathering from Christian philosophy, as it was shown he did from the philosophy of the ancients, belief that the universe is governed by unvarying law.

The literary bearing of Poe's interest in ancient and Christian philosophies may now be made apparent. There is reason to believe that his study was connected in his mind with the needs of literature. He is of the opinion that the study of philosophy is the great want of American letters.[93] He is so deeply impressed with this fact, he says, that he "could not help suggesting briefly the various points of view from which its importance may be viewed." It has already been noted that he expressed himself strongly of the belief that study,—and in all probability by study he meant philosophic study,—would increase a writer's chances for a permanent reputation.

Evidence points to the fact that Poe felt the art of rhetoric to be philosophic in its nature and bearings. From the principle of unvarying law which he found in philosophy, both ancient and

[91]*S. L. M.*, vol. 2, p. 573. *Pinakidia.*

[92]*Ibid.*, vol. 2, p. 580.

[93]*Ibid.*, vol. 2, p. 233. *The Classics.*

Christian, he seems to have worked out a literary theory that included suggestions for both subject-matter and technique. From Coleridge, too, as the "Biographia Literaria" reflected Platonic doctrines, he may have derived help for his conception of poetry springing from philosophic truth.[94] In developing this idea, Poe maintains that he can recognize in poetry a double nature; it may be regarded in the light of its imaginative element, its ideality; it may also be viewed in its every-day acceptation, as the poetry of words. He states it as his opinion that these aspects are very intimately related to each other; that the imaginative element arises from and is a test of the latter; and that both views are differing sides of the same question. Nowhere does Poe seem more conscious of this difference than in the following passage: "A poem," he says, "is not the Poetic faculty but *the means* of exciting it in mankind."[95]

The imaginative element in poetry, Poe denominated the poetic sentiment. Christian philosophy, I have already noted, affirms reverence and veneration to be man's natural instinct to worship superiority in the Deity, a state of mind which seemed to Poe a quality of the sentiment he deemed poetical. Plato's Dialogues[96] appeared to him an expression in greater detail of the same feeling. Indeed, Poe's known acquaintance with Plato's writings, the frequent verbal similarities between his work and that of the Greek philosopher, as well as their striking parallels in ideas, all lead

---

[94]The pages of the *Biographia Literaria*, which as has been shown, Poe knew, make the point that Dynamic philosophy is applicable to criticism in the Fine Arts. Coleridge states the point thus: "In the third treatise of my Logosophia, announced at the end of this volume, I shall give *(Deo volente)* the demonstrations and constructions of the Dynamic Philosophy scientifically arranged. It is, according to my conviction, no other than the system of Pythagoras and of Plato revived and purified from impure mixtures. . . . The science of arithmetic furnishes instances that a rule may be useful in practical application, and for the particular purpose may be sufficiently authenticated by the result, before it has itself been fully demonstrated. It is enough, if only it be rendered intelligible. This will, I trust, have been effected in the following Theses for those of my readers who are willing to accompany me through the following chapter, in which the results will be applied to the deduction of the imagination; and with it the principles of production. . . ."

[95]*S. L. M.*, vol. 2, p. 328. Review of Drake's *Culprit Fay.*

[96]The *Dialogues of Plato*, translated into English with Analyses and Introductions by B. Jowett, M.A. Oxford, 1892.

one to assume that he was recalling Plato's doctrines for this aspect of literary art.

A comparison of these similarities suggests that Poe may have drawn his notion of the poetic sentiment from Plato's discourse on love, put into the mouth of Socrates.[97] In both cases Plato and Poe agree that the soul by nature longs for true beauty. Socrates speaks "in a figure" which is "composite," of the soul as a "pair of winged horses and a charioteer," of the soul which "with exceeding eagerness" longs to behold "true being."[98] From a natural impulse it tends to "soar aloft and carry that which gravitates downwards into the upper region, which is the habitation of the gods," there to obtain the vision of heavenly beauty.[99] Elsewhere, in the same discourse, Socrates affirms that human souls, like the souls of the gods, long after the upper world and he goes on to say that "in the way of nature, every soul of man at one time has beheld true being,"[100] and longs to recall the vision. Poe does not adopt Plato's figure of the soul in the likeness of the charioteer with the winged horses, but he does stress the Platonic idea of the natural impulse of the soul to long for beauty. Man has, by nature, he says in his essay on Longfellow's Ballads, a "thirst unquenchable" for the "beauty above"; this burning thirst belonging to the immortal essence of man's nature. And in "The Poetic Principle," he speaks of "the struggle to apprehend the supernal Loveliness."

A further similarity may be the fact that both Plato and Poe consider this longing to be attended by dissatisfaction, even by depression and sadness. Socrates says that when the soul is separated from true beauty, it is oppressed, irritated, and uneasy, a state which he likens to "the irritation and uneasiness in the gums at the time of cutting teeth." It "can neither sleep by night nor abide in her place by day."[101] Poe expresses much the same idea in the following passage:—

"And thus, when by poetry . . . we find ourselves melted into tears—we weep then—not as the Abbate Gravina supposes—through excess of pleasure, but through a certain, petulant, impatient sorrow at our inability to grasp *now*, wholly, here on

[97]Plato, *op.cit.*, vol. 1, p. 452. *Phaedrus.*
[98]*Ibid.*, vol. 1, p. 454.
[99]*Ibid.*, vol. 1, p. 453.
[100]*Ibid.*, vol. 1, p. 456.
[101]*Ibid.*, vol. 1, p. 458.

earth, at once and for ever, those divine and rapturous joys, of which *through* the poem, or *through* the music, we attain to but brief and indeterminate glimpses.''
The beauties of earth and heaven, both agree, encourage man to long for supernal beauty. In the first place, in reminding one of true beauty, the beauties of earth and heaven are the ambrosia which nourishes the poet's soul. Socrates, in describing the god-like charioteer, makes him put up his horses ''at the stall'' and give them ambrosia to eat; he makes even the human soul feed on the divine nourishment. The hope of this nourishment it was which encouraged and kept alive all souls in their striving to find that ''pasturage.''[102] Poe is likewise of the opinion that the beauties of earth and heaven, inspiring in man the true poetical effect, are the ''ambrosia which nourishes his soul.'' And in the following passage he enumerates these beauties:—[103]

''He recognizes the ambrosia which nourishes his soul, in the bright orbs that shine in Heaven—in the volutes of the flower—in the clustering of low shrubberies—in the waving of the grain-fields—in the slanting of tall, Eastern trees—in the blue distance of mountains—in the grouping of clouds—in the twinkling of half-hidden brooks—in the gleaming of silver rivers. . . .''
Moreover, both Plato and Poe agree that these higher beauties of earth affect the lover and poet[104] with a shuddering awe. Plato says that when one views the ''earthly namesake'' of the true beauty, if his ''initiation is recent,'' he feels running through him a shudder and stealing over him ''the old awe.''[105] With perhaps the same meaning Poe speaks of ''an earthly harp'' producing in one a ''shivering delight,'' for its notes ''*cannot* have been unfamiliar to the angels.''[106]

Both Plato and Poe also agree that this longing for absolute beauty is, on the part of the lover and the poet, a longing for immortality, and that therefore the soul struggles to create. The

---

[102]*Ibid.*, vol. 1, p. 454. *Phaedrus.*

[103]*Works*, vol. 14, p. 290. *The Poetic Principle.*

[104]Plato, in Agathon's speech in the *Symposium*, identifies Love with the poet (p. 566). ''In the first place he [Love] is a poet, . . . and he is also the source of poesy in others, which he could not be if he were not himself a poet. And at the touch of him everyone becomes a poet, even though he had no music in him before; this also is a proof that Love is a good poet and accomplished in all the fine arts.''

[105]Plato, *op.cit.*, vol. 1, p. 457. *Phaedrus.*

[106]*Works*, vol. 14, p. 275. *The Poetic Principle.*

tale of Diotima in the "Symposium" unfolds to Socrates the natural instinct which the soul possesses to long for immortality. The
instructress in love informs him that mortal nature seeks "birth
in beauty" and that souls seek to perpetuate themselves in beauty
as well. Such creators, she explains, are "poets and all artists
who are deserving of the name inventor."[107] Poe is also of the
opinion that the longing for the beauty above indicates a longing
for immortality. It is, he says, a consequence and an indication of
perennial life. He considers that a necessary consequence proceeding from this longing for immortality is the desire to create.
Poets, therefore, "struggle to invent novel combinations among
those forms of beauty which already exist, or by novel combinations
of those combinations which our predecessors, toiling in chase of
the same phantom, have already set in order."[108]

The theme in poetry is also discussed in a similar vein. In certain parts of this discussion one may even detect identities in
phrasing. Love, the elevation of the soul, or true beauty, is,
both Plato and Poe agree, the most worthy subject for
the poet's attention. "What a strange thing it is,"
Eryximachus says in quoting Phaedrus,[109] "that, whereas other
gods have poems and hymns made in their honor, the great and
glorious god, Love, has no encomiast among all the poets who are
so many . . . to this day no one has ever dared worthily to
hymn Love's praises!" Still quoting from Phaedrus, Eryximachus
scoffs at some of the themes that have been thought appropriate
for a speaker's eloquence. Of one in particular he is especially
scornful, saying: "What is still more extraordinary, I have met
with a philosophical work in which the utility of salt has been
made the theme of an eloquent discourse." The company then
proposes, each in his turn, to make a series of speeches, all in the
honor of love, Phaedrus giving the first speech. Poe, without, however, using Plato's story form, embodies the same idea in his criticism. Love is, he says, "the purest and truest of all poetical
themes."[110] He, as well as Eryximachus and Phaedrus, scoffs at
certain themes that have been thought poetical. Take for example
his strictures on the didactic themes in poetry. He gives it as his

[107]Plato, op.cit., vol. 1, p. 579. Symposium.
[108]Graham's Magazine, vol. 20, p. 249. Review of Longfellow's Ballads.
[109]Plato, op.cit., vol. 1, p. 547. Symposium.
[110]Works, vol. 14, p. 290. The Poetic Principle.

opinion "that Mr. Longfellow's conception of the aims of poesy is erroneous."[111]   And he speaks with especial contempt of such a subject as "carious teeth" as a theme in poetry.[112]

But Phaedrus, it seems although choosing the best theme for praising love, has yet, in the opinion of Pausanias, spoken in an "indiscriminate manner."   He has not taken into consideration that there are two loves, one high and the other low; one Heavenly, Aphrodite, the daughter of Uranus, the other, common, the daughter of Zeus and Dione.   The daughter of Uranus, it is, who has "nothing of wantoness in her; but the love of the daughter of Zeus and Dione is such as the meaner sort of men feel . . . and is of the body rather than of the soul."   Pausanias contends that the poet should devote his praises to this goddess of love, the heavenly Aphrodite.   Poe distinguishes, as does Pausanias, between the nature of the two loves.   In identical phrasing, it may be noted, he expresses himself thus . . . "love—the true, the divine Eros—the Uranian, as distinguished from the Dionaean Venus."   He likewise agrees with Pausanias that the Uranian goddess is the love which elevates the soul, while the Dionaean Venus fills the lover with passion and keeps him bound to the earth.   With Pausanias, he insists, too, that a poet should praise the heavenly love.   In all probability, enough has now been said to make the Platonic elements stand out in the following explanation that Poe gives of the poetic sentiment:—

"Thus, although in a very cursory and imperfect manner, I have endeavored to convey to you my conception of the Poetic Principle. It has been my purpose to suggest that, while this Principle itself is, strictly and simply, the Human Aspiration for Supernal Beauty, the manifestation of the Principle is always found in *an elevating excitement of the soul*—quite independent of that passion which is the intoxication of the Heart . . . .   For, in regard to Passion, alas! its tendency is to degrade, rather than to elevate the Soul.   Love, on the contrary—Love—the true, the divine Eros—

[111]*Graham's Magazine*, vol. 20, p. 249.   Review of *Longfellow's Ballads*.

[112]The *American Quarterly Review* for 1834 also discusses the propriety of "*diseased teeth*" as a subject for poetry.   Although the criticism is entitled *Decline of Poetry*, the reviewer only mildly censures the poet's choice of the theme.   *Op. cit.*, vol. 15, p. 463.   The *New York Mirror* of Jan. 25, 1834, prints the poem to which the *American Review* refers.   In the *Mirror*, Eleazar Parmly, dentist, has taken the trouble to add to Solyman Brown's poetical efforts, "notes, practical, historical, illustrative, and explanatory."

the Uranian, as distinguished from the Dionaean Venus—is unquestionably the purest and truest of all poetical themes."[113]

Passing from consideration of the imaginative element in poetry,
we come to the poetry of words, or the second aspect of literary
form that Poe feels springs from philosophy. Poe distinguishes
this aspect from the former in that it is the practical result of that
sentiment. So evident is his conviction that a distinction exists
between these two aspects, that he is of the opinion that one may
even be found without the other.

"The *Poeta Nascitur,*" he says in explaining this point, "which
is indisputably true if we consider the Poetic Sentiment, becomes
the merest of absurdities when we regard it in reference to the
practical result. We do not hesitate to say that a man highly
endowed with the powers of Causality—that is to say, a man of
metaphysical acumen—will, even with a very deficient share of
Ideality, compose a finer poem (if we test it as we should by its
measure of exciting the Poetic Sentiment) than one who, without
such metaphysical acumen, shall be gifted, in the most extraordinary degree, with the faculty of Ideality."[114]

From Christian philosophy he appears to have derived the idea
of form in the sense of divine adaptation. How closely he followed
Dr. Dick in this idea may be judged from the following parallel
columns:—

Dick	Poe
The Christian Philosopher	*S. L. M.,* vol. 2, p. 113
p. 27	
"In surveying the system of nature with a Christian and a philosophic eye, it may be considered . . . as manifesting his Wisdom, in the nice adaptation of every minute circumstance to the end it was intended to accomplish."	". . . Thus its effect will depend, [he is discussing the poetry of Mrs. Sigourney] in a very large degree, upon the perfection of its finish, upon the *nice adaptation* of its constituent parts."

---

[113]Poe makes the same point in regard to Mrs. Welby's poems. *Works,
Marginalia,* vol. 16, p. 56. A passionate poem, he says there, "is a contradiction in terms." Professor Prescott notes that Poe gives Coleridge credit
for affirming Poetry and passion to be discordant. But as Professor Prescott says, the idea does not appear to come from Coleridge, who distinctly
states that poetry always implies passion. Passages in Coleridge, however,
Prescott adds, vaguely indicate that poetry arises in the control of passionate
feeling.—Notes to *The Poetic Principle,* Poe's *Critical Essays,* p. 345. From
the above evidence, which I have just cited in the text, it seems reasonable
to think that Plato and not Coleridge was Poe's source for the idea.

[114]*S. L. M.,* vol. 2, p. 328. Review of Drake's *Culprit Fay.*

In other instances Poe states practically the same thought, with a slightly different wording. For instance, in the criticism of "George Balcombe," by Judge Tucker, he says: "Its *interest* is intense from beginning to end. . . . Its most distinguishing features are invention, vigor . . . and exceeding ingenuity and finish in the adaptation of its component parts."[115] In the following example, in his criticism of Halleck's "Marco Bozzaris," he uses the term "circumstances" to designate the parts of a piece, a point similar to the Christian philosopher's mode of expression. "Force is its prevailing characteristic— . . . a force consisting . . . in a well-ordered and sonorous arrangement of the metre, and a judicious disposal of what may be called the circumstances of the poem."[116] In another criticism of this period, one can again see the influence of Christian philosophy. "In regard to the story, or that chain of fictitious incident usually binding up together the constituent parts of a Romance, there is very little of it in this book."

From Plato he seemed to discover further ideas on technique in the explanation of "the Many and One in Nature." He obviously sees in the myth of heavenly beauty, the same principles of art that Plato himself affirms that he found in it. Turning to Plato, we find Socrates explaining to Phaedrus that the myth of the longing of the soul for heavenly beauty really contained rules for the art of rhetoric. The myth had, in his mind, a serious meaning.[117] "In these chance fancies of the hour," he said, "were involved two principles of which we should be too glad to have a clearer description if art could give us one." These principles were first, he explained, unity of particulars in a single note; and, secondly, that of "division into species." Socrates acknowledges that he is a "great lover of these processes of division and generalization." And he goes on to say that they help him to think and to speak; that if he finds "any man who is able to see a 'One and Many' in nature" him he follows and he walks " 'in his footsteps as if he were a god'." Socrates also speaks, in describing "the fourth kind of madness," of this ability to generalize from particulars. He says that a "man must have intelligence of universals, and be

---

[115]*Ibid.*, vol. 3, p. 58. Review of *George Balcombe, a Novel.*
[116]*Ibid.*, vol. 2, p. 334.
[117]Plato, *op.cit.*, vol. 1, p. 474. *Phaedrus.*

able to proceed from the many particulars of sense to one conception of reason."[118]

Following Poe, in his evident indebtedness to Plato's explanation of the "Many and One in Nature," makes it evident that the question resolves itself in his mind into a common protest against imitation in literature. Both Plato and Poe on the basis of this principle are determined to drive out the imitating poet.[119] They both agree with at least one identity in phrasing that exact repetition, as in a mirror, is not the highest type of art. Socrates, in his dialogue with Glaucon concerning the nature of imitation, ridicules the apparent creations of him who creates by repeating exactly what is before him. That way, he says, is easy enough. In fact, "there are many ways in which the feat might be quickly and easily accomplished, none quicker than that of turning a mirror round and round." Such a method, he assures Glaucon, would soon make the sun and heavens, the earth, animals and plants.[120] Poe also maintained that exact repetition is not poesy. The "eyes of Amaryllis" being repeated in the mirror, the "living lily in the lake," or the "forms and colors and sounds and sentiments" being merely *recorded*, while undoubtedly productive of pleasure, will not produce a true poetic effect.[121] The poet, therefore, Poe says in the "Landscape Garden," will not concern himself with the details of Nature; he will not endeavor to "imitate the colors of the tulip."[122] As a summary of his stand against exact repetition may be cited the following from the Review of "Longfellow's Ballads": "He who shall merely sing with whatever rapture, in harmonious strains, or with however vivid a truth of imitation, of the sights and sounds which greet him in common with all mankind—he, we say, has yet failed to prove his divine title."[123] In his article on the "Poetic Principle," with the same intention of

---

[118]*Ibid.*, vol. 1, p. 455. Doubtless this explanation of the rules of rhetoric is what Plato means further on in *Phaedrus* where he speaks of the true rhetoric's being that which is "acceptable to God." He says (p. 483), "rhetoric has a fair beginning here." In the closing pages of the *Republic*, Plato hints at the possibility of poetry attaining to this perfection.—Plato, *op.cit.*, vol. 3, p. 322.

[119]*Ibid.*, vol. 3, p. 322. *The Republic.*

[120]*Ibid.*, vol. 3, p. 308.

[121]*Graham's Magazine*, vol. 20, p. 248. Review of *Longfellow's Ballads and Other Poems.*

[122]*Works*, vol. 4, p. 265. *Landscape Garden.*

[123]*Graham's Magazine*, vol. 20, p. 248.

criticizing exact repetition on the poet's part, Poe changes the phrase "truth of imitation," to "truth of description."[124] It may now be seen that the idea of "The Many in One" presents suggestions that will help a writer to avoid imitation. Both Plato and Poe give the same remedy, which, if applied, Plato says, will permit "our sweet friend . . . to exist in a well-ordered State."[125] The remedy suggested consists in proving his title to the name of poet,[126] not by imitating the world of sense, but by being inspired by the beatific vision, the interpretation of which myth, Plato explained[127] as involving an understanding of the principle of unity in variety.[128] Poe suggests the same remedy to the imitating poet. The poet, he says, using Plato's words, must "prove his divine title." To give this proof, the poet should not, as he shows that Longfellow does, fail to understand true beauty and content himself with exact repetition of the details of nature's loveliness; but he should work from a basis which constitutes true beauty, that is, he should not "demur at the great labor requisite for the stern demands of high art." He should not demur at the

---

[124]*Works*, vol. 14, p. 273.
Coleridge expresses very much the same idea and doubtless drew on Plato for the point: ". . . images, however beautiful, though faithfully copied from nature, and as accurately represented in words, do not of themselves characterize the poet. They become proofs of original genius only as far as they are modified by a predominant passion; or by associated thoughts or images awakened by that passion; or when they have the effect of reducing multitude to unity, or succession to an instant. . . ."—*Biographia Literaria*, p. 153.

[125]Plato, *op.cit.*, vol. 3, p. 322. *The Republic.*

[126]Perhaps the "ancient quarrel between philosophy and poetry" to which Plato refers, and which he cites as a reason for excluding the poet from the Republic, may be settled according to the remedy Plato himself suggests.—*Ibid.*, vol. 3, p. 322.

[127]*Ibid.*, vol. 3, p. 217.

[128]It is suggested that Plato's allegory of the underground cave may have the same interpretation as his myth of the soul longing for the vision of heavenly love. In both the soul attains to *realities*, leaving the world of sense. —*The Republic*, p. 217. In both the soul ascends to the intellectual world and in both it attains the vision of heavenly beauty.—The myth in *Phaedrus* is explained as involving principles applicable to rhetoric. The allegory of the cave may then perhaps be said to have this meaning. On this supposition, Plato may mean that the imitating poet, if mindful of rules of true art, —these rules which are a part of human nature, which produce the many from one, or, in other words, which see variety in uniformity,—may be welcomed into a "well-ordered State."—*Ibid.*, vol. 3, p. 322. *The Republic.*

"unremitting toil and patient elaboration which, when soul-guided, result in the beauty of Unity, Totality, and Truth."[129]

Poe has learned from philosophy to enlarge his understanding of unity. He has philosophized on unity as he had found it explained in the drama until it becomes a principle pervading the universe, operating as unvarying law. He is then seen to translate this abstraction back into a guide for the writer. Thus the *Many in One*, the philosophic bearings of argument, and the "nice adaptation of constituent parts," help him, as Socrates testified to the first of the trio, to combine a mass of particulars under a single note, to imitate, by skillful contrivance of detail, the perfect design of the Deity. Indeed, with a slight variation in phrasing from the words of the Greek philosopher, he has learned how "to think," and, as a consequence, to write.

But, as with *Blackwood* and with law methods, Poe is again convinced that his study has not been final. Philosophy, he contends, does not bring to a writer all that his art demands. The further help that Poe sought in natural science will be discussed in the following chapter.

---

[129] *B. G. M.*, vol. 5, p. 227. Review of Longfellow's *Hyperion, a Romance.*

CHAPTER V
UNITY, A SCIENTIFIC LAW IN THE PHYSICAL WORLD

Unity which Poe felt, from his study of ancient and Christian philosophy, to be a philosophic truth, he now apparently wishes to see as a scientific fact, as a law operating in the physical world. Evidence shows that he recognized the insufficiency of philosophy as a sole guide to a working principle. Take, for example, on this point, his critical review of Taylor Lewis' edition of *Plato's Laws*, in which he replies to the professor's contemptuous remarks on "this noisy Baconianism, about which there is kept up such an everlasting din."[1] While he appreciates, he says, the "purity and nobility of the Platonian soul," he yet "vastly prefers even the noise of Bacon . . . or the nebular star-dust of Nichols, to what Dr. Lewis will insist on terming the 'clear, simple, common-sense philosophy of Plato'." In fact, in the light of a sole guide, he values the Platonian philosophy, as "exactly nothing at all." Observe, also, what he says of the insufficiency of Christian philosophy to set forth the idea of plan or design on the part of the Creator. He makes a statement to the effect that, in order to carry out the plan proposed in the Bridgewater Treatises, a scheme at once impracticable and impossible, would be necessary: "Every object in creation, from an ant to an elephant, every member of every animal would require a separate volume, before the plan would be complete." Such works on philosophy are only useful, the review contends, for what they may contain of "positive information."[2]

Not only is Poe of the opinion that philosophy alone cannot explain law as he now sees it, but he grows more and more insistent

---

[1]*Broadway Journal*, vol. 1, p. 393. *Plato contra Atheos*. Plato against the Atheists; or the 10th Book of the Dialogue on Laws. Taylor Lewis was professor of Greek Language and Literature, in the University in the City of New York.

[2]*Ibid.*, vol. 1, p. 78. Review of *Chemistry, as Exemplifying the Wisdom and Beneficence of God*. By George Fownes, Ph.D., F.R.S. Harrison does not list this short review as Poe's work. It follows, however, the same line of thought as Poe's review given above, and, moreover, appears in the same magazine at very nearly the same time.

on the need of scientific proof. Again and again he declares that
what he intuitively feels to be a law pervading the universe, receives corroborating testimony from science; that what he feels
to be unity, is to him as certain in its existence and in its operation
as is the working of any science to a scientist. He says in "The
Landscape Garden," in discussing the principle of unity by which
the artist arranges his material, that these sentiments of art afford
as absolute a demonstration as does the science of mathematics to
the mathematician.[3]

Before attempting, however, to ascertain Poe's method of comprehending unity as a scientific law of the universe, it may be well
to review what is known of his interest in scientific matters. One
is inclined to the supposition that with Poe, science was, at an early
date, an awakening interest. Two of the most important pieces
of evidence on this point are, first that in 1829 he makes his fanciful poem "Al Aaraaf" center around a scientific observation, that
of the discovery of a star by Tycho Brahe; and that, in the same
year, in a short poem, "Science," bearing as a sub-title, "Preface
to Al Aaraaf," he discusses, though not with sympathy, in fact
with what might be called alarm, the influence that science has in
preying on "the poet's heart." And it is with apparent reproach
that he thus apostrophizes science :—

"Hast thou not dragged Diana from her car,
And driven the Hamadryad from the wood
To seek a shelter in some happier star?"

In 1833 his scientific interests take on a more determinate tone.
They are testified to by Sara S. Rice in her "E. A. Poe Memorial
Volume,"[4] where she states these facts in the words of John H. B.
Latrobe, who gives, according to the author of the "Memorial
Volume," an account of his conversation with Poe concerning the
basis for the story of "Hans Phaall—A Tale."[5] Poe spoke most
enthusiastically, Mr. Latrobe says, of certain scientific research
he had made for the story of his voyage to the moon. He entered
into—

---

[3]*Works*, vol. 4, p. 266.

[4]Rice, Sara S., *Edgar Allan Poe, A Memorial Volume*, Baltimore, 1877, p. 61.

[5]*S. L. M.*, vol. 1, p. 565. *Hans Phaall—A Tale.* That this conversation took
place in 1833 is testified to by the fact that Latrobe speaks of it being on
the Monday following the publication in the paper, the *Saturday Visitor*, of
the *MS. Found in a Bottle*, the tale which received the hundred dollar prize,
Oct. 12, 1833. Mr. Latrobe was one of the three members of the committee
that awarded the prize.

"a somewhat learned disquisition upon the laws of gravity, the height of the earth's atmosphere, and the capacity of balloons. . . . Presently, speaking in the first person, he began the voyage, after describing the preliminary arrangements, as you will find them set forth in one of his tales, called 'The Adventures of Hans Phaall,' and leaving the earth and becoming more and more animated, he described his sensation, as he ascended higher and higher, until, at last, he reached the point in space when the moon's attraction overcame that of the earth, when there was a sudden bouleversement of the car and a great confusion among its tenants." Poe's account was so realistic, Mr. Latrobe says, that he quite fancied himself on an actual voyage to the moon.

Between 1835 and 1840, he is discovered to be studying the *Philosophical Transactions of the Royal Society of London*, a compilation of scientific papers dating from the year 1665. From these volumes, he appears to have copied notes, which he afterwards used as material for a second presentation of his story referred to above.[6] Comparing this later form of "Hans Phaall," which appeared in 1840, with these notes, many identical passages come to light, as the following parallel columns will show:

Poe's Unpublished Notes *Works*, vol. 16, p. 347	Hans Phaall—A Tale *Works*, vol. 2, p. 96
"He observed the moon when 2¾ days old, in the evening soon after sunset, before the dark part was visible, and continued to observe it till it became visible. The two cusps appeared tapering in a very sharp faint prolongation, each exhibiting its farthest extremity faintly illuminated by the solar rays be-	"I had been strengthened in my opinion [of lunar atmosphere] by certain observations of Mr. Schroeter, of Lilienthal. He[7] observed the moon when two days and a half old, in the evening soon after sunset, before the dark part was visible, and continued to watch it until it became visible. The two cusps

----

[6]Harrison publishes these notes with the title *Poe's Unpublished Notes*. (*Works*, vol. 16, p. 347). He says: "These MS. notes were found in Poe's handwriting among the MSS. in possession of Mrs. W. M. Griswold, Cambridge, Mass. . . . The notes are legible and neatly written with a pencil on both sides of four and a half sheets (the last being torn) of ordinary memorandum paper." Harrison is of the opinion that these notes refer principally to *Eureka*, Poe's work of 1848, although he says they may be outgrowths of Poe's studies for *Hans Phaall*. He says that "Notes on Eureka" is endorsed on the MSS. in handwriting not Poe's. That they were started with a revision of *Hans Phaall* in mind seems probable since they furnish material for the 1840 form of the tale which the 1835 form as printed in the *S. L. M.*, did not possess. *Works*, vol. 2, p. 330.

[7]Harrison makes the point that in the opening sentence of Poe's notes—

fore any part of the dark hemisphere was visible. Soon after the dark limb appeared illuminated. This prolongation of the cusps beyond the semicircle, he thinks, must arise from the refraction of the sun's rays by the moon's atmosphere. He computes, also, the height of the atmosphere, which refracts light enough into its dark hemisphere, to produce a twilight more luminous than the light reflected from the earth when the moon is about 32° from the new to be 1356 Paris feet; and that the greatest height capable of refracting the solar ray is 5376 feet.''

appeared tapering in a very sharp, faint prolongation, each exhibiting its furthest extremity faintly illuminated by the solar rays, before any part of the dark hemisphere was visible. Soon afterward, the whole dark limb became illuminated. This prolongation of the cusps beyond the semicircle, I thought, must have arisen from the refraction of the sun's rays by the moon's atmosphere. I computed, also, the height of the atmosphere (which could refract light enough into its dark hemisphere, to produce a twilight more luminous than the light reflected from the earth when the moon is about 32° from the new), to be 1356 Paris feet; in this view, I supposed the greatest height capable of refracting the solar ray, to be 5376 feet.''

Another long passage in Poe's notes, beginning ''Hevelius writes that he has several times found in the skies perfectly clear . . . .'' appears, too, in the form of the author's notes, in the later form of ''Hans Phaall.''[8]

Indications pointing to the fact that these notes were drawn from the pages of the *Philosophical Transactions*, are first, the credit, in one instance, that Poe, in the person of Hans Phaall, gives the 82nd volume of these Transactions for a certain point which regulated the preparation for the passage to the moon.[9] In his notes, he makes another reference to the *Philosophical Transactions*, giving in this instance the ''82nd vol. pr. 2, art. 16'' as his source.[10] And further, an investigation extending beyond the 82nd volume, reveals that Poe was even more indebted to the *Transactions of the*

''He observed the moon when 2¾ days old'' . . . ''it is not clear to whom reference is made.'' The column above, in the text under *Hans Phaall*, shows, however, that Poe by ''he'' is referring to Mr. Schroeter of Lilienthal, who, it seems, was a scientist of considerable repute.

[8]*Works*, vol. 16, p. 351. *Poe's Notes*. Cf. *Ibid.*, vol. 2, p. 96. *Hans Phaall*.
[9]*Ibid.*, vol. 2, p. 96.
[10]*Ibid.*, vol. 16, p. 347. *Poe's Unpublished Notes*.

Royal Society than one might have supposed from his reference just quoted. The following columns indicate the nature of Poe's dependence on these scientific papers:

Philosophical Transactions vol. 17, p. 450	Poe's Unpublished Notes Works, vol. 16, p. 353
Of an Appearance of Light, like a Star, seen in the Dark Part of the Moon, on Friday the 7th of March, 1794, by Wm. Wilkins, Esq., at Norwich.	"On March 7, 1794, a few minutes before 8 in the evening, Mr. Wilkins of Norwich, an eminent architect, observed,
"When I saw the light speck, . . . a few minutes before 8 in the evening, I was very much surprised; for at the instant of discovery I believed a star was passing over the moon, which on the next moment's consideration I knew to be impossible. I remembered having seen, at some periods of the moon, detached lights from the serrated edge of light, through a telescope; but this spot was considerably too far distant from the enlightened part of the moon; besides, this was seen with the naked eye. I	with the naked eye,
was . . . rivetted to the spot where I stood, during the time it continued, and took every method I could imagine to convince myself that it was not an error of sight; and 2 persons, strangers, passed me at the same time, whom I requested to look, and they said it was a star. I am confident I saw it 5 minutes at least; but as the time is only conjectural, it might not possibly be so long. The spot appeared rather brighter than any other enlightened part of the moon. It was there when I first looked. The whole time I saw it, it was a fixed, steady light, except the moment before it disappeared, when its brightness increased. . . . "	a very bright spot upon the dark part of the moon; it was there when he first looked at the moon. The whole time he saw it, it was a fixed steady light, except the moment before it disappeared, when its brightness increased—he saw it about five minutes."

Another part of Poe's notes is found to come from an article following the one just given. A point about Mr. Wilkins, that of his being an architect, referred to in column 2 above occurs in this article. The observations in both cases are those of Thomas Stretton, or as Poe has it, of Mr. T. Stretton.

Philosophical Transactions vol. 17, p. 451	*Poe's Unpublished Notes* Works, vol. 16, p. 353
An account of an Appearance of Light, like a Star, seen lately in the Dark Part of the Moon by Thomas Stretton, in St. John's Square, Clerkenwell, London; with remarks on this Observation, and Mr. Wilkins's. Drawn up, and communicated by the Rev. Nevil Maskelyne, D.D., F.R.S., and Astronomer Royal.	"The same phenomenon was observed by Mr. T. Stretton in St. John's Sq. Clerkenwell, London, on April 13, 1795."
"Not doubting but the phenomenon, seen by Thomas Stretton, in St. John's Square, was the same as was seen by Mr. Wilkins at Norwich, ..."	

Philosophical Transactions vol. 16, p. 255	*Poe's Unpublished Notes* Works, vol. 16, p. 353
Of 3 Volcanoes in the Moon. By Wm. Herschel, LL.D., F.R.S.	"Apr. 19, 1787, Dr. Herschel discovered 3 volcanoes in the
"April 19, 1787, 10^h 36^m sidereal time, I perceive 3 volcanos *(sic)* in different places of the dark part of the new moon. Two of them are either already nearly extinct, or otherwise in a state of going to break out . . . . The 3d shows an actual eruption of fire, or luminous matter. . . .	dark part of the moon. 2 of them seemed to be almost extinct, but the 3rd showed an actual eruption of fire, or luminous matter, resembling a small piece of burning charcoal covered by a very
"The appearance of what I have called the actual fire or eruption of a volcano, exactly resembled a small piece of burning charcoal, when it is covered by a very thin coat of white ashes, which frequently adhere to it when it has been some time ignited; and it had a degree of brightness, about as strong as	thin coat of white ashes:

that with which such a coal would be seen to glow in faint daylight. All the adjacent parts of the volcanic mountain seemed to be faintly illuminated by the eruption, ... This eruption resembled much that which I saw on the 4th of May, in the year 1783; ..."

It had a degree of brightness about as strong as that with which such a coal would be seen to glow in faint daylight. The adjacent parts of the mountain seemed faintly illuminated by the eruption. A similar eruption appeared on May 4, 1783."

From Dr. Dick's works, Poe also appears, as in the case of the *Philosophical Transactions*, to be gathering data concerning the solar system. The following parallel columns reveal a study of Dick, especially of his, "The Celestial Scenery":—

Dr. Dick, *op.cit.*, Page 52

"This planet [Juno] is of a reddish color, and is free from any nebulosity; yet the observations of Schroeter render it probable that it has an atmosphere more dense than that of any of the old planets of the system. A remarkable variation in the brilliancy of this planet has been observed by this astronomer, which he attributes to changes that are going on in its atmosphere, and thinks it not improbable that these changes may arise from a diurnal rotation performed in twenty-seven hours."

Poe's Unpublished Notes Works, vol. 16, p. 348

"Juno is free from nebulosity in appearance yet, according to Schroeter, it has an atmosphere more dense than that of any of the old planets of the system— variable atmosphere."

Page 53

"The following are some of the observations of this planet by Schroeter and Herschel. The atmosphere of Pallas, according to Schroeter, is to that of Ceres ... nearly as two to three. It undergoes similar changes, but the light of the planet exhibits greater variations."

Page 353.

"The atmosphere of Pallas, according to Schroeter, is to that of Ceres as 2 to 3; it undergoes great changes."

Dr. Thomas Dick's "Christian Philosopher" appears to be a source for "Eureka."

Christian Philosopher
Chapter: *Omnipotence of
the Deity*, p. 17

"Were we to take our station on the top of a mountain, of a moderate size, and survey the surrounding landscape, we should perceive an extent of view stretching 40 miles in every direction, forming a circle 80 miles in diameter, and 250 in circumference, and comprehending an area of 5,000 square miles. In such a situation, the terrestrial scene around and beneath us—consisting of hills and plains, towns and villages, rivers and lakes—would form one of the largest objects which the eye, or even the imagination, can steadily grasp at one time. But such an object, grand and extensive as it is, forms no more than the *forty thousandth part* of the terraqueaous globe; . . . were a scene, of the magnitude now stated, to pass before us every hour, until all the diversified scenery of the earth were brought under our view, and were twelve hours a-day allotted for the observation, it would require nine years and forty-eight days before the whole surface of the globe could be contemplated, even in this *general* and *rapid* manner."

Page 20

"The earth contains a mass of matter equal in weight to at least 2,200,000,000,000,000,000,000, or more than 2 thousand trillions of tons, supposing its mean density to be only about 2½ times greater than water. To move this ponderous mass, a single inch beyond its position, were it fixed in a quiescent state,

Eureka
Works, vol. 16, p. 281

"If we ascend an ordinary mountain and look around us from its summit, we behold a landscape stretching, say 40 miles, in every direction; forming a circle 250 miles in circumference; and including an area of 5,000 square miles. The extent of such a prospect, on account of the *successiveness* with which its portions necessarily present themselves to view, can be only very feebly and very partially appreciated:—yet the entire panorama would comprehend no more than one 40,000th part of the mere *surface* of our globe. Were this panorama, then, to be succeeded, after the lapse of an hour, by another of equal extent; this again by a third, after the lapse of another hour; this again by a fourth after lapse of another hour—and so on, until the scenery of the whole Earth were exhausted; and were we to be engaged in examining these various panoramas for twelve hours of every day; we should nevertheless, be 9 years and 48 days in completing the general survey."

Page 282

"But if the mere surface of the Earth eludes the grasp of the imagination, what are we to think of its cubical contents? It embraces a mass of matter equal in weight to at least 2 sextillions, 200 quintillions of tons. Let us suppose it in a state of quiescence; and now let us endeavor to conceive a mechanical would require a mechanical force almost beyond the power of numbers to express. The physical force of all the myriads of intelligences within the bounds of the planetary system, though their powers were far superior to those of men would be altogether inadequate to the production of such a motion.''

The Solar System
Page 80

"Of this system, the SUN is the center and the animating principle, ... This vast globe is found to be about 880,000 miles in diameter. . . . Were its central parts placed adjacent to the surface of the earth, its circumference would reach two hundred thousand miles beyond the moon's orbit, on every side . . . . Even at the rate of 90 miles a-day, it would require more than 80 years to go round its circumference.''

force sufficient to set it in motion! Not the strength of all the myriads of beings whom we may conclude to inhabit the planetary worlds of our system —not the combined physical strength of *all* these beings— even admitting all to be more powerful than man — would avail to stir the ponderous mass *a single inch* from its position.''

Page 283

"The diameter of . . . the Sun is 882,000 miles. An inhabitant of the latter, travelling 90 miles a day, would be more than 80 years in going round a great circle of its circumference. . . . Now, were the Sun placed upon the Earth, centre over centre, the body of the former would extend, in every direction, not only to the line of the Moon's orbit, but beyond it, a distance of 200,000 miles.''

An interesting bit of evidence also testifying to Poe's scientific interest is that of his making a scientific experiment the basis of his story, "The Conversation of Eiros and Charmion.'' Dr. Dick in the "Christian Philosopher'' describes an experiment whereby combustion is seen to follow the total extraction of nitrogen from the air, saying that in all probability that was the method prophesied by the Scriptures for the fiery destruction of our world. Dr. Dick suggests that by the aid of chemical apparatus, we can perform experiments "on a *small scale,* similar in kind, though infinitely inferior in degree, to the awful event under consideration.''[11]

The following parallel columns will show that Poe in declaring, as he does, that it was the "extension of the idea, which had engendered awe,''[12] was following Dr. Dick's scientific experiment as prophetic of the means for accomplishing the terrible catastrophe.

---

[11]Dick, *Works*, vol. 2, p. 135. *The Christian Philosopher.*
[12]*Works*, vol. 4, p. 7. *Eiros and Charmion.*

Christian Philosopher
Page 32

"The atmosphere is now ascertained to be a compound substance formed of two very different ingredients, termed *oxygen gas,* and *nitrogen gas.* Of 100 measures of atmospheric air, 21 are oxygen and 79 nitrogen. The one, namely, oxygen, is the principle of combustion and the vehicle of heat, and is absolutely necessary for the support of animal life, and is the most powerful and energetic agent in nature; the other is altogether incapable of supporting either flame or animal life. Were we to breathe oxygen air, without any mixture or alloy, our animal spirits would be raised. . . .

"If the nitrogen were extracted from the air, and the whole atmosphere contained nothing but oxygen or vital air, combustion would not proceed in that gradual manner which it now does, but with the most dreadful and irresistable rapidity . . . . "

Chapter: *General Conflagration,* p. 135

". . . should the Creator issue forth his Almighty fiat—'Let the nitrogen of the atmosphere be completely separated from the oxygen, and let the oxygen exert its native energies without control, wherever it extends';—from what we know of its nature, we are warranted to conclude, that instantly a universal conflagration would commence throughout all the kingdoms of nature. . . ."

Eiros and Charmion
Works, vol. 4, page 7

"It had been long known that the air which encircled us was a compound of oxygen and nitrogen gases, in the proportion of twenty-one measures of oxygen, and seventy-nine of nitrogen, in every one hundred of the atmosphere. Oxygen, which was the principle of combustion, and the vehicle of heat, was absolutely necessary to the support of animal life, and was the most powerful and energetic agent in nature. Nitrogen, on the contrary, was incapable of supporting either animal life or flame. An unnatural excess of oxygen would result . . . in just such an elevation of the animal spirits as we had latterly experienced. It was the pursuit, the extension of the idea, which had engendered awe. What would be the result of a total extraction of the nitrogen? A combustion irresistible, all-devouring, omniprevalent, immediate;—the entire fulfilment, in all their minute and terrible details, of the fiery and horror-inspiring denunciations of the prophecies of the Holy Book."

To sources other than the *Philosophical Transactions of the Royal Society* and Dr. Dick's "Christian Philosopher," Poe was likewise indebted during the early period of his search for scientific knowledge. He speaks in his notes for "Hans Phaall" of his need of reading Brewster's edition of "Ferguson's Astronomy";[13] and in the passage following this reference, that dealing with the phosphorescence of the moon, he appears to be quoting from that source. At the end of the "Notes," he again refers to Brewster, mentioning Brewster's "Selenography."

Poe seems also to have read a life of Kepler by John Drinkwater Bethune. In "Eureka," he writes in rapturous strain of Kepler's intuitively grasping "with his soul" the law that governs "the machinery of the Universe."[14] Comparing Poe's passage with Kepler's exulting words, as Bethune gives them, I shall quote considerably from the latter that it may be seen how nearly Poe preserved the tone of his source. It may be observed that Poe in making his quotations has transposed some sentences, that he really summarizes a long discussion, and that he prefaces his actual borrowing by several remarks of his own on Kepler: Kepler, he says, is "essentially a *theorist;* . . . that divine old man. . . ."

Kepler	Poe
Life of Kepler, by Bethune	*Eureka*

"What I prophesied two and twenty years ago as soon as I discovered the five solids among the heavenly orbits [Kepler is referring to the law connecting the mean distances with the periods of their revolution about the Sun, a law which Kepler says is expressed mathematically, as, the squares of the times vary as the cubes of the distances] what I firmly believed long before I had seen Ptolemy's 'Harmonics'—what I had promised my friends in the title of this book, which I named before I was sure of my discovery—what sixteen years ago I urged as a thing to be sought—

---

[13]*Works*, vol. 16, p. 349. *Poe's Unpublished Notes.*
[14]*Works*, vol. 16, pp. 197, 198. *Eureka.*

that for which I joined Tycho Brahe, for which I settled in Prague, for which I have devoted the best part of my life to astronomical contemplations, at length I have brought to light, and have recognized its truth beyond my most sanguine expectations. Great is the absolute nature of Harmonics with all its details, as set forth in my third book; it is all found among the celestial motions, not indeed in the manner which I imagined (that is not the least part of my delight) but in another very different, and yet most perfect and excellent. It is now eighteen months since I got the first glimpse of light, three months since the dawn, very few days since the unveiled sun, most admirable to gaze on, burst out upon me. Nothing holds me: I will indulge in my sacred fury; I will triumph over mankind by the honest confession, that I have stolen the golden vases of the Egyptians.'' A note says, ''In allusion to the Harmonics of Ptolemy to build up a tabernacle for my God far away from the confines of Egypt. If you forgive me, I rejoice; if you are angry I can bear it; the die is cast, the book is written; to be read either now or by posterity, I care not which; it may well wait a century for a reader, as God has waited six thousand years for an observer.''[15]

''*I care not whether my work be read now or by posterity. I can afford to wait a century for readers when God himself has waited six thousand years for an observer. I triumph. I have stolen the golden secret of the Egyptians. I will indulge my sacred fury.*''

---

[15]It is doubtless permissible to think that Poe read and copied from this life of Kepler, for not only does this identity of phrasing exist, but he also appears to refer to the volume containing the passage in his *How to Write a Blackwood Article*. In this satirical sketch, he praises in a mocking way the *Society for the Diffusion of Useful Knowledge*, calling it, for short, S. D. U. K. Bethune's life of Kepler is bound up in the series, *Library of Useful*

It may also be well to examine the probabilities of any connection Poe may have had with a series of articles in the *S. L. M.* of 1838, entitled "New Views of the Solar System," "New View of the Tides," "Review of 'New Views of the Solar System'," "Notice to the Reviewer of 'New Views of the Solar System'," and "The Reviewer of 'New Views of the Solar System' Reviewed." The time, the periodical, and the general nature of the subject-matter, all speak for the likelihood of Poe's having been an attentive reader of these articles. Detailed interest in the subject-matter makes a stronger plea. In fact, it may even suggest, that with the exception of the piece, "Review of 'New Views of the Solar System'," Poe was himself their author. I had first, after reading letters from G. W. Eveleth to Poe, entertained the possibility of John William Draper's authorship,[16] but from facts learned later I have been led to abandon this view. These facts are the following: Eveleth and Prof. Draper, in an exchange of letters, spoke of Poe with reference to his editorship of the *S. L. M.;* of this editorship being partly at a time when he (Draper, who was now discussing with Eveleth new astronomical ideas) wrote certain reviews for it. From this point and from the fact that Prof. Draper's lectures on science delivered at Hampden Sydney College were noticed in the *Messenger* for 1836, lectures which gave evidence of Draper's scientific attainments, one may suppose that Draper's own writing for the *Messenger,* that he was now recalling to Eveleth, under the name of "reviews," was critical work on astronomical subjects. From the facts, too, that one of the series of articles in question is a long review on "New Views of the Solar System," that it was known to have been written by a professor of mathematics,[17] and that the author of "New Views" styles himself a

---

Knowledge, a series which bears in a note on the title-page, "Published under the Superintendence of the *Society for the Diffusion of Useful Knowledge,*" the first letters of which title resolve the series into what may possibly be the *S. D. U. K.* of Poe's source.

[16]Mabbott, Thomas Ollive, *The Letters from George W. Eveleth to Edgar Allan Poe.* The New York Public Library, 1922, p. 23. John William Draper was professor of natural philosophy and chemistry in Hampden Sydney College and later in the University of New York.

[17]*S. L. M.,* vol. 5, p. 105; vol. 4, p. 747. While it is true that Draper was professor of natural philosophy and chemistry in Hampden Sydney College, Allibone gives the information that he published Treatises on "mixed mathematics," a point that might possibly explain the reference made by the author of "New Views of the Solar System."

novice in the field of astronomy, it would seem that Draper did not write the series on the solar system, but that he may have written the long critical review calling their validity in question. I had entertained, too, the probability of Eveleth's authorship, but the following facts would dispute his claim. Eveleth, in 1849, frankly calls Poe "the starter" of an effort to "change" views of metaphysics and physical science.[18] Eveleth's own idea on the rotation of the heavenly bodies, that, in 1849, he refers to as a "bit," written out for and sent to *Silliman's American Journal* and to Prof. Draper (of whom mention has already been made), "two or three months ago,"[19] could not have been so elaborately presented in 1838 as were "New Views" at that time. Clearly, then, Eveleth could not have been the author of the articles on the solar system in the *Southern Literary Messenger*. No attempt, however, will be made to press Poe's claim for their authorship beyond the exhibition of striking similarities between his scientific interests and those held by the author of the articles; and of the sympathetic relation that these scientific views bear to what is known to be Poe's literary criticism and practice of the years preceding and following the publication of these articles. One may recall, too, in this connection, that 1838, the time of their appearing, coincides with what we have every reason to believe was the time of Poe's renewed study of science for the revised form of "Hans Phaall" as it appeared in 1840.

While the principle of unity seems to be the idea which offers most striking points of contact, a similarity which will be reserved for later discussion, there appear, also, to exist other definite converging lines of interest. In the first place, both authors make use of the same sources. The writings of Sir David Brewster, as they affected Poe, have already been noted. The author of "New Views of the Solar System" also quotes from Brewster in regard to the "absolute motion of the solar system," and "the discovery of the *means*" by which it is bound together.[20] A further similarity in sources, regarded negatively, is the fact that for astronomical data, neither Poe in his early study as testified to by his Notes, nor the author of "New Views" appears to depend on Newton and

[18]Mabbott, *Letters from George W. Eveleth to Edgar Allan Poe.* p. 20.
[19]*Ibid.*, p. 22.
[20]*S. L. M.*, vol. 5, p. 267. *The Reviewer of "New Views of the Solar System" Reviewed.*

Laplace as unquestioned authority. Poe at that time makes mention only once of Kepler and then with but a slight notice of a certain lunar observation.[21] Of Newton and of Laplace, by name, at least, he also seems oblivious. With the author of "New Views," writing as we have seen, at about the same time in which Poe took his notes, Newton is inconsistent, and Laplace, while "a reasoning man and a philosopher," does not give facts "their true bearing upon the tidal phenomena."[22] Both authors likewise weigh the merits for source material of the practical views and the physical views of the astronomer, both evincing deep interest in experimental work of the former. Three years at least before the publication of the articles on the solar system, Poe makes Hans Phaall "purchase . . . some volumes of Mechanics and Practical Astronomy," and devote "every spare moment to their perusal."[23] The author of "New Views" is of the opinion that the practical astronomer alone states conditions as they really exist in the astronomical world. He it is, and not the physical astronomer, who can suggest the true cause lying back of gravitation. His system "requires *exact data.*"[24] Again, to Poe in his Notes and to the author of "New Views," Herschel speaks with the voice of authority. The above parallel columns exhibited Poe copying from Herschel's articles in the Philosophical Transactions. The writer on the solar system speaks contemptuously in answer to his reviewer of what is, in his opinion, false knowledge of the mathematicians in regard to the exact distance of the earth from the sun. He knows, he says, in apparent triumph, what Sir John Herschel thinks of the mathematician's "ill-conditioned triangles." In another instance he regards Herschel's opinion as settling contradictory information concerning the revolution of Venus on her axis.[25] And in still another place, speaking of consulting Newton and Laplace, he announces his intention of "drawing largely . . . on a still later astronomer than either, Sir John Herschel."[26]

[21]*Works*, vol. 16, p. 351. *Poe's Unpublished Notes.*

[22]*S. L. M.*, vol. 4, p. 748. *New View of the Tides;* vol. 5, p. 224. *Notice to the Reviewer of "New Views of the Solar System."*

[23]*Ibid.*, vol. 1, p. 567. *Hans Phaall—a Tale.*

[24]*Ibid.*, vol. 5, p. 267. *The Reviewer of "New Views of the Solar System" Reviewed.*

[25]*Ibid.*, vol. 4, p. 750. *New View of the Tides.*

[26]*Ibid.*, vol. 5, p. 224. *Notice to the Reviewer of "New Views of the Solar System."*

In addition to the similarity in sources between Poe's notes for the revised form of "Hans Phaall," his lunar story, and the articles on the solar system and the tides, an obvious identity of purpose also exists. Poe makes at least seven-eights of these notes relate to the moon; they show as we have seen, investigation of its motions, conditions, and gravity. The author of "New Views of the Tides" is of the opinion that a satisfactory understanding of the solar system is obtained by a new comprehension of the moon in her relation to our earth.[27]

There are also indications that "New Views of the Solar System" and "New View of the Tides" are connected with Poe's later work, and that they thus may be regarded as one step in a progressive study of astronomy, beginning with "Hans Phaal—A Tale," and ending with "Eureka." In the first place, with both authors the work is throughout strikingly like that of a novice in the field of astronomy. Poe in the progress of his work frequently corrects former theories and as frequently admits errors of statement. In his *Addenda* to "Eureka,"[28] he says that, since announcing an opinion as to the origin of the satellites, he has been led, by "closer analysis" to modify somewhat that view. He likewise shows a startling reversal of statement in regard to the motion of the moon. In his notes for "Hans Phaall" he has collected data giving the moon the same space of time in rotating on her axis that she has in revolving round us in her orbit.[29] But in his *Addenda* to "Eureka" he adopts a contrary view. He holds now, he says, "to the idea that the moon must rotate upon her axis oftener than she revolves round her primary." And he adds that the same must be the case of the moons which accompany Jupiter, Saturn, and Uranus.[30] The author of the articles on the Solar System also proclaims himself a novice. He acknowledges that he is but a volunteer, and that, too, without any authority from those who might, in the opinion of some, be considered as a source of unquestioned

---

[27]*S. L. M.*, vol. 4, p. 747. *New View of the Tides.*

[28]*Works*, vol. 16, p. 339.

Poe may have owed his changed opinion to Eveleth. Cf. Mabbott, *Letters from George W. Eveleth to Edgar Allan Poe.* p. 22.

[29]*Works*, vol. 16, p. 351. *Poe's Unpublished Notes.*

[30]*Ibid.*, vol. 16, p. 339.

authority.[31]   And, again, he corrects a statement, saying that he had spoken "unreflectingly."[32]

Not only is the work in both instances that of a novice, but both authors acknowledge that, in support of their theory, they are depending, somewhat, at least, on intuitive processes of the mind. Poe's whole theory of the universe, as he developes it in "Eureka," is an exaltation of man's intuition.[33]   The author of "New Views" likewise depends on his intuition.   The intuitive recognitions of the mind have led him, he says, to the opinion that, since Jupiter's moons describe orbits round their primary concave to the sun, so must the paths of all planets be equally concave to some more distant center.[34]

The articles on the solar system also appear to have a logical place in a chain of what is known to be Poe's predictions of new astronomical views.   Taking these predictions chronologically, we find first, in 1835, in "Hans Phaall," Poe writing of the intelligence to be imparted by the returned voyager from the moon, to the "private ear of the States' College of Astronomers."[35]   "Much —very much," Hans Phaall has to communicate, of the climate of the planet, and "above all, of those dark and hideous mysteries which lie in the outer regions of the moon—regions which, owing to the almost miraculous accordance of the satellite's rotation on its own axis with its sidereal revolution about the earth, have never yet been turned, and, by God's mercy, never shall be turned, to the scrutiny of the telescopes of man."   In 1838, the author of "New Views" also promises future astronomical information.   He begins his article on the tides with the following paragraph:—

"We see and we acknowledge the vast improvements which have been made in the arts and sciences within the last half century.   In these improvements the Americans have signally participated; and can it be now said, with any degree of propriety, that any one has reached the limit beyond which none can penetrate into the fields of improvement and discovery?   Or, that all that can be known, is known?"

His theory regarding the solar system which he promises soon to present to the world "will clear up all difficulties respecting these

---

[31]*S. L. M.*, vol. 4, p. 750.   *New View of the Tides.*

[32]*Ibid.*, vol. 5, p. 265.   *The Reviewer of "New Views of the Solar System" Reviewed.*

[33]*Works*, vol. 16, pp. 197, 212, 252, 266.

[34]*S. L. M.*, vol. 4, p. 750.   *New View of the Tides.*

[35]*Ibid.*, vol. 1, p. 579.   *Hans Phaall—A Tale.*

bodies.''[36]   He speaks, too, of "another place and another time" being suitable for showing "the entire insufficiency of our astronomers' *gravitations* and *attractions* to produce such effects.''[37]   By the theory which he now presents to the world, he hopes "to *wake up* American philosophers from the bewildering opiates administered to the scientific world by the mathematicians of the last century." And Poe, several years before 1843, adds predictions to those he had already suggested in "Hans Phaall." He attempts in these views, which he calls "A Prediction," to amend Laplace's theory of the nebular hypothesis. "As soon as the beginning of the next century," he says, "it will be entered in the books" that the Sun was originally condensed at once (not gradually according to the supposition of Laplace) to his smallest size."[38]   In 1848, appeared "Eureka," which may doubtless be the culmination of preceding prophecies. In the second place, the articles in question appear not only to take their place in a series of predictions, but to be also part of Poe's progressive study of astronomy, in that they contain certain points common to his literary and scientific views, other than those of a basis for unity, which law, it must be again remembered, is reserved for a later discussion. Both authors stress the idea of equality in nature. They both appear to conceive of equality or the balancing force in nature, as common to all steps

---

[36]*S. L. M.*, vol. 4, p. 770. *New Views of the Solar System.*

A study might be made of a serial story that runs through the *American Museum* during the time the author of *News Views of the Solar System* is publishing his pieces. The story is entitled, *The Atlantis.* It presents many points that are congenial to both Poe and the writer of the articles we are considering. For example, *The Atlantis* dwells with apparent delight on the alacrity with which in the Utopian island, scientists and philosophers are willing to investigate new views. It also stresses the fact that literature betrays a sad need of scientific study. Whoever may be the author, he is, to all intents and purposes, the Pope of American letters, for he draws largely on Pope's *Art of Sinking in Poetry* for the stand he takes against ignorant writers. Compare in this instance Poe's *How to Write a Blackwood Article* with Pope's *Martin Scriblerus.*

[37]*S. L. M.*, vol. 4, p. 750. *New View of the Tides.*

[38]*Works*, vol. 16, p. 337. *Addenda to Eureka.* Poe writes to G. W. Eveleth, February 29, 1848, that several years before writing *Eureka* he had penned but never printed some views on astronomy to which he gave the heading, *A Prediction.* Harrison prints this letter from the *Methodist Review* of January, 1896.

Cf. also Eveleth's letter to Poe, March 9, 1848. Mabbott, *Letters from George W. Eveleth to Edgar Allan Poe*, p. 19.

of what we are supposing to be a consistently increasing effort to comprehend the solar system. It will later be shown that Poe expounded his scientific views in "Eureka" with equality as his general law.[39] It will likewise be seen in the latter part of this chapter, that he made use of the idea of equality in literary criticism, especially as that principle was the basis of the metrical art. The author of "New Views" also contends for equality. It is to establish this point that he hazards his new theory of the solar system,[40] a theory by which he hopes to explain equality in the motion of the planets.

Philosophy appears to have influenced both writers in maintaining their principle of equality. Poe is of the opinion that the philosophic conception of a balancing force in nature is no other than the scientific fact of the laws of repulsion and gravitation. The philosopher as well as the scientist speaks in 1836 when he confounds Empedocles' profession of the system of four elements, to which two more were added, called by the names, *"principium amicitiae"* and *"principium contentionis,"* with the laws of attraction and repulsion.[41] As a philosopher, too, it has been noted, he discussed equality as the "root of all Beauty,"[42] and consistently throughout "Eureka" he endeavors to see as one, the philosophic and the scientific explanation of the universe.[43] Kepler, he says in "Eureka," drew inspiration for scientific conclusions from "the nebulous kingdom of Metaphysics."[44] As a philosopher, the author of "New Views of the Solar System" also discusses equality in nature. To the bitter attack on his theory, he replies that the reckonings of his reviewer may be mathematically correct, but that they are not so *"philosophically."*[45] His reviewer, he thinks, in another instance in refusing to investigate the new theory ad-

---

[39]*Works*, vol. 16, p. 253. *Eureka.*

Poe definitely states that *unity* is the law, and that *variety* has the meaning of variations from that law. On this score he criticizes Leigh Hunt's terming the law unity *in* variety. Prescott, *op. cit.*, p. 179.

[40]*S. L. M.*, vol. 4, p. 769. *New Views of the Solar System.*

[41]*Ibid.*, vol. 2, p. 581. *Pinakidia.*

[42]Cf. Chapter on Philosophy.

[43]*Works*, vol. 16, p. 266. *Eureka.*

[44]*Ibid.*, vol. 16, p. 197.

[45]*S. L. M.*, vol. 5, p. 265. *The Reviewer of the "New Views of the Solar System" Reviewed.* The attack referred to appeared in *S. L. M.*, vol. 5, p. 105: Review of 2 Pieces entitled *New Views of the Solar System.*

vanced, has shown himself to be most unphilosophical. A further point in common between the two writers is that magnetism is the cause back of gravitation. Poe says that Newton, "while boldly grasping the Law itself, shrank from the principle of the Law"; and that "Laplace had not the courage to attack it."[46] He advances the theory that magnetism, or electricity, though he admits an unsatisfactory explanation of the force, since it counterbalances a tendency towards the center, is yet as suitable a term as can be found for the principle of whose "awful character" he speaks with reverence.[47] He says further that he has received much help in trying to solve this question from dynamics. That particular science renders unquestionable aid, he thinks, in recognizing matter to have not only tended towards a center, but in admitting it to have one time existed in a state of diffusion, and this state he consistently explains to be the result of magnetic or electric force.[48] The author of "New Views of the Solar System" appears to be working along the same line for an understanding of the cause back of gravity. He, too, admits gravitation to be an "undefined force."[49] He is aware, he says, that Newton has hinted at its real nature; but he feels confident that the *Principia* offers no suggestions of "the *means*" by which planetary bodies hold their course.[50] Brewster he likewise reports as propounding the question of "the means by which the Almighty has bound the whole" together.[51] He ends his account of his investigation of the cause back of gravitation by saying, as did Poe, that it is upon the science of dynamics that he bases all his views, and that by showing how the planets and satellites are wielded by electro-magnetic machinery, new discoveries, exceeding even those following the discovery of steam, may come to light.[52]

From the foregoing evidence, one may doubtless with reason admit at least that Poe was familiar with the contents of the articles on the solar system, and, with like reason, one might even be will-

---

[46]*Works*, vol. 16, p. 223. *Eureka*.

[47]*Ibid.*, vol. 16, pp, 212; 213. *Eureka*.

[48]Considerations of dynamics are to be found in *Eureka;* pp. 237; 245.

[49]*S. L. M.*, vol. 5, p. 264. *Reviewer of "New Views of the Solar System" Reviewed.*

[50]*Ibid.*, vol. 5, p. 224. *Notice to Reviewers of "New Views of the Solar System."*

[51]*Ibid.*, vol. 5, p. 267. *Reviewer of "New Views of the Solar System" Reviewed.*

[52]*Ibid.*, vol. 5, p. 267.

ing to entertain the idea of his being their author. Attention remains to be called to the method both authors have of working out from astronomy a principle of unity. Unvarying law, which, as has been shown,[53] Poe felt in 1836 and 1837 to be a philosophic truth, the author of "New Views" in 1838 attempts to see operating under the processes of science.

The author of "New Views" endeavors to show that the principle of unity governs the movements of the planets about the sun. He advances the general theory that the velocity of the planets is equal, while the number of their revolutions about their primary varies. Disregarding the elaborate mathematical calculations by which he tried to prove this idea, I shall state only the main points with which he attempted to substantiate his claim. He takes the revolution of the moon around the earth as an example of equality in motion among the heavenly bodies. The mechanism of this system, he says, shows that the revolutionary progress of our earth is equal to the progressive velocity of its attending body. The progress of the earth he emphatically says must limit the progress of the moon.[54] As another example of equal motion in the heavenly bodies, he cites the motion of Jupiter's satellites around their center. The velocity of Jupiter's "retinue of little worlds," he notes, is equal, limited in their progress as they are, by the course of their primary. But in this equality of motion, he expresses himself as conscious of a variety of motion also. From a suppositional case, he first attempts to prove this point. Suppose, he says, in his article on the tides, that we had an additional moon; the inner moon because of the greater contraction of its orbit, would make more revolutions around the earth than the outer one, and would therefore appear to move faster. Then, from an actual case, that of the action of Jupiter and his satellites, he tries to verify his supposition. Jupiter's attending bodies describe varying revolutions around their center. This he thinks a just illustration of the law he is considering. He expresses himself as satisfied that in both of the cases cited exists the operation of the law of equality with the variation from the law. Then, viewing the evidence of the small systems, and reasoning from analogy, he next attempts to see equality and variability governing the whole solar system. The mechanism of Jupiter's little worlds, he says, in the same article,

---

[53]Cf. Chapter on Philosophy.
[54]*S. L. M.*, vol. 4, p. 747. *New View of the Tides.*

gives a "conclusive idea of the mechanism not only of the greater system of our sun,[55] but of all the systems composing the universe." And again, he speaks of Jupiter and his moons representing "in miniature" all the systems that exist. He now announces it to be his belief that the sun carries his planets as Jupiter does his moons.[56] In evident justification for thus transferring this law of action from the smaller system to the greater, he elaborately discusses the theory of the progressive sun.[57] It is now generally admitted, he says, "by astronomers in England, France, and Germany, that the Sun is not a stationary body," but moves on in his grand orbit. Maintaining the sun to be progressive, he then attempts to attach equal velocity to the whole revolving planetary system. No one planet, he says, can advance ahead; none can remain behind. They are all limited in their progress by their luminous leader.[58] He promises to show, mathematically, that the differing velocities as heretofore given cannot be correct—that Jupiter moves with the same velocity that Mercury, Venus, the Earth, and Mars do.[59] A necessary condition of this theory of equal velocity and as the logical consequence of a progressive sun, he believes to be the theory of concave planetary orbits. In this supposition, he takes the cases of our earth and her moon, and of Jupiter and his satellites as indicative of the kind of orbit described by all the planets and their attending bodies. "It is evident," he says, "that Jupiter's moons describe orbits round their primary, invariably concave to the sun, and it is equally evident . . .

---

[55]*Ibid.*, vol. 4, pp. 747-750. *New View of the Tides.*

[56]*Ibid.*, vol. 4, p. 433. *New Views of the Solar System.*

[57]*Ibid.*, vol. 4, p. 750. *New View of the Tides.* The author of New Views mentions Dr. Wilson of Glasgow as the first one who advanced this theory. *The Philosophical Transactions of the Royal Society of Edinburgh*, vol. 10, p. 296, gives a biographical account of Dr. Alexander Wilson. The theory referred to is there attributed to the son of Dr. Wilson, Patrick Wilson. The Reviewer of *New Views of the Solar System*, who, as has been said, may possibly be Prof. Draper of Hampden Sydney College, mentions three other propounders of the same theory, Mayer, in 1760, Lalande in 1776, and Herschel in 1780, the first two of whom in his opinion, having back of the assertion no more than analogical reasoning, and the last supposing he has discovered the proof of translation. The reviewer advises the author of *New Views* to convince himself of these facts by reading: Biot's Astronomie, vol. 3, chap. 3, and Delambre's Astronomie, vol. 3, chap. 32.

[58]*S. L. M.*, vol. 4, p. 434. *New Views of the Solar System.*

[59]*Ibid.*, vol. 4, p. 435.

that the planets describe the same kind of orbits, and equally concave to some more distant center, around which the sun himself
is describing a similar orbit.''[60]

But even without a progressive sun and concave planetary orbits,
the author further professes the ability to demonstrate that the
velocity of the planets is equal. Whether the sun is a stationary
or traveling body makes no difference at all, he says in the article
on the tides, when the question is that of equal motion of the
planets. Even with "orbits returning into themselves," he still
maintains equal planetary motion. This proof he contends rests
on a consideration of the times of the planets, and he attempts to
demonstrate equality by the periods of the planets in their revolutions. "I shall . . . proceed at once to show," he says in
his second article on the solar system, "that the planets must have
the same velocity, even to a second of time, or their periods would
be very different from what they are." In other words, he is apparently convinced that an error in the number of revolutions will
arise if different velocities are assigned to the planets. In his
calculations which follow this statement, he considers the case of
Mercury and Venus; first supposing the condition of equal motion. He divides the time of Venus, which "for greater convenience" he has reduced to hours, by the time of Mercury, similarly
reduced, and announces the result as showing two periods and
nearly one-half of another for Mercury, and one period for Venus.
This result, he says, corresponds to the actual facts as demonstrated.
He then supposes the condition of unequal velocities, the velocities
that are "stated in our books . . . and taught in our schools,"
and attempts to show that, by this calculation, an error in the number of revolutions will result. By giving the velocities of these two
planets according to our mathematical teachings, he says, Mercury would make only one revolution and part of another, while
Venus makes one. He then takes the earth and Jupiter and, as he
did with Mercury and Venus, computes the number of their revolutions, first on the basis of equal and then of unequal velocities.
In the latter case, he says, the number of revolutions given the
earth is incorrect; the earth is made to revolve a little more than
five times while Jupiter revolves once. In the former case, he asserts, the computation, resting on equal velocity, the "number of

---

[60]*Ibid.*, vol. 4, p. 750. *New View of the Tides.*

revolutions of the Earth, corresponds to a second of time to the
real facts, as they exist in relation to these two planets, in the
system, as it came from the hands of its Creator.''[61]

Variability in rotatory motion, he likewise discusses. He advances the theory that the planets give rotation to the sun, and the
moons to the planets. The force producing motion is, he says,
electro-magnetic pressure, and, being unequal as the densities of
the bodies differ, the rotatory motion is unequal also. Such a
theory he acknowledges to be original.[62] But it is, he thinks, on that
score, none the less true. In attempting to substantiate his contention, he first claims the existence of electro-magnetic force. It
is equally easy, he says, in the first article on the solar system, to
conceive the Deity creating elastic materials and specifically applying them, as to conceive the creation of our globe in any terms
at all.[63] He notes the fact that Newton acknowledged the pressure
of magnetic fluid, although in a state of diffusion and without specific offices to perform. He differs, therefore, he says, from Newton, solely in giving this electric material certain definite functions.[64] Can it be possible, he asks, that such materials can be
without agency? And he replies to his own question by stating his
conviction that one of these offices is to produce rotatory motion.
He tries to prove his point by describing what he feels to be the
true nature of the influence of the moon on the earth. From the
small case, he then forms, as before, in considering equality of motion, a general notion of existing conditions in the solar system at
large. He first assumes the existence of elastic, magnetic spheres,
explaining that the sun, the planets and their satellites are surrounded by magnetic material. These spheres, he says, act and
react upon each other, and in no way is this interaction to be attributed to the planets themselves. He then considers the pressure of these spheres. Knowing that the theory of tides admits
the pressure of the moon on the earth, he expresses his conviction
that this pressure will result in something more than a depression
of the water's surface.[65] It will result, he thinks, in rotary or

[61]*Ibid.*, vol. 4, p. 770.   *New Views of the Solar System.*
[62]*Ibid.*, vol. 4, p. 435.   *New Views of the Solar System.*
[63]*Ibid.*, vol. 4, p. 433.   *New Views of the Solar System.*
[64]*Ibid.*, vol. 5, p. 266.   *Reviewer of ''New Views of the Solar System'' Reviewed.*
[65]*Ibid.*, vol. 4, p. 749.   *New View of the Tides.*

axillary motion of the earth also. The west-to-east motion of the earth he further explains from his theory that the moon, moving faster than its primary, throws greater pressure on the eastern portion of our globe and hence causes it to rotate always in that direction. He then announces the general notion that he has deduced from the individual case—that of the moons causing the planets to rotate, and the planets, the sun.[66] In this rotation caused by pressure, he then notes variability of motion. He hopes that the great difference between the rotation of the earth and the moon may excite the attention of his learned readers.[67]

Coming now to the work acknowledged to be Poe's, one finds the same effort to comprehend unity as a scientific principle that characterized the preceding work.

In the "Addenda to Eureka" Poe starts with the notion of equality and then sees in that equality the existence of variability also. Equality appears to be the effort to view under the same head the two motions of rotation and revolution. He seems also to give it the meaning of unity. An evident emphasis and perhaps a possible indication that he had derived the idea from some source, may be seen in the fact that, in one instance, in referring to the rotation and revolution of a planet, he places in quotation marks the expression *both under one*.[68]

As an example of this idea of equality, or perhaps of unity, he takes first the motion of the sun. The sun, he says, after its condensation[69] rotated on its axis, but this axis not being the center

---

[66]*Ibid.*, vol. 4, p. 433. *New Views of the Solar System.*

[67]A series of articles entitled *Curiosities of Science*, written by John Lofland, called the Milford Bard, have certain points in common with *New Views of the Solar System*. They speak of the sun as a galvanic battery; of the planets being moved by electricity; and of electricity being the "grand cause of all the phenomena or operations of nature." It does not seem reasonable, however, to think that Lofland could have written *New Views*, for his ideas are scattered and disconnected, and he does not seem to be working with any principle in mind; rather to be detailing certain knowledge chiefly from his own experimentation, which he considers curious and interesting. He does not exploit, moreover, the main contention of *New Views*, namely, equal velocity of the planets. Lofland, John, *Curiosities of Science*, Baltimore, 1853.

[68]*Works*, vol. 16, p. 338. *Poe's Addenda to Eureka.*

[69]*Ibid.*, vol. 16, p. 337. Poe affirms here that he differs from Laplace in thinking that the sun was originally condensed at once, and not gradually, as in the Nebular Hypothesis.

of the figure, it not only rotated but revolved also. Poe appears to feel that he has given sufficient reason for concluding that the two motions of the sun are a unit, for he adds: "Rotation and revolution are one, but I separate them for convenience of illustration."[70] With the same evident meaning, he speaks also of Neptune's making his rotation a revolution; and of Neptune's moon rotating and revolving "both under one." As was done in "New Views of the Solar System," he now endeavors, from analogy, to make the smaller case prove the greater. He says that he has doubtless given enough, without referring to the other planets, to make his point plain.[71] In this unity he sees variability also. He recognizes diversity in the rotatory motions of the planets and then tries to account for it. It had been affirmed, it will be remembered, that rotation was due to pressure of the electro-magnetic spheres— those of the moons on the planets and those of the planets on the sun.[72] The author of "New Views" had remarked, too, on the striking difference between the rotations of the moon and the earth. Poe now appears in his "Addenda to Eureka" to offer a suggested explanation of this diversity. Disregarding as before elaborate mathematical calculations, and his frequent assumptions of his use and interpretation of Newton's and Kepler's laws,[73] I shall try to give what seem to be the main steps in his reasoning. He notes the general tendency of planets in condensing to approach the sun.[74] This tendency to *approach the center* may have the same meaning as had the former term "pressure," though in the "Addenda" Poe does not definitely so state it. If we grant this to be the case, the progressive steps in this article of his explanation of variability of rotation appear to be consistent with the first steps in "New Views." He seems to be desirous in the "Addenda" of making the difference in rotation of the planets depend on the difference in their density.[75] He understands density to be governed by distance from the sun, since, as he says, a planet falls nearer in proportion as it condenses. The degree to which the planet approaches the sun would, therefore, indicate the degree

[70]*Ibid.*, vol. 16, p. 338.
[71]*Ibid.*, vol. 16, p. 339.
[72]Cf. note 65.
[73]*Works*, vol. 16, p. 342.
[74]*Ibid.*, vol. 16, p. 343.
[75]*Ibid.*

of its pressure. Consequently, when he maintains, as has just been shown, that the velocity of rotation depends on density, he doubtless means, as did the former article, that rotation depends on pressure.

Poe, in his effort to find equality governing the physical world, appears to carry his attempted proof into still other fields. Though at no time does he deny that the sun is a moving body, he does not, as did the author of "New Views," insist on making that theory the principal basis of his assumption of equality of forces. It will be remembered that even the author of those articles advanced the theory of equal velocity of the planets from the standpoint of a stationary sun.[76] That author said he was only endeavoring to invite scientific investigation of his views, but beyond the attacks already referred to his theory met with no response. Poe, on his part, now decides to contend for equality on still another score. In "Eureka" he tries to demonstrate that this principle is the law controlling the creation, present condition, and destiny of the material and spiritual universe. He is of the opinion now that Laplace's Nebular Hypothesis gives the most satisfactory explanation of the creation of the solar system.[77] It is no doubt a fact that he speaks as the philosopher as well as the scientist, when he terms it "beautifully true," and as being "far too beautiful . . . not to possess Truth as its essentiality."[78] He proceeds, then, to outline Laplace's theory, saying that he gives it as its author himself conceived it. During the course of this outline, it will be noted that Poe stresses the operation of unity and the variation from that law, evidently convinced that the theory covers the working of these two factors. In the first place, the theory recognizes, he says, variety and uniformity in the nebulous mass from which creation sprang. It then assumes matter as diffused in a state of

---

[76]Cf. note 61.

[77]Poe's dependence in *Eureka* on Laplace's theory when, if we consider him the author of *New Views*, he had there appeared to have only a slight acquaintance with that astronomer, is quite consistent with the progressive nature of his study, his acknowledgement of being only a novice in astronomical learning, his frequent corrections of his own mistakes, and his assertion that, despite his conviction that Laplace's knowledge was wanting in certain fields, he intended at a future time, to draw largely on him for material. *S. L. M.*, vol. 5, p. 224. *Notice to the Reviewer of "New Views of the Solar System."*

[78]*Works*, vol. 16, p. 252.

heterogeneous nebulosity.[79]   The planets, says the theory, were
whirled from the sun, and, as that body continued to condense,
they, composed like their parent body of heterogeneous material,
lost their form as rings and became broken into an infinity of separate pieces.[80]   Poe at this point in his outline expresses himself
strongly of the opinion that Laplace felt the necessity of assuming
heterogeneous material in the nebulosity.   In no other way, he
thought, could the French astronomer account for the breaking up
of the rings, since they could not have broken had they been
homogeneous.   He maintains that he reaches the same result as
Laplace, that of heterogeneous material, although he reaches it,
he says, by another assumption, that of predicating heterogeneity
to the atoms that compose the mass.[81]

The theory likewise provides for uniformity, according to Poe's
rendering.[82]   The rings whirled from the nebulous mass, possessed, in their heterogeneous nature, at the same time, a constitution nearly uniform.   In addition to this general character, the
rings when broken into separate pieces showed a tendency to become absorbed by that portion which is superior in mass, a tendency therefore toward oneness.   Thus the creation of Neptune,
Jupiter, Uranus, and the other planets is hypothetically accounted
for, under the law of unity and the variation from it.   Poe then
outlines the Nebular Hypothesis as it explains the origin of the
moons.   Neptune threw off a ring of un-uniform material which
developed the same tendency to break up and the pieces the same
desire to cluster about the center of the heaviest of their number.
In this manner, Neptune threw off another ring, with the same
result.   Neptune thus came to have his two moons, and, as the
planets continued to condense, Uranus was finally attended by three
lunar bodies, Saturn by seven, Jupiter by four, and our Earth by
its one.

As he continues to detail the points of Laplace's Hypothesis, it
can be noted that Poe stresses equality in the rotatory motion of
the planets.   The theory assumes that the velocity of a planet's
revolution around the sun is equal to the rotary velocity of the sun.
With Neptune as an example, this equality is explained, first, when

[79]Ibid., vol. 16, pp. 245-252.
[80]Ibid., vol. 16, p. 247.
[81]Ibid., vol. 16, p. 248.
[82]Ibid., vol. 16, p. 247.

that planet existed as the ring thrown from the nebulous mass. "The ring . . . *revolved*," Poe relates, in quoting from Laplace, "*as* a separate ring, with just that velocity with which, while the surface of the mass, *it rotated*." Later, when the ring settles into a planet, the same equality is preserved. The theory likewise assumes equality between the tangential and gravitating forces.

Though expressing himself as satisfied in the main with Laplace's theory, Poe is still of the opinion that the theory needs certain emendations and certain modifications. In the "Addenda to Eureka," he had declared his wish to guard against the interpretation of adhering in detail to Laplace's entire view.[83] He also says, later, that his assumptions imply important differences from the Nebular Theory as given by Laplace. The Nebular Hypothesis, he felt convinced, made no provision for the Newtonian law of gravitation. It is true, he says, that Laplace assumed such a law, but, according to the explanation that atoms extend in unlimited succession throughout space, he had no logical right for the assumption.[84] It is not surprising, then, considering his conviction of the need of revision and his custom, as has been noted, of offering new views, that he should now advance a theory of his own that would attempt an explanation of the plan and method he professes to feel in the creation of the universe. He appears to be desirious of justifying his right to suggest a theory, first, on the grounds that the greatest truths have been brought to light by judicious *guesses*. Plato, he says, gives proof of the safety of occasional guessing.[85] Kepler grasped "with his soul" the secret of the principle of the machinery of the universe.[86] Laplace, whose

---

[83]*Works*, vol. 16, p. 337. *Poe's Addenda to Eureka.*

[84]Poe's words, on this point, are *(Works*, vol. 16, p. 266): "His [Laplace's] most unwarranted assumption was that of giving the atoms a movement towards a center, in the very face of his evident understanding that these atoms, in unlimited succession, extend throughout the Universal space. . . . Under such circumstances, there could have occurred no movement at all; and Laplace, consequently, assumed one on no more philosophical ground than that something of the kind was necessary for the establishment of what he intended to establish."

[85]*Works*, vol. 16, p. 279. *Eureka.*

It is suggested that a study might be made of Poe's detective story in the light of his knowledge of law, in general, of medical jurisprudence, and of what he has to say concerning the relation between data and the hypothesis.

[86]*Ibid.*, vol. 16, p. 197. Vol. 14, p. 187. *A Chapter of Suggestions.*

hypothesis he has just related, deduced an absolute truth from no better start than mere speculation. In fact, the original idea to which Laplace owed his theory was derived, Poe thinks, from a compound of the "true Epicurean atoms with the false nebulae" of Laplace's own time.[87] He also tries to justify his right to theorize on so stupendous a subject as the universe by bringing forth a mass of scientific facts to substantiate his claim. Before entering, however, into these facts in Poe's attempted proof of his own hypothesis, I shall first give the main points of his theory, with its essential differences from that of Laplace.

Poe appears to construct his theory, first, in imitation, perhaps, of Laplace's example, on the atomic theory he had learned from ancient philosophy,[88] and to this pagan belief, he joined the conception of the Deity as the Creator, a conception which, as we have seen, he had found so elaborately explained in the pages of Christian philosophy.[89] His purpose seems to be to discover and to demonstrate the true meaning of gravity, the point which he has asserted to be not provided for in Laplace's theory. No one, he says, "up to this date" has any understanding of what lies behind the essential characteristics of this principle. He states his proposition thus: "*Unity* is the *source* of the phenomenon."[90] It will be remembered that in the "Addenda" Poe had asserted that the differing forces of rotation and revolution should be viewed under one head, and that before that date, in "New Views of the Solar System" the author had tried to maintain equal velocity of the planets. In the theory about to be explained it will be seen that Poe is now claiming equality for two other forces, and furthermore, that he is assuming an identity of source for the two. In other words, he is claiming, first, that the diffusive force originates in unity; secondly, that the diffusive force equals the attracting force, or gravity; and, thirdly, that gravity also has unity for its source.

---

[87]*Ibid.*, vol. 16, p. 266.

[88]Cf. Chapter on Philosophy.

[89]G. W. Eveleth, in writing to Poe, Mar. 9, 1848, praises warmly this starting-point that he (Poe) has chosen. He admits the chance of some opposition on the ground that the starting-point is "but an off-spring of the imagination"; but he professes himself satisfied with it since it is supported "to full maturity." Mabbott, *Letters from G. W. Eveleth to Edgar Allan Poe*, p. 19.

[90]*Works*, vol. 16, p. 217. *Eureka.*

In advancing this theory, Poe starts with God, whom he chooses to consider under the light of Divine Volition. "As our starting-point," he says, "let us adopt the *God-head*," who, "by dint of his Volition," created, out of nothing, matter "in its utmost conceivable state of . . . *Simplicity.*"[91] This starting-point Poe affirms to be his sole assumption in the theory which he advances. Oneness he predicates of this originally created matter. It is a particle, he says, "of *one* kind—of *one* character—of *one* nature—of *one size*—of one form." He is of the opinion that the universe was made from this particle. The atoms were irradiated spherically from this center, with equal diffusion. *One* was thus forced into *Many,* and the atoms presented an appearance, from their difference in size and their equi-distance between centers of quantity, of a particular un-uniformity, though, in general, there was uniformity in design. But the force was determinate and ceased. Reaction, therefore, set in, a "*satisfiable* tendency of the disunited atoms to return into *One.*" But the lapsing into one is not to be allowed until certain ends are accomplished. A "separate something," Poe says, will, while permitting "up to a certain epoch" atoms to coalesce with one another, at the same time prevent a total coalition. Thus he describes the two forces as held in balance. When the Divine purposes are fulfilled, however, then the repulsive influence will yield to the tendency toward the center, and all atoms will return to the one from which they sprang. The above, briefly stated, is Poe's theory.

Poe then attempts to bring forward scientific proof for his theory. He must find, he says, some scientific phenomenon, some phenomenon whose law is known and whose validity is unquestioned which will be a precise parallel to the condition this theory assumes; namely, absolute unity as a source, and *equal* diffusion from that center. He must find some third idea, an idea science stamps as true, which will be a link between unity and diffusion as his theory gives them.

Poe is of the opinion that irradiation of light will illustrate both the points he needs, and therefore will be the link he is seeking. He is aware, he says, that light particles radiate equally from a luminous center. He affirms then, that unity is the source of their diffusion. He is also aware that the scientific law governing this phenomenon is that irradiation varies as the squares of

---

[91]*Ibid.,* vol. 16, pp. 205-206.

the distances from the centre, or, that irradiation proceeds in direct proportion to the squares of the distances. He then states the converse of the idea and says he is further aware of the scientific law governing concentralization or gathering together of light particles towards their centre. This law he states to be: Concencentralization varies *inversely* as the squares of the distances.

From the scientific illustration of light showing equal diffusion from a centre, Poe then forms a hypothetical method of diffusion, which will, he thinks, correspond exactly with it. He imagines a hollow sphere of glass, the interior surface of which will receive a stratum of atoms equally diffused by a force resident in the centre. A second and inferior exercise of the same force he then imagines as infusing a second layer on the first. A third and still inferior force deposits a third layer on the second, and so on until the glass sphere is filled. Poe is of the opinion that his imaginative illustration parallels exactly the process in light radiation. He has preserved, he thinks, the same condition; namely, equable diffusion from a center; and, therefore, he expresses himself as justified in assigning to his method of diffusion the law governing light and says the forces of irradiation of atoms are directly proportional to the squares of the distances.

Poe's next step is an attempt to find an analogy between his imaginary irradiation of atoms and the diffusion of rings from the sun according to Laplace's theory. In seeking this analogy, he again resorts to a suppositional case. Confining himself to results, he says, and not to the process in both instances, he considers what the results of the processes of being whirled from the center would be if one were able to view them all at once. He imagines what conditions would exist if all the rings whirled from the sun—the rings which in time became Neptune, Saturn, Uranus, etc—remained entire until the final discharge of that ring which gave birth to Mercury. He can picture to himself, he says, a series of co-existent, concentric circles. Between this condition for which, though imaginary, he still claims a scientific starting-point, and his wholly imaginary distribution of atoms in the glass sphere, he claims a correspondence. He is of the opinion that they agree in results; that is, in arrangement of atoms in the one case and of rings in the other. He is also of the opinion that, from this similarity, he is justified in affirming that the forces which threw off each concentric circle varied as the squares of the distances.

Poe puts in the step, that, in his imaginary experiment with the glass sphere, the number of atoms diffused on the interior surface and the succeeding circles, are in direct proportion with the forces which diffused them.

Poe has shown, following light radiation, that the diffusive force originates in unity. The planet and his atoms, therefore, he thinks, are radiated from a centre, and are both governed by the same law. He now wishes to point out, first, that the force of gravity equals the diffusive force; and, secondly, that it originates in unity as well as does the diffusive force. He inspects Newton's law of gravity and states it to be thus: "All bodies attract each other with forces proportional to their quantities of matter and inversely proportional to the squares of their distances." He re-states Newton's law, giving it as he says a more philosophical phraseology, though by no means modifying its meaning.[92] "Every atom, of every body, attracts every other atom, both of its own and every other body, with a force which varies *inversely* as the squares of the distances between the attracting and attracted atom." He then notes certain correspondences. First, the law governing the irradiation of light: that controlling the diffusion of his atoms in the glass sphere; and that guiding the concentric circles and therefore the planets as they were whirled from the sun —that law is identical, he says, in all cases. The force of irradia-tion in all these phenomena varies as the squares of the distances. Secondly, the law governing the return of light particles corres-ponds with the return of atoms to their centre, or, in other words, to gravity. In both cases the forces vary *inversely* as the squares of the distances. He is, therefore, of the opinion that gravity is the reaction, or action conversed, of the diffusive force and is, as a consequence, equal to it.

For the final part of his proposition, namely, that gravity has its source in unity, Poe now tries to advance scientific proof. He tries to fortify his position by quoting from Herschel and Hum-boldt to the effect that a movement toward a center among the heavenly bodies is, at least, not an untenable idea. Herschel ad-mits, though reluctantly, Poe says, that the systems of the uni-verse are in a state of progressive collapse.[93] Humboldt expresses

[92]*Works*, vol. 16, p. 215.
[93]*Ibid.*, vol. 16, p. 297.

the belief that we have no data at hand to dispute the possibility of such a movement toward a center.[94]   Dr. Nichol, from whom Poe professes to maintain a wide difference of opinion in regard to cosmical conditions, makes on this point, he says, remarks pertinent to the question.[95]   According to Dr. Nichol, the observations taken through Lord Rosse's high-power telescope reveal not circular masses of nebulae, but a condition quite the reverse. Volumes of stars, Dr. Nichol says, "stretch out apparently as if they were rushing towards a great central mass in consequence of the action of some great power." Poe is of the opinion that the circular masses alluded to are the variations in the absolutely rectilinear path of the planets to their centre. The *general* path would be a straight line, he says,[96] and the infinity of curves the local deviations from the general uniform motion. From such evidence as he has just brought to bear, Poe appears to feel that he has sufficiently developed the thesis of his discourse to entitle him to assert that gravity is the "tendency to collapse,"[97] and that it is the law under which atoms, planets, stars, and clusters of stars seek their original unity.

Of what use to Poe, one asks, was his scientific study? Doubtless it was owing to his interest in science that changes and additions found their way into his literary theory and practice. I shall try to show, first, that it varied the nature of the critical art from what he had hitherto conceived it; secondly, that it enlarged and enriched his theory in such matters as a new comprehension of plot structure, the necessity of the dénouement, a basis for the metrical art, and the understanding of verisimilitude; and, thirdly, that it produced striking changes in his practice.

Criticism, in Poe's mind, seems to have passed through successive stages. Recall, for example, what he had to say on the almost utter lack of critical acumen in an English review. He had found mainly, he said, the expression of mere opinion. Recall too, his efforts, in the days of his study of law, to make his criticism judicial. But in this last stage, the period of his scientific training, he comes to view criticism as a science. In one instance he

---

[94]*Ibid.*, vol. 16, p. 299.
[95]*Ibid.*, vol. 16, p. 298.
[96]*Ibid.*, vol. 16, p. 299.
[97]*Ibid.*, vol. 16, p. 301.

definitely gives it that name;[98] ·in another, he expresses surprise
that critics can so complacently pronounce judgment without the
slightest knowledge of determinate principles on which to base
their sentence.

Natural science, it has just been said, strengthened Poe's understanding of plot structure. It has already been noted that A. W.
von Schlegel's "Lectures on Dramatic Art and Literature"[99] and
Aristotle's *Poetics* had each its influence in forming the character
of his plot. It has also been seen that philosophy had a bearing
in determining its nature.[100] Indeed, the sureness with which a
change in source re-acts upon this particular interest invites one's
attention. The method of telling a story as a logical sequence of
events bound together by no outstanding idea beyond the oneness
of effect produced by an overwhelming mass of sensations, certainly by no emphasis on arrangement of parts—the plot of the
Blackwood days, gave way, as we have seen, under Schlegel's influence, to the comprehension of the plot in the light of totality of
interest. The latter idea grew under the influence of Aristotle's
unity of action, an idea which to Poe came to mean the plot as an
organism of mutually dependent parts. But it is in all probability
not too much to say that the greatest strength of Poe's conception
of plot structure lay in his study and appreciation of Newton's
law of gravitation.

Poe suggests an analogy between plot structure and the universe. He states this idea, in one instance, in the following words:
"The Universe is a plot of God."[101] In attempting to carry out
this parallelism, he stresses first of all the idea of the atomic nature
of the plot. For example, he thinks that a plot may be appreciated
by all *in its atoms*, but taken as a whole, it is of far too ideal a
nature to be a popular interest.[102] In another instance he views
plot structure as being atomic, saying that Bulwer's workmanship
shows an ability to adapt the very numerous atoms of his story,[103]
and he seems to carry the analogy further in referring to the plot
as a "mass."[104]

---

[98]*Works*, vol. 11, p. 1. *Exordium.*
[99]Cf. Chapter III. *Unity in the Drama and Fine Arts.*
[100]Cf. Chapter IV. *Unity in Terms of Philosophy.*
[101]*Works*, vol. 16, p. 292. *Eureka.*
[102]*Ibid.*, vol. 10, p. 120. Review of Bulwer's *Night and Morning.*
[103]*Ibid.*, vol. 10, p. 117.
[104]*Ibid.*, vol. 13, p. 45. *The American Drama.*

The parallel between the universe and the plot in literature appears to be likewise stressed in the attempt to identify the mutual dependence of part on part, or of atom on atom, especially as Newton's law of gravity gives the idea, with the mutual dependence in the structural formation of the plot. Newton's law of gravity, it will be remembered, Poe had interpreted to mean: "Every atom of every body, attracts every other atom, both of its own and every other body, with a force which varies inversely as the squares of the distances between the attracting and the attracted atom." So greatly does Poe appear to be impressed with this scientific truth of mutual dependence, that he declares his mind is overwhelmed with the idea. An atom displaced, he says, would affect the whole universe.—

"If I venture to displace, by even the billionth part of an inch, the microscopical speck of dust which lies now upon the point of my finger, what is the character of that act upon which I have adventured? I have done a deed which shakes the Moon in her path, which causes the Sun to be no longer the Sun, and which alters forever the destiny of the multitudinous myriads of stars that roll and glow in the majestic presence of their Creator."[105]

It is not surprising, then, that with so profound a conviction of the scientific truth of mutual dependence of atom on atom, that he should express the same idea in literary practice. He makes a distinction between the plot as he understood it from his study of Aristotle's definition, between the plot as an organism, and the plot as an outgrowth of science. He is of the opinion that Aristotle's plot calls for only slight dependence of parts in comparison with one springing from scientific knowledge. The difference he places in the degree of injury resulting from the removal of any one of the incidents making up the structure. In the former case, he says, the removal or displacing of any one of the leading incidents would prove a *detriment* to the whole; in the latter, not one part, not the most minute incident, can be displaced without *ruin* to the mass. He further illustrates the dependence by affirming that the withdrawal of any part from its rightful place in plot structure would "overthrow the fabric" as completely as would the changing of the position of a single brick in a building. The idea of the most delicate mutual dependence continues throughout

---

[105] *Ibid.*, vol. 16, p. 218.

Poe's literary criticism. On its basis, he declares a stanza of poetry to be a unit, one line of which removed would ruin the whole.

Further intensifying his idea of mutual relationship, Poe even insists on plot structure showing reciprocal action between cause and effect. It is very probable that he had met this idea of reciprocity as a philosophic truth in the *Bridgewater Treatises*.[106] He may also have found it in Kant's "Critique of the Judgment."[107] But he also discusses the point of mutuality of adaptation on the basis of his own hypothesis. He first inspects, scientifically and mathematically, the question of mere adaptation. Newton's law shows, he says, that forces are directly proportional to the amount of matter projected;[108] his own hypothesis supposes the diffusive force directly adapted to the number of atoms diffused.[109] But his own hypothesis appears to add a further step. The mutual relationship between cause and effect, it is highly probable, originated in his idea of gravity and diffusion counterbalancing each other and both having their source in the same center, a condition which Divine Volition, according to his theory, made possible. He maintains that it is from stand-points such as these that the plot in fictional literature should be viewed. The pleasure, he says in *Eureka*, which one derives from plot structure, is in the ratio of its approach to this species of divine reciprocity. And he adds that, in constructing the plot, one should "aim at so arranging the incidents that we shall not be able to determine of any one of them, whether it depends from any one other, or upholds it."[110]

The necessity of the dénouement also rests on a scientific basis. Poe had attempted to demonstrate, it was noted, that gravity has its origin in unity, and, at the same time, from its progressive return to its source, carries within itself the necessity of an end. On this latter point, Poe had, it was also noted, laid great stress on Herschel's admission of the universe presenting a state of pro-

---

[106]Poe read, according to his own statement, the article on the *Bridgewater Treatises* in which mutuality of relation between cause and effect is discussed, though with no scientific explanation. It is surprising, then, to find him saying, in his article on the *American Drama*, and in *Eureka*, that the *Bridgewater Treatises* have overlooked this point.

[107]Cf. Chapter IV. *Unity in Terms of Philosophy*. Cf. note 79.

[108]*Works*, vol. 16, p. 215. *Eureka*.

[109]*Ibid.*, vol. 16, p. 231.

[110]*Ibid.*, vol. 16, p. 292.

gressive collapse;[111] a state which he identifies with gravity and hence with return to unity. He is of the opinion that an obvious analogy exists between the law of gravitation and a dénouement brought about by incidents springing from the main subject of a piece. The end of a piece, he says, must be brought about by events originating in the ruling idea, and springing from the bosom of the thesis.[112] Should one not conceive of the universe as having an end, Poe further says, in continuing the analogy, creation would impress one with the same sense of dissatisfaction we experience from the dénouement in an imperfect plot, brought about by interposed incidents foreign to the subject.

Poe admits, however, that the plot as he sees it in its scientific sense is a standard in criticism, rather than a possibility to be attained by human skill. The universe as the "plot of God," is an ideal or perfect plot, conceived by science in its strictest sense. The artist should, however, he maintains, hold this plot in mind when he is fashioning his tale, and approach its perfection as nearly as he can.

Poe also endeavors to treat metrical art with a scientific hand. He claims the discovery of what he calls the true method of scanning and of what he conceives to be the real nature of the caesura.[113] The latter has been used, he says, "time out of mind" by all poets, but with no knowledge of the character he gives it. The whole subject of versification he has treated more thoroughly, he maintains, than any other living grammarian, critic, or essayist.

A chronological survey of Poe's interest in metrical art will reveal somewhat of his sources and the development of his theory. An early evidence presents itself in a letter from Judge Tucker to Poe in December, 1835, the content of which indicates that he and the jurist exchanged critical opinions[114] on the question of versification. Judge Tucker commends Poe's frequent success in the art and, at the same time, asks for criticism in return. "I will try to write out from memory a few rude lines," he says; "I send them on one condition. You are to judge them candidly."[115] The letter further indicates that the correspondents had different

---

[111]*Ibid.*, vol. 16, p. 301.
[112]*Ibid.*, vol. 16, p. 306.
[113]*Works*, vol. 11, p. 229. Review of *Poets and Poetry of America*.
[114]*Letters*, p. 21. Judge Tucker's letter to Poe.
[115]*Ibid.*, p. 24.

standards for judgment. Judge Tucker writes of the lines to which reference has just been made: "Reject them if they do not come up to either my standard or yours. Let me know which." Ruggedness is apparently the standard which Poe, at this time, has in mind. A mere flow of mellifluous lines, he had evidently said, according to Judge Tucker's letter, by no means fulfills the demands for metrical art.[116] He seems also to have complained that a certain poem of the jurist's was faulty, because too "faultless". Tucker replies to this criticism of his lines:—

"Not that I could not have made them rugged, but because I did not think myself master of that sort of 'grace beyond the reach of art,' which so few can snatch. I have seen something analogous to it in the features and in the carriage of persons who were the handsomer for not being perfectly handsome, and the more graceful for a little awkwardness."[117]

Judge Tucker's standard, however, differing from Poe's ruggedness, appears to be equality in time, an equality in which he is also aware of irregularities. The time of the bar, he says, must be the same, no matter how many notes are in it. He requires, he adds, that the notes must be uttered in due time and that the presence of nine, of eleven, or even of twelve syllables should not affect the time but should rather render a relief from "the mawkish sweetness which by continuance becomes nauseous." He considers that Moore, Pope, and Byron can throw a few syllables out of or into their verse and yet preserve the rhythm without interruption. This art, he thinks, is the secret of Moore's charm. And he points out to Poe that one of his own (Poe's) pieces does not measure up to this standard. He refers to what Poe had evidently called a fragment, and insists that there are in it lines which cannot in any way be forced into time. Take, he says, Baldazzar's speech, at the bottom of the first column of p. 15.[118]

In 1835, Poe was in fair way, as has just been seen, of learning from Judge Tucker certain notions of the charm of equality with irregularity of beat in versification. There are indications during the years 1836 and 1837 that Poe tried to account for the charm of equalized cadence in verse; and to analyze the pleasure that comes from the rhythmic flow of lines varied though not retarded by irregular beat. Judge Tucker had offered him no explanation

---

[116]*Ibid.*, p. 21.

[117]*Ibid.*, p. 22.

[118]*S. L. M.*, vol. 1, p. 15. This fragment to which Judge Tucker refers is evidently Poe's *Politian*, called an unfinished drama.

of this charm. "I do not know," writes the jurist in the letter of 1835, "to what to liken those occasional departures from regular metre which are so fascinating." Though he suggests that they may be likened to grace notes in music, he only vouches, he says, for the accuracy of his ear. But it was into the field of philosophy and science that Poe took his investigation for laws lying back of this spell. Poe had found in philosophy, it will be remembered, the principle of unity,[119] for in 1836, Coleridge had taught him an understanding of this principle as it lay back of the creative imagination. His own philosophic research beginning, as we have seen, in the latter days of 1836, had also brought to him an added comprehension of the principle. The Platonic sense of proportion and the conception of *Many in One,* had, on Socrates' recommendation, been for him a rich store for rhetorical needs.[120] He had, moreover, found in science, as the present chapter has detailed, what seemed to him ample illustration of unity with its attendant variations in the physical world. He now seems to be of the opinion that the same principles in philosophy and science may be applied to metrical art,—that in them may lie the secret of the charm which he and Judge Tucker were discussing. In furtherance of this supposition may be cited his review in 1837 of Bryant in which he uses for a metrical theory the exact philosophic terms he had been working on the preceding year. He warmly praises Bryant for being able to equalize his measures. And in the same review he cites Pope as an example of the same ability.

The true method of scansion, Poe says, is based in processes of natural law.[121] Equality is its underlying principle. He considers,

---

[119]Cf. Chapter on Philosophy.

[120]Cf. Chapter on Philosophy.

[121]*Works,* vol. 14, p. 218. *Rationale of Verse.*

Mr. Mabbott, in his work on Poe's *Politian,* suggests that Poe's prosody is in need of a thorough study. Mabbott, Thomas Ollive, *Politian, An Unfinished Tragedy, by Edgar A. Poe. Including the Hitherto Unpublished Scenes from the Original Manuscript in the Pierpont Morgan Library, Now First Edited with Notes and Commentaries.* The Collegiate Press, George Banta Publishing Co., Wisconsin, 1923.

While the study that I am presenting does not claim in any sense to be thorough, it does, I believe, give the basic principle on which Poe founded his verse. It shows, too, that Poe's later poetry, for example, the *Raven,* was preceded by a study of theory. Mr. Mabbott's statement, then, that the student must remember that Poe always practiced first and theorized afterwards, seems not wholly justified. Mabbott, *Politian,* p. 83.

therefore, that all English prosodists have been laboring under a misconception in placing the secret of scansion somewhere in the study of feet, metres, rhythms, and rules in *"ancient"* verse.[122] It is a mistake, he insists, to take the Iliad as a starting-point, instead of Nature and common sense. Indeed, the mere fact that he attempts to rationalize the subject shows, it would seem, an effort on his part to see the art in its scientific relations. His very obvious desire to establish an analogy between what he calls the development of verse and a scientific hypothesis of creation places little doubt in the assumption that, to him, versification was a matter of science. The effort to seek this analogy is apparent in that his proposition for the growth of verse forms is in tone strongly reminiscent of his outline of Laplace's theory and of his general comprehension of scientific law. He says for example, in summing up the details of metrical development, that he believes the processes he gives to be "nearly if not accurately those which *did* occur in the gradual creation of what we now call verse."[123] As if to call attention to the progressive nature of this creation, he puts within inverted commas the term *processes*. And he seems to be desirous of further carrying out the analogy by stating that both are atomic. Poe gave Laplace's explanation, it will be remembered, of the very start of creation being the meeting of two atoms in space.[124] The beginning of verse, or, as he calls it, the rudiment, results, he thinks, from "the very germ of a thought seeking satisfaction in equality of sound" from words of two syllables.[125] He places the spondee, therefore, at the beginning of the process of verse development, and says that his idea is corroborated by the fact that spondees are most frequent in ancient tongues. A certain parallelism between science and verse appears to continue in the character of the gradual growth in both cases. The two atoms, according to the scientific theory, were joined by others, until an aggregation was formed.[126] The second step, Poe says,

[122]*Ibid.*, vol. 14, p. 217. *Rationale of Verse.*
[123]*Ibid.*, vol. 14, p. 229. Cf. vol. 16, p. 260. *Eureka.*
[124]*Ibid.*, vol. 16, p. 246. *Eureka.*
[125]*Ibid.*, vol. 14, p. 220. *Rationale of Verse.*
[126]*Ibid.*, vol. 16, p. 246. *Eureka.*

in verse creation was the collocation of two spondees; the third, the juxtaposition of three of such words.[127]

Both hypotheses likewise agree that mass, the aggregation of atoms in the one instance, and the collection of spondees in the other, reaches a point where it seeks relief from "excess of self." In "Eureka" he describes the mass of the sun "needing relief"[128] when its equilibrium was disturbed, and its consequent throwing off of material from its equatorial region. In the hypothetical development of verse, he speaks of the spondees seeking relief from too great predominance of their own material.[129] And he seems to have in mind the same means for relief in both cases. The introduction of variety appears to be the remedy. While the parallel in its details in this regard cannot be too closely insisted upon, yet both theories deal so consistently with relief in consequence of variety, that one is led to think the metrical was suggested by the scientific. The planets whirled from the sun, and, at a later period, from planets themselves, Poe had chosen, in furtherance of his theory, to consider as so many gigantic atoms. These atoms displayed a particular difference in size and form, each from each, though there was always, he thought, a general equality preserved.[130] Although he does not definitely state the connection between variety and the attempt of the planet to obtain relief from its too great predominance of material, it can be seen that he makes the inference plain. In the metrical theory, the perception arises, he says, that relief is needed from excess of spondees; there is too great monotony felt. A variety of forms is therefore resorted to. Words of two syllables, though differently accented, appear; that is to say, iambuses and trochees are introduced.[131] And in like manner and from a like cause, anapaestic and dactylic *words* came in further to relieve monotony.[132]

Then the line appeared.[133] With considerable minuteness Poe

---

[127]*Ibid.*, vol. 14, p. 220. *Rationale of Verse*. In one instance Poe makes use of this term in discussing one of the forms of verse as it developed. It will be noted later in the chapter.
[128]*Ibid.*, vol. 16, p. 249. *Eureka*.
[129]*Ibid.*, vol. 14, p. 223. *Rationale of Verse*.
[130]*Ibid.*, vol. 16, p. 269. *Eureka*.
[131]*Ibid.*, vol. 14, p. 220. *Rationale of Verse*.
[132]*Ibid.*, vol. 14, p. 222. *Rationale of Verse*.
[133]*Ibid.*, vol. 14, pp. 223-226. *Rationale of Verse*.

explains this step in verse development, a step which repeats, only on a larger scale, the same search of relief through some phase of variety. Laplace's two atoms meeting in space, suggestive of the construction of the spondee, now propose lines equal in the number of their feet. To secure a desired variety, the number of feet will show difference: one line will be twice the length of another; and, lastly, numerous proportions will appear.

Rhyme takes its place as one part of the "processes," it being, Poe feels convinced, an outgrowth of the introduction of lines. Again the same development is seen: namely, from simple forms to those of greater complexity. Those rhythms with the concluding syllable long, he deems the more simple and, for this reason, will show the earliest approach at rhyme. But, in due course of time, the two remaining rhythms, the trochaic and dactylic, will result in double and triple rhymes. He gives the following lines as an example of his meaning:

> "Virginal Lilian, rigidly, humblily dutiful;
> Saintlily, lowlily,
> Thrillingly, holily
> Beautiful!"

Then he analyzes as follows the lines into absolute, proximate, and proportional equalizations, each one of which, he says, will be recognized by the cultivated ear. "Absolute equalities:

(1)   Between the long syllable of each dactyl and the two short conjointly;

(2)   Between each dactyl and any other dactyl;

(3)   Between the two middle lines;

(4)   Between the first line and the three others taken conjointly;

(5)   Between the last two syllables of the respective words "dutiful" and "beautiful;"

(6)   Between the last two syllables of the respective words "lowlily" and "holily."

Proximate equalities:

(1)   Between first syllable of "dutiful" and first syllable of "beautiful";

(2)   Between first syllable of "lowlily" and that of "holily".

Proportional equalities:

(1)   Of five to one, between the first line and each of its members, the dactyls;

(2)   Of two to one, between each of the middle lines and its members, the dactyls;

(3)   Of five to two, between the first line and each of the two middle;

(4)   Of five to one, between first line and the last;

(5)   Of two to one, between each of the middle lines and the last;

(6)   Of four to one, as concerns number, between all the lines, taken collectively and any individual line.''

The next and final step in verse development and one which appears preëminently reminiscent of Poe's understanding of scientific law governing the universe is the stanza. May he not at this point have held in mind Herschel's and Nichol's hint of a movement of all heavenly bodies towards a center; and also his own interpretation of this theory as a complete surrender to the most perfect satisfaction, the accomplishment of a perfect unity? The following points at least suggest this connection.

Poe calls the stanza a ''mass,'' and says it owes its ''birth'' to the completion of a perfect or proportional equality ''between all the lines, taken collectively and any individual line.'' Such a ''mass,'' he claims, in its primitive sense, at least, would possess absolute unity.   Indeed, (and here his wording reverts to Aristotelian terms, which, as we have seen, he came to view in scientific relations) he asserts that the ''removal of one of its lines would have rendered it imperfect.'' Then he discusses the steady tendency in all the proportions detailed, to give rise to this perfect satisfaction in unity. All the equalizations are apparent, he says, to a sensitive ear, and they journey to their end with a ''progressive increase.''

Of course it cannot with any certainty be said that Poe took as a model the creation of the universe for the development of verse forms, but that he may have done so suggests itself from the similarities between the two that I have detailed, and the hint that Poe throws out to the effect that he *could* go ''behind the idea of equality,'' and show ''how and why'' it is that satisfaction arises from it. Moreover, his continued willingness to rest what he chooses to call the ''processes'' in the gradual development of verse, on a hypothetical basis, speaks, it would seem, for their dependence on the scientific theory.

Then Poe states it as his opinion that scanning by time is but the appreciation of scientific law. He even endeavors, as will be seen, to work out his system mathematically, giving numerical values to long and short syllables as he conceives of varied beats being forced into equal time. In attempting to explain this method as it is most fully detailed in "The Rationale of Verse," it seems most understandable, if one keeps in mind the philosophic and scientific laws which have just been referred to. The meaning, then, of what Poe calls his general proposition, will be quite plain. He says:—

"In all rhythms, the prevalent or distinctive feet may be varied at will, and nearly at random, by the *occasional* introduction of equivalent feet—that is to say, feet the sum of whose syllabic times is equal to the sum of the syllabic times of the distinctive feet."[134] Various admonitions follow this proposition, such as that one should take care not to introduce so many variations that distinctive feet no longer exist; and such as that one should take care to wait before introducing any variation, until the ear has become accustomed to what is intended for the distinctive feet. That the variation should correspond with the sense of the piece, he likewise suggests. Pope, he thinks, has fine instances of this care. Having made these suggestions, he then starts to explain and illustrate what he means by his general proposition. He begins by fixing on a standard of measurement, choosing the long syllable as the unit,[135] and considering the short syllable as having a certain proportion to that length. He then takes up the question of the substitution of equivalent feet. A trochee is equal to an iambus, both being equal to three short syllables.[136] Another instance of the substitution of different equivalent feet, he maintains, is the caesura. He considers this foot[137] the most important of all feet, and, as we said at the outset of this discussion, he claims the merit of discovering the character about to be detailed. According to his explanation, it is the best illustration of unity and variety. In fact, he makes it a variable foot, always equal in the sum of its syllable-time to the prevailing foot. He differs, he says, from all prosodists in the nature of its use, though he agrees with them that it is a "pause."[138] In opposition to the prosodists who introduce

---

[134]*Ibid.*, vol. 14, pp. 234-235.

[135]*Ibid.*, vol. 14, p. 249.

[136]*Ibid.*, vol. 14, p. 234.

[137]Poe very plainly calls the caesura a foot. It is, he says, "a perfect foot." *Ibid.*, vol. 14, p. 216.

[138]*Works*, vol. 11, p. 228. *Poets and Poetry of America.*

it between two members of the same verse, by which one is contrasted with the other, he maintains that it should be used as a pause to give force. Its use is also, he thinks, to allow a stepping over into another species of foot without producing the slightest discord. He marks the caesura with a waved line in order to express variability of value. In the following line, the caesura, he says, is *son*, and it equals three short syllables:—

> "I have a little stepson of only three
> years old."

Gray, the caesura, equals four short syllables in:—

> "Pale as a lily was Emily Gray."

A further example of variation he gives as the bastard foot. This foot is illustrated, he says, in the recognition that a precise number of syllables does not have to be adhered to, provided the time required for the whole foot is kept intact.[139] He gives as an example of a bastard iambus:—

> "or laugh | and shake | in Rab | e lais ea |
> sy chair, | "

He wishes to make the three syllables *e lais ea* equal in time the two syllables composing any one of the other feet, and he thinks it can be done by pronouncing the syllables *e lais* in double quick time. *elais* is therefore a bastard iambus. On this basis, he condemns *blending*, or the effort to force several syllables into a fewer number of beats. In the line:—

> "See the delicate footed reindeer"

delicate should not be pronounced "del'cate." Every syllable should be pronounced in full. But the syllables *licate* should be made to occupy the time of a short syllable and so must be said twice as quickly as any other of the short syllables in the line. *Delicate* has, in time, therefore, the value of a long and a short syllable, and he calls it a bastard trochee. He now brings forward what he considers a bolder variation, or bolder substitution of equivalent feet. In the line:—

> "Many are the thoughts that come to me"

he considers the syllables *ny are the* as equal only to a short syllable, and if pronounced in the time of the other short syllables in the line, will make the foot, not a bastard trochee, he thinks, but what he calls a "quick trochee".

---

[139]*Ibid.*, vol. 14, p. 232. *Rationale of Verse.*

He then proceeds to give numerical values to syllables. He takes again the line:—

"Many are the thoughts that come to me."

The long syllable is the unit. The prevailing foot is the trochee. Therefore *that* and *to* will be pronounced in one-half the time of *thoughts* and *come*. *Ny are the* taken together will be said in one-half the time of *Ma*, each syllable of the triplet being equal to one-sixth. *Me* he regards as a caesura and allots it the time of three short syllables. Writing the line again and giving it Poe's figures, we find it to be:—

Many are the | thoughts that | come to | me$^{3/2}$.
      6 6 6   2   2

Poe now considers that the value of his system of scanning by time could be no better tested than by taking a case where usual scansion has failed to agree on the proper mode. He advances the theory that a stanza should be scanned as though it were one continuous verse. As an example he cites the instance of a poem that to the ear is perfectly harmonious, but to the eye is a puzzle to scan. The last word in the first line of Byron's "Bride of Abydos" has, he says, always been a matter of mystery to the prosodists.[140] The line was meant for dactylic and the foot at the end was irregular and therefore confusing. In a similar way, the first word of the second line also proved a stumbling-block. It prevented the line from being scanned according to the foot that was obviously the poet's intention. This word, said some prosodists, according to Poe, was evidently the poet's blunder. Some even demanded that it be cut from the line. Poe now offers to show that scanning by time in one continuous verse without reference to line will clear up the difficulty. In his scansion the ensuing points may be noted. First, that unity as it exists with variations will be seen to be the law followed; that the dactyl is the prevailing foot, or four short syllables; that the caesura has the value of four short syllables. Two spondees in a measure, being equal to two long, are also equal to four short syllables.

"Know ye the | land where the | cypress and | myrtle Are |
emblems of | deeds that are | done in their | clime Where the |
rage of the | vulture the | love of the | turtle Now | melt into |
softness now | madden to | *crime* | Know ye the | land of the |

---

[140]*Ibid.*, vol. 14, p. 243. *Rationale of Verse.*

cedar and | vine where the | flowers ever | blossom the |
beams ever | shine Where the, | etc.''

Another influence of Poe's scientific interest on his literary work
is its obvious effect on his understanding of the power of reality
to produce an impression. The question grows in his mind into a
comprehension of verisimilitude. His changed attitude in this regard is interesting to follow. In the ''Letter to B—'', in 1831, he
had apparently wholly discredited the place of real life in the
poet's art. He spoke at that time with contempt of ''Peter Bell''
and quoted with enthusiasm from Ossian the passages which,
in his opinion, Wordsworth had unjustly criticized. In ''Genius,''
written some time before 1836, he again doubts that realism can
satisfy the poet's fancy. ''The dull scenes of real life,'' he says
there in this connection, ''can never be suffered to chill the ardor
of the romantic imagination.'' While it is true in this early period
of writing he imitated the detailed method of the physician and
the sensation story-writer as they presented their material in *Blackwood,* it is not until he has passed through a long period of scientific thinking that he has much to say on the subject of real
life. Then, as a student of natural science, he explains his meaning.

Plausibility of a story rests, says Poe, on the faithfulness with
which a writer adheres to minute detail. Especially is this true,
he adds, in fiction whose ground-work is science. In this case the
detail must be eminently scientific as far as observation and analogy
can carry it.[141] In a note appended to the revised form of ''Hans
Phaall'' he explains that Locke, the author of the ''Moon Hoax,''
in attempting to give plausibility by scientific detail, owing to
astronomical blunders, had failed in being credited with belief.
Among other errors, Locke had, it seems, quoted Herschel errone-
ously to the effect that with high magnifying lens one could see
flowers on the surface of the moon and even detect the color and
shape of the eyes of small birds. Poe goes on to examine other
stories of similar nature to the ''Moon Hoax.'' As in the former
case, he attributes the lack of plausibility in ''L'Homme dans la
lune, ou le Voyage Chémerique fait au Monde de la lune,'' to scientific errors. In spite of its author's claiming a knowledge of natural science, the book exhibits only fanciful theories of his time.

---

[141]*Works,* vol. 2, p. 103. Note to *Hans Phaall.*

For example, the seventeenth century writer maintains that "gravitating power" extends but a short distance from the earth's surface; and that the motion of our globe is "from the east to the west." But plausibility by a strict adherence to fact, Poe maintains, is exemplified in his own "Hans Phaall." He has so aimed at verisimilitude, he says, by making every minute detail in the passage from the earth to the moon accord with the views of the most eminent astronomers, that the unreal element in the thesis of the story becomes an accepted reality. Unbelief is suspended.

Even in critical opinions dealing not at all with scientific subjects, Poe also shows the influence of training in natural science. Art criticism, in 1836, appealed to him chiefly as the principle of unity he had learned in the drama. In 1845, however, he gives full expression in art comments to what he calls truth—the truth of expression, the perfection of proportion. Recall what he said on the anatomy of the figure in the "Ivory Christ" being well wrought out.

The drama, he thinks, furnishes striking proof of the need of verisimilitude. In his article on "The New Comedy" he is attempting to account for what, as he says, is usually spoken of as the decline of the drama. He is of the opinion that the drama has not declined; it has simply not advanced. "Our fault-finding," he says, "is on the score of deficiency in verisimilitude—in natural art, that is to say in art based in the natural laws of man's heart and understanding." He cites as an example the answer one character makes to every remark addressed to him, that "he is indifferent to flowers." Such a reply is not only absurd, Poe thinks; it has not even the redeeming feature of a farcical element. He gives other instances in which real life is little displayed. "Also in the same category, we must include the rectangular crossings and recrossings of the *dramatis personae* on the stage; the coming forward to the foot-lights when anything of interest is to be told; the reading of private letters in a loud, rhetorical tone; the preposterous soliloquizing; and the even more preposterous 'asides.' "[142]

A curious instance in this connection is what Poe has to say on Scriptural prophecies carrying out a scientific method. He professes himself struck with the fact that the Scriptures in their predictions do not depend for belief on general statements, but trust their truths to minute details. The Christian and the philosopher,

---

[142]*Broadway Journal*, vol. 1, p. 205.

he says, will understand him when he attributes to the Deity a
conscious intention of providing for the evidence of the fulfillment of the word of scripture, an intention manifested in the smallest detail.[143] He expresses his conviction of what he conceives to
be the wisdom of this plan, saying: "No general meaning attached
to a prediction, no general fulfilment of such prediction, could
carry to the reason of mankind inferences so unquestionable as its
particular and minutely incidental accomplishment. General statements, except in rare instances, are susceptible of misinterpretation
or misapplication; details admit no shadow of ambiguity."

It remains now to suggest in what way Poe's practice was affected by his interest in science. We have already noted instances
of his taking over scientific material as subject-matter. For example, Dr. Dick's predicted destruction of the world resting on a
carefully detailed experiment becomes as we have seen part of Poe's
text in "Eiros and Charmion;" and experimental work in the
Philosophical Transactions appears in his story of the flight to the
moon. But his scientific training also extends into realms that
have nothing to do with science. Perhaps the best way of noting
this influence in his practice is to contrast former ways he employed to produce an effect with those of later time. In early
work he adopted such measures as the human-like body of the ship
in the "MS," the gruesome teeth of Berenice, the mystic eyes of
Ligeia, the recurring of the name, Morella, ghostly in its echo, the
horrors of the charnel-house, some climactic instances of metempsychosis, to strike the attention and to prolong the impression.
While it is true that at all times he shows an aptness to return to
these means, a growing desire to depict reality becomes apparent
in his work. This effort seems to manifest itself, first, in a wav-
ering attempt to draw on nothing but real life. For example, the
end of his long realistic tale of 1838, the "Narrative of Arthur
Gordon Pym," is curiously confused with certain points and with
the general tone of his mystic tale of the "MS," the early effort
of 1831. The brig in the "Narrative" rushing with hideous velocity into the southern polar gulf, a shrouded human figure in
the pathway, almost, one might say, tells again of the phantom
ship in the "MS" sweeping into the current flowing northward
and whirling dizzily in the circles of the whirlpool. Then a more
consistent depicting of real life reveals itself in 1846 in the "Cask

---

[143]*Works*, vol. 3, p. 9. Review of Stephens' *Arabia Petraea.*

of Amontillado." In fact, this tale shows an absolute change in method. It may not be too much to say that all the training science had given him both in choice of subject-matter and in technical method appears in this story. In it, Poe shows himself a scientific writer. He finds his thesis in real life and presents a plot of mutually dependent parts, each "atom" of which appears to spring irresistibly from the bosom of the thesis. The main points of the story will, I think, make his intention plain.

Revenge is the thesis. Montresor exclaims as the opening words: "The thousand injuries of Fortunato I had borne as best I could, but when he ventured upon insult, I vowed revenge."

The working out of the thesis follows the events as given:

Dusk of an evening in Italy.

During madness of carnival season.

Montresor and Fortunato meet.

Fortunato garbed in motley, with bells that tinkle from the top of his cap.

Drunk, blear-eyed, unsteady, but eager still for adventure.

Montresor tells of his vaults filled with choice Amontillado.

Hints he may ask Luchresi to test it for him.

Fortunato, stung to jealousy at slight of his connoisseur-ship, and eager for his favorite wine, insists on descending with his companion to depths of underground passages where are the vaults of the Montresor palace.

Palace at this hour empty of attendants.

Fortunato at Montresor's suggestion notes damp walls where nitre hangs moss-like; dank air of the crypt in which the flame of the torches only glows instead of flames;

listens to Montresor's description of arms of Montresor family:

"A human foot d'or, in a field azure; the foot crushes a serpent rampant whose fangs are embedded in the heel."

They pass on in search of the Amontillado.

Come to another crypt less spacious.

Three walls lined with human bones piled to vault overhead. "From the fourth side the bones had been thrown down, and lay promiscuously upon the earth, forming at one point a mound of some size. Within the wall thus exposed by the displacing of the bones," was a still interior crypt or recess, in depth about four feet, in width three, in height six or seven.

Fortunato steps unsteadily into this crypt. In an instant he is chained by his enemy to wall of granite at the back.

Shrieks for help.

No aid comes.

Montresor starts to wall up victim.

As he places the last stone in its position he calls Fortunato's name, but he hears only faint jingling of bells.

The "atoms" in the story show a tendency, as evidently was Poe's intention, to point, or as the scientific theory expressed it, to rush back to their origin—to their original oneness from which they sprang, and the complete satisfaction in revenge remains to impress as the faint tinkling of the bells on Fortunato's cap tells that the victim is crushed. Thus the dénouement, following the scientific theory, is a matter of supreme necessity.

CONCLUSION

Poe may be said to have reached a point in his critical thinking wherein he saw that effect as the object of a writer's art is produced by an appreciation of the orderly nature and working of law, and he felt that the secret of impressive writing lies in the use of natural processes. As regards the stages by which he reached this conclusion, it is apparent that the particular interests he found in his reading came to transmute themselves in his mind into one consistent way of thinking. Each of these interests, we have seen, has played its part in making his literary theory,—a theory which guided his choice of subject-matter and formed his technical method.

From his reading Poe taught himself to choose material that of itself possessed a compelling interest. Although he never wholly abandoned as subject-matter for his own experimentation the mystic and the supernatural, he yet confessed to a growing conviction that real experience will best touch the heart of humanity. He selected then from *Blackwood* and other foreign periodicals, from scientific journals, from Plato, and from other sources, what he found to be the most likely themes for producing an impression. Such material as youthful beauty afflicted with disease, either mental or physical, and condemned to die a lingering death; sensations that irresistibly arise from sad situations; and emotions that are common to the heart of all mankind, found their way into his poems and stories.

Moreover, from his reading he learned a method of dealing with this subject-matter. To this end he considered effect in the manner that writers in *Blackwood* and that Augustus Wilhelm von Schlegel had conceived it, and dwelt upon such points as adaptation of constituent parts, a pre-established design, the doctrine of the Many-in-One, and the need of brevity in the way that philosophy explained them. He acquired some degree of understanding of the processes of civil law, of the fundamental principles of the drama, and, finally, he attempted to see in all these lines of his study so many instances of the functioning of science. Unity, therefore, became to him a law which a writer may use both as a test for excellence and as a means whereby he may attain to an excellent standard.

And this technique and content which were the outgrowth of his reading he explained as varying aspects of the same question. For subject-matter in his hands, became, in its philosophic meaning, not only a theme to elaborate but also a method of development. Beauty, as Plato had explained it, he found, was not only a suitable theme for poetry, but, again on Plato's recommendation, it also furnished a method of making that beauty felt by others. And this union of technique and content he likewise professed to see embodied in the field of realism. Disease was not only a fascinating subject for successful tales, but it also suggested, in a scientific diagnosis of its symptoms, a means of producing horror in the reader. In fact, he considered that any real experience of universal interest, if depicted with the method learned from nature, could not fail to be impressive. This copying from nature had in his mind no vagueness in its application, but was, the text has attempted to show, a conscious effort on a writer's part to imitate in his poem or story, the order of natural law, as that law manifests itself in perfect adjustments, in short, in scientific unity. Thus, Poe taught himself that the matter and method of fitting together details of beauty and disease, of adapting to each other sensations overwhelming some unhappy victim, of delicately adjusting emotions, determined the effect of the piece. He taught himself, as he said, to advance, some steps at least,in the science of criticism; and, as he also stated, to use this critical principle in its meaning of verisimilitude.

Such critical dicta then, as Poe gives for the guidance of poets in the Philosophy of Composition, and of writers of the short story in the review of Hawthorne's Tales, could not have been merely exaggerated statements detailed at the end of some finished product, either poem or story, merely to describe, as an afterthought, methods he had used unconsciously. On the contrary, we have seen that his ideas had a long period of growth, that they began in the early days of his study of British periodicals, and that they passed through other and varying influences,—law, the drama and fine arts, philosophy, and science,—each of which added to them richness and depth of meaning. Moreover, Poe was forever conscious of his method.

It now remains only to be said that there are certain materials which have been studied as possible additions to the Poe canon. Some of these pieces, as has been pointed out in the text, have been already ascribed to Poe, although no detailed weighing of the cases has hitherto been offered; other pieces are, I believe, mentioned for the first time in this paper as possibly the work of Poe. It may be useful to enumerate these works in this place:— "Genius" (in vol. 2 of the *Southern Literary Messenger*), "The Philosophy of Antiquity" (parts 1-3, in vols. 2 and 3 of the *Messenger*), "The Classics" (in vol. 2 of the *Messenger*), "New Views of the Solar System," "New View of the Tides" (in vols. 4 and 5 of the *Messenger*), "Half an Hour in the Fine Arts Gallery in Philadelphia" (in vol. 5 of *Burton's Gentleman's Magazine*), and several articles of art criticism referred to in the text.

BIBLIOGRAPHY

Alison, Archibald. "Essays on the Nature and Principles of Taste." Edinburgh, 1825.
American Museum, vols. 1-2. Baltimore, 1839.
  Poe's contributions are noted in the text.
American Quarterly Review, vol. 15, pp. 448-73. "Decline of Poetry." Philadelphia, 1834.
Aristotle. "Treatise on Poetry," trans. by Thomas Twining. London, 1789.
Bacon, Francis. *Works*, vols. 1-2. London, 1825.
Baker, H. T. "Coleridge's Influence on Poe's Poetry." *Mod. Lang. Notes*, vol. 25, pp. 94-5. Baltimore, 1910.
Baldwin, S. "The Aesthetic Theory of Poe." *Sewanee Review*, vol. 26, pp. 210-21. New York, 1918.
Beatty, Arthur. "William Wordsworth, His Doctrine and Art in Their Historical Relations." Madison, 1922.
Beck, T. R. "Elements of Medical Jurisprudence." Albany, 1823.
Bethune, J. E. D. "Life of Galileo Galilei." Boston, 1832.
Birch, Thomas. "The History of the Royal Society of London." 4 vols. London, 1756.
Blackwood's Edinburgh Magazine. Edinburgh.
  Vol. 1. 1817. "Fragment of a Literary Romance," pp. 382-87.
  "Gree˙ Tragedy. No. I," pp. 40-2.
  "Greeκ Tragedy. No. IV," pp. 593-96.
  "Lalla Rookh," pp. 503-10.
  "Marlow's Tragical History of the Life and Death of Doctor Faustus," pp. 388-94.
  "Modern Greece," pp. 515-18.
  Vol. 2. 1818. "Analytical Essays on the Early English Dramatists," pp. 21-30.
  "Analytical Essays on the Early English Dramatists. No. IV," pp. 656-62.
  "Notices of the Acted Drama in London," pp. 664-69.
  "Remarks on the Periodical Criticism of England," pp. 670-79.
  Vol. 3. 1818. "Letter to the Rev. Professor Laugner," pp. 689-95.
  "Notices of the Acted Drama in London. No. V," pp. 207-11.
  "Notices of the Acted Drama in London. No. VI," pp. 329-31.
  "Remarks on Schlegel's History of Literature," pp. 497-511.
  Vol. 4. 1818. "On the Early English Dramatists. No. VI," pp. 66-74.
  "Remarks on the Poetry of Thomas Moore," pp. 1-5.
  1819. "The Opera," pp. 715-20.
  Vol. 6. 1819. "Notices of the Acted Drama in London. No. XI," pp. 51-55.
  1820. "Analytical Essays on the Old English Dramatists. No. VIII," pp. 409-17.
  "Notices of the Acted Drama in London. No. VIII," pp. 386-89.
  Vol. 7. 1820. "Notices of the Acted Drama in London. No. XV," pp. 182-85.
  "Notices of the Acted Drama in London. No. XVI," pp. 307-11.
  Vol. 10. 1821. "Buried Alive," pp. 262-64.
  "Man in the Bell," pp. 373-75.
  "Modern British Drama," pp. 53-60.
  Vol. 12. 1822. "Bowles' Grave of the Last Saxon," pp. 71-8.
  "Milman's Belshazzar," pp. 25-40.
  "Noctes Ambrosianae," pp. 100-14.

Vol. 13.   1823.   "Confessions of An English Glutton," pp. 86-93.
"Hints for Jurymen," pp. 673-85.
"Horae Germanicae," pp. 3-14.
"Noctes Ambrosianae. No. VIII," pp. 592-611.
"Remarks on Mr. Alison's Theory of Beauty, as Explained by Mr. Jeffrey," pp. 385-90.
"Remarks on Mr. Barry Cornwall's New Poems," pp. 532-41.
Vol. 14.   1823.   "Chapter on Goblins," pp. 639-46.
"Horae Germanicae. No. XVI," pp. 377-96.
"Modern Dramas and Dramatic Writers," pp. 555-60.
"On the Sources of the Picturesque and Beautiful," pp. 249-54.
"Popular Tales of the Northern Nations," pp. 293-94.
Vol. 15.   1824.   "Goethe's Wilhelm Meister," pp. 619-32.
Vol. 16.   1824.   "The Devil's Elixir," pp. 55-67.
"Letters of Timothy Tickler, Esq., to Eminent Literary Characters. No. XVIII," pp. 291-304.
Vol. 17.   1825.   "Beck and Dunlop on Medical Jurisprudence," pp. 351-52.
"Horae Germanicae," pp. 673-81.
"A Letter to Charles Kemble on the Present State of the Stage," pp. 727-31.
Vol. 18.   1825.   "Analytical Essays on the Modern English Drama. No. III," pp. 119-30.
"Horae Hispanicae XI," pp. 83-92.
"Note-Book of a Literary Idler. No. II," pp. 233-40.
Vol. 19.   1826.   "Noctes Ambrosianae. No. XXIV," 211-27.
"On the Dramatic Powers of the Author of Waverley," pp. 158-60.
"Prodigality of Words," pp. 578-87.
Vol. 20.   1826.   "Horae Hispanicae. No. XIII," pp. 559-72.
Vol. 21.   1827.   "Horae Germanicae. No. XXII," pp. 214-26.
"Horae Germanicae. No. XXIII," pp. 464-82.
"Le Revenant," pp. 409-16.
Vol. 22.   1827.   "The Epicurean; a Tale by Thomas Moore," pp. 376-482.
"Noctes Ambrosianae. No. XXXIV," pp. 105-34.
Vol. 24.   1821.   "Elements of Rhetoric," pp. 885-908.
Vol. 25.   1829.   "First and Last Crime," pp. 303-10.
"Noctes Ambrosianae," pp. 525-48.
Vol. 26.   1829.   "First and Last Sacrifice," pp. 444-52.
Vol. 27.   1830.   "Noctes Ambrosianae. No. XLIX," pp. 802-32.
Vol. 28.   1830.   "The Iron Shroud," pp. 364-71.
"Passages from the Diary of a Late Physician," pp. 322-38; 474-95.
"Passages from the Diary of a Late Physician; the Man About Town," pp. 921-40.
Vol. 29.   1831.   "Passages from the Diary of a Late Physician," pp. 105-27.
Vol. 30.   1831.   "Greek Drama. No. I," pp. 350-90.
"Sotheby's Homer," pp. 93-125.
Vol. 31.   1832.   "Sotheby's Homer. Critique V," pp. 145-80.
Vol. 32.   1832.   "Passages from the Diary of a Late Physician," pp. 279-99.
Vol. 42.   1837.   "Involuntary Experimentalist," pp. 487-92.
"Passages from the Diary of a Late Physician," pp. 248-92.
Vol. 45.   1839.   "Our Pocket Companions," pp. 130-44.
Blake, W. B.   "Edgar Allan Poe: A Centenary Outlook." *Dial*, vol. 46, pp. 103-4.   Chicago, 1909.
————   "Commemorations of Poe." *Dial*, vol. 47, pp. 118-20.   Chicago, 1909.

Blair, Hugh. "Lectures on Rhetoric and Belles Lettres." London, 1823.
Boileau-Despréaux, Nicolas. "Art of Poetry." Boston, 1892.
Brewster, David. "The Martyrs of Science; or, The Lives of Galileo, Tycho Brahe, and Kepler." New York, 1847.
———— "Life of Sir Isaac Newton." London, 1875.
———— "Letters on Natural Magic Addressed to Sir Walter Scott." London, 1832.
Broadway Journal, vols. 1-2. New York, 1845-46. Poe's contributions are noted in the text.
Bulwer-Lytton, Edward. "Night and Morning." Boston, 1893.
Burke, Edmund. "A Philosophical Enquiry Into the Origin of Our Ideas on the Sublime and Beautiful." London, 1798.
Burnet, Thomas. "The Sacred Theory of the Earth." London, 1759.
Browning, Mrs. E. B. "Lady Geraldine's Courtship." Boston, 1900.
Campbell, Killis. "Poe." *The Cambridge History of American Literature*, vol. 2, pp. 55-69. New York, 1918.
———— "New Notes on Poe's Early Years." *Dial*, vol. 60, pp. 143-46. Chicago, 1916.
———— "The Poe Canon." *Mod. Lang. Assoc. Pub.*, vol. 27, pp. 325-53. Baltimore, 1912.
———— "The Poe-Griswold Controversy." *Mod. Lang. Assoc. Pub.*, vol. 34, pp. 436-64. Baltimore, 1919.
"Miscellaneous Notes on Poe." *Mod. Lang. Notes*, vol. 28, 1913.
———— "Gleanings in the Bibliography of Poe." *Mod. Lang. Notes*, vol. 32, pp. 267-72. Baltimore, 1917.
———— "Poe's Indebtedness to Byron." *Nation*, vol. 88, pp. 248-49. New York, 1909.
———— "Poe and the *Southern Literary Messenger* in 1837." *Nation*, vol. 89, p. 9. New York, 1909.
———— "Bibliographical Notes on Poe." *Nation*, vol. 89, pp. 623-24; 647-48. New York, 1909.
———— "The Source of Poe's 'Some Words With a Mummy'." *Nation*, vol. 90, pp. 625-26. New York, 1910.
———— "News for Bibliophiles." *Nation*, vol. 93, pp. 362-63. New York, 1911.
———— "Some Unpublished Documents Relating to Poe's Early Years." *Sewanee Review*, vol. 20, pp. 201-12. New York, 1912.
Canby, H. S. "The Short Story in English." New York, 1909.
Cobb, Palmer. "The Influence of E. T. A. Hoffmann on the Tales of Edgar Allan Poe." New York, 1908.
———— "Edgar Allan Poe and Frederick Spielhagen: their Theory of the Short Story." *Mod. Lang. Notes*, vol. 25, pp. 67-72. Baltimore, 1910.
Cody, Sherwin. "Poe—Man, Poet, and Creative Thinker." New York, 1924.
Coleridge, S. T. "Biographia Literaria." London, 1817.
De Quincey, Thomas. "Collected Writings of Thomas De Quincey." Vol. 11, pp. 156-221. Edinburgh, 1910.
Dick, Thomas. *Complete Works*. Cincinnati, 1855.
D'Israeli, Isaac. "Curiosities of Literature." London, 1823.
Edinburgh Review. Edinburgh.
   Vol. 2. 1803. "Traité Medico—Philosophique sur l'Alienation Mentale, ou le Manie," pp. 160-72.
   Vol. 3. 1804. "Récherches et Expériences Médicales et Chimiques sur le Diabéte Sucré," pp. 410-22.
   Vol. 5. 1804. "Abernethy's Surgical Observations," pp. 168-79.
   Vol. 8. 1806. "Essays on the Anatomy of Expression in Painting," pp. 365-78.
   Vol. 11. 1807. "Southey's Specimens of English Poetry," pp. 31-40.

Vol. 24. 1814. "Waverley—a Novel," pp. 208-43.
Vol. 26. 1816. "Schlegel on the Drama," pp. 67-107.
Vol. 40. 1824. "Posthumous Poems of Percy Bysshe Shelley," pp. 494-514.
Vol. 58. 1834. "Astronomy and General Physics Considered with Reference to Natural Theology," pp. 422-57.
Ewers, H. "Edgar Allan Poe." New York, 1916.
Fontaines, André. "La Vie d'Edgar A. Poe." Paris, 1919.
Gentleman's Magazine, (Burton's) vols. 1-6. Philadelphia, 1837-39. Poe's contributions are noted in the text.
Glanvil, Joseph. "Essays on Several Important Subjects in Philosophy." London, 1676.
———— "Lux Orientalis; or An Enquiry into the Opinion of the Eastern Sages Concerning the Preëxistence of Souls." London, 1662.
———— "Scepsis Scientifica; or, Confest Ignorance, the way to Science." London, 1885.
Godwin, Francis. "The Strange Voyage and Adventures of Domingo Gonsales to the World in the Moon." London, 1768.
Godwin, William. "The Adventures of Caleb Williams; or, Things as they are." London, 1831.
———— "Lives of the Necromancers." London, 1876.
Graham's Magazine. Philadelphia, 1841-43. Poe's contributions are noted in text.
Gray, Thomas. Letters. Vol. 1. London, 1900.
Gruener, Gustav. "Notes on the Influence of E. T. A. Hoffman upon Edgar Allan Poe." Mod. Lang. Assoc. Pub., vol. 19, pp. 1-25. Baltimore, 1904.
Harrison, J. A. "Complete Works of Edgar Allan Poe." New York, 1902.
Hazlitt, W. A. "Sketches of the Principal Picture Galleries in England." Works, vol. 9, pp. 7-81. London, 1903.
———— "Contributions to the Edinburgh Review," vol. 10. London, 1904.
Herschel, William. "Of 3 Volcanoes in the Moon." Philosophical Transactions of the Royal Society of London, vol. 16, p. 255. London, 1809.
Humboldt, Alexander von. "Cosmos." New York, 1850.
Hunt, Leigh. "The Indicator and the Companion." 2 vols. London, 1834.
"How to Write a Grim Story." Indicator, London, 1819.
Kames, H. H. "Elements of Criticism." Edinburgh, 1774.
Kant, Emanuel. "Criticism of the Judgment." London, 1892.
Lauvrière, Emile. "Edgar Poe." Paris, 1911.
Leigh, Oliver. "Edgar Allan Poe: The Man, The Master, The Martyr." Chicago, 1906.
Lessing, Gotthold. "Laocoon." Boston, 1910.
Locke, John. Works, vols. 1-3; 9. London, 1801.
Lockhart, John. "Memoirs of the Life of Sir Walter Scott." 5 vols. Boston, 1902.
Lofland, John. "The Milford Bard." Baltimore, 1853.
Mabbott, T. O. "The Letters from George W. Eveleth to Edgar Allan Poe." New York Public Library, 1922.
———— "Politian, An Unfinished Tragedy, by Edgar A. Poe." The Collegiate Press, George Banta Publishing Co., Wisconsin, 1923.
Mackenzie, Shelton. "Noctes Ambrosianae by John Wilson." New York, 1863.
Maskelyne, Nevil. "An Account of an Appearance of Light, like a Star, seen lately in the Dark part of the Moon . . ." Philosophical Transactions of the Royal Society of London, vol. 17, p. 451. London, 1809.
Mathews, Brander. "Short-story; Specimens Illustrating its Development." New York, 1907.
Maturin, C. R. "Melmoth the Wanderer." Edinburgh, 1821.

Medico-Chirurgical Review and Journal of Practical Medicine. vol. 28, p. 245.
Minor, B. B. *The Southern Literary Messenger.* New York, 1905.
Moore, C. L. "The Case of Poe and His Critics." *Dial,* vol. 47, pp. 367-70. Chicago, 1909.
New York Mirror, vol. 10. New York, 1832. Poe's contributions are noted in the text.
Oliphant, Mrs. T. K. "William Blackwood and his Sons." Edinburgh, 1897.
Plato. *The Dialogues of Plato,* ed. by Jowett, vol. 1, pp. 431-89; 541-94; vol. 4, pp. 45-106. Oxford, 1892.
Pope, A. "M. Scriblerus; or, The Art of Sinking in Poetry." *Works,* vol. 6. London, 1760.
Prescott, F. C. "Selections from the Critical Writings of Edgar Allan Poe." New York, 1909.
Quarterly Review. London.
    Vol. 44. 1831. "Origin of the Homeric poems," pp. 124-68.
    Vol. 50. 1834. "Astronomy and General Physics considered with Reference to Natural Theology," pp. 1-34.
Radcliffe, Mrs. Ann (Ward). "The Italian; or, The Confessional of the Black Penitents." London, 1811.
———— "The Mysteries of Udolpho." London, 1820.
———— "The Romance of the Forest." London, 1792.
———— "A Sicilian Romance." London, 1809.
Ransome, Arthur. "Edgar Allan Poe. A Critical Study." New York, 1910.
Rice, S. S. "Edgar Allan Poe, a Memorial Volume." Baltimore, 1877.
Robertson, J. M. "New Essays towards a Critical Method." New York, 1897.
Robertson, J. W. "Edgar A. Poe: a Study." San Francisco, 1921.
Schlegel, A. W. von. "Lectures on Dramatic Art and Literature." London, 1894.
Scott, Walter. "On the Supernatural in English Fiction." *Foreign Quarterly Review,* vol. 1, p. 72. London, 1827.
———— Essay on the Drama. *Encyclopedia Britannica.* 8th ed., pp. 133-69. Boston, 1855.
Shelley, Mrs. M. W. (G) "Frankenstein; or, The Modern Prometheus." London, 1849.
Simms, W. G. "Beauchampe; or, The Kentucky Tragedy." New York, 1882.
Southern Literary Messenger, vols. 1-5. Richmond, 1834-38. Poe's contributions are noted in the text.
Stewart, Dugald. "Elements of the Philosophy of the Human Mind." New York, 1814.
Tennemann, W. G. "A Manual of the History of Philosophy," trans. by Arthur Johnson. London, 1852.
Trent, W. P. "William Gilmore Simms." Boston, 1896.
Tucker, Abraham. "The Light of Nature Pursued." London, 1805.
Tucker, George. "Voyage to the Moon." New York, 1827.
Whewell, William. "History of the Inductive Sciences, from the Earliest to the Present Times." London, 1837.
———— "On the Philosophy of Discovery, Chapters Historical and Critical." London, 1847.
Whitty, J. H. "Complete Poems of Edgar Allan Poe." Boston, 1917.
Wilmer, L. A. "Our Press Gang; or, A Complete Exposition of the Corruption and Crimes of the American Newspapers." Philadelphia, 1859.
Woodberry, G. E. "Edgar Allan Poe." Boston, 1885.
Wordsworth, William. *The Prose Works of William Wordsworth.* London, 1876.

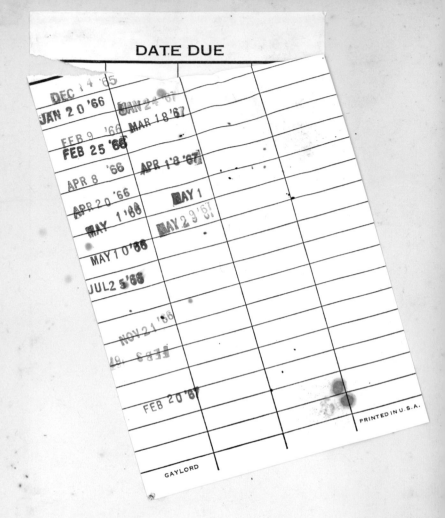